The Mount Lemmon Highway twists through the Santa Catalinas north of Tucson, leading to a recreation bonanza including skiing, fishing, camping, and hiking. George Stocking

the Back Roads

ARIZONA HIGHWAYS

Watson Lake reflects a line of
textured granite boulders in the
Prescott area's Granite Dells area.
Randy A. Prentice

Text by Sam Negri
With Additional Text By *Arizona Highways* Contributors

Photography by *Arizona Highways* Contributors

the Back Roads

Arizona Highways

The Back Roads

Text: Sam Negri

Additional Text: *Arizona Highways* Staff and Contributors as indicated

Photographs: *Arizona Highways* Contributors

Photography Editor: Richard Maack

Copy Editor: Evelyn Howell

Maps: Gus Walker

Interns/Researchers: Brian Minnick, Carley Partridge

Book Design: Bill Greaves, Concept West

Book Production: 1106 Design

Production Coordinator: Annette Phares

Book Editor: Bob Albano

Library of Congress Control Number 2007924185

ISBN 978-1-932082-77-7

First printing, 2007. Printed in China.

Published by the Books Division of *Arizona Highways*® magazine, a monthly publication of the Arizona Department of Transportation, 2039 West Lewis Avenue, Phoenix, Arizona 85009. Telephone: (602) 712-2200. Web site: www.arizonahighways.com

Publisher: Win Holden

Editor: Robert Stieve

Managing Editor: Bob Albano

Associate Editor: Evelyn Howell

Director of Photography: Peter Ensenberger

Production Director: Michael Bianchi

Production Assistants: Diana Benzel-Rice, Ronda Johnson, Annette Phares

ARIZONA HIGHWAYS

Built as a mining town on Cleopatra Hill, Jerome seems to teeter on the steep hillsides as it glows in the first light of the day.
George Stocking

Contents

A rare winter bloom of Mexican goldpoppies carpets a slope below the Superstition Mountains.
Randy A. Prentice

Scholz Lake graces the Garland Prairie area, with the San Francisco Peaks on the horizon. Tom Bean

The Babbitt Building and Hotel Monte Vista stand out on a snowy evening in Flagstaff. Tom Bean

Getting the Most From This Book

The *Back Roads* continues the *Arizona Highways* tradition of helping people "discover" the beauty of the land, not to conquer it, but to be at peace with it, to appreciate it. Point toward the unknown horizon with your arms flung back—or take the next step with quiet awareness. Travel these back roads and you will be introduced to quiet places where you can listen to the birds, smell the flowers, touch the earth, watch the sunset, and learn something of Arizona's ancient past and pioneer roots. You can still feel the adrenalin rush of roaming off the beaten track to mountain views and canyon precipices and to lakeside playgrounds where you may frolic, fish, or just forget the outside world.

You'll discover you can reach many of Arizona's most-scenic wonders and historic treasures that are off the well-traveled highways. Apache Trail, Hannagan Meadow, ghost towns, Indian cliff dwellings, and historic cavalry posts—all these and many more adventures await you along Arizona's byways.

Take plenty of water, your camera, your fishing gear, your bird books, mountain bikes, and—especially—your sense of adventure. You really haven't seen how amazing Arizona is until you've turned onto its delightful back roads. A good map of the area in which you are traveling will also stand you in good stead.

The 40 drives in this book are grouped into nine regions identified in the map on Page 11. Accompanying each drive are a map and a route finder, giving detailed directions and contact information for various agencies and attractions you may want to visit. Bear in mind that mileages specified in the route finders are approximate—odometer readings vary, depending on the vehicle, size of its wheels, distance being measured, and other factors. Also bear in mind that some roads have more than one name, and maps can list them differently. For example, in the Phoenix-Central Arizona chapter, the wildflowers drive into the Superstition Mountains includes Hewitt Station Road, also called Forest Service Road 357; in the Arizona Strip chapter, the drive to Timp Point lists Forest Service Road 22, which is listed on some older maps as Forest Service Road 422 and on some maps as West Side Road.

We suggest that you bring with you a detailed map or gazetteer covering the area in which you plan to travel. Also, it's a safety practice to leave your itinerary information with a friend, who could alert authorities if you do not return home by your scheduled time.

Most of these drives are tours that you can complete in one unhurried day while carefully driving the family sedan; speeds of 25 miles per hour or less are reasonable on unpaved roads, even on well-maintained roads in dry weather. (Each tour specifies high-clearance or four-wheel-drive vehicles where challenging road conditions warrant it.) Each region's opening summary provides an overview of the region, a list of the drives, and towns and sites that the drives will take you to or near.

Be forewarned: Most of these tours are not Sunday drives over paved highways. Passing drivers may be few and far between, and your cell phone signal may disappear entirely as you drive through mountains and down canyons. For long stretches, you may drive without seeing any eateries and service stations, so start each trip with a full tank of gasoline and all the food you will need for a minimum of two days. Always carry at least a gallon—or more—of water per person; even when you are driving a mountain tour (rather than a desert one), it's still dry country out there.

Steep grades and rough roads can use up a lot of gas, so always fill up before leaving a populated area; and check your oil and tire pressure. Make sure your spare tire is properly inflated. In some extremely remote areas, like the Arizona Strip in northern Arizona, it may take hours for a tow truck to reach a disabled vehicle—assuming you've been able to summon one on your cell phone or with the help of a rare passerby. The Strip's regional land manager, the federal Bureau of Land Management (BLM) has told travelers that it's not unreasonable in that rocky area to carry two spare tires.

Some small settlements have never had an ATM, so be financially prepared for small emergencies that require cash. You'll find campgrounds on many of these tours, as well as fishing, boating, and hiking trails. Just remember to pack along whatever gear and provisions you'll need to safely enjoy such outdoor opportunities.

Arizona's back country is still unspoiled, so take a few extra moments to leave it that way for the next explorer. Pick up any litter you might spot and bring it out with you. Put out any campfires. For both today and tomorrow, resolve to leave this land better than you found it. Who knows ... you might return to the area!   ⋀⋀

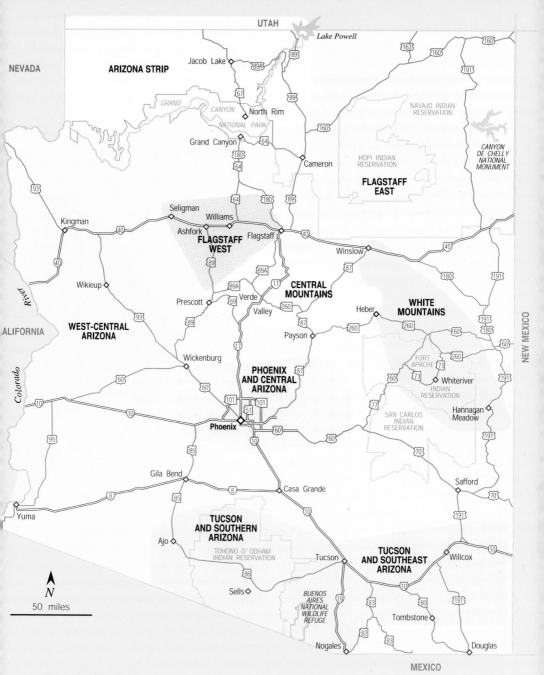

The 9 Regions

A setting sun and a storm cast shadows over the Lost Dutchman State Park on the eastern edge of metropolitan Phoenix.
Randy A. Prentice

Hannagan Meadow, decorated here with woolly mullein and ox-eye daisies, lies along the Coronado Trail in eastern Arizona's White Mountains.
Randy A. Prentice

Rising dramatically from the inner depths of the Grand Canyon, the massive 7,633-foot Wotan's Throne greets the morning light.
Colleen Miniuk-Sperry

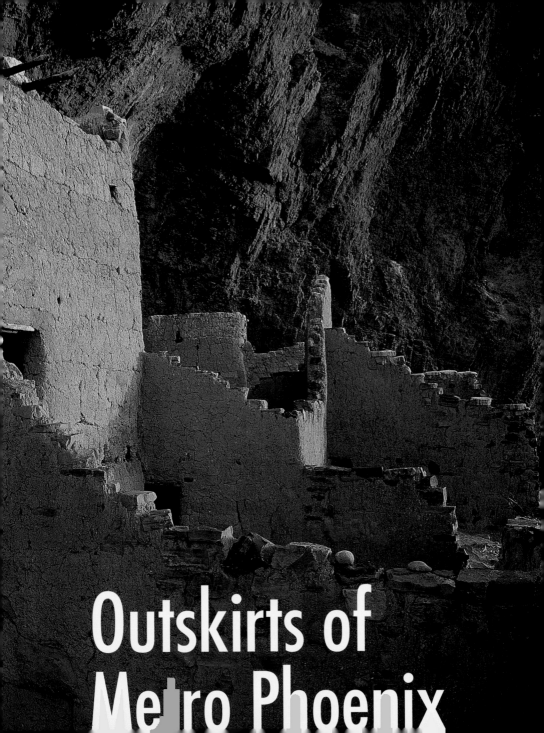

Outskirts of
Metro Phoenix

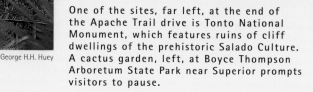

One of the sites, far left, at the end of the Apache Trail drive is Tonto National Monument, which features ruins of cliff dwellings of the prehistoric Salado Culture. A cactus garden, left, at Boyce Thompson Arboretum State Park near Superior prompts visitors to pause.

History and Wilds Are Close By

• Overview

The next time you're crawling in traffic on the Black Canyon or Superstition freeway, refresh yourself with this thought: You don't need to drive a hundred miles or more to become a free-range human. This chapter is devoted to five drives that begin on the edges of metropolitan Phoenix. They'll take you far from the city—in a sense— to areas teeming with history, great scenery, mountains, and desert, while keeping you close to amenities such as restaurants, gas stations and even shopping. Most of the time in most places on these trips your cell phone probably will work.

• The Drives

• Towns and Sites

Morristown, Lake Pleasant, Apache Junction, Theodore Roosevelt Dam, Tonto National Monument, Maricopa, Seven Falls, Middle Verde River, Boyce Thompson Arboretum State Park, Superior, and the Superstition Mountains.

Related to the cardinal but with grayish sides and less red, the pyrrhuloxia is a common Sonoran Desert bird. G.C. Kelley

The springs at Castle Hot Springs produce about 340 gallons of 131-degree mineralized water a minute. Richard K. Webb

Drive 1

Morristown to Castle Hot Springs and Carefree

A desert is by definition a place where rivers often have no surface water, rainfall is scarce, and the fishing is terrible. That's what most people believe, but take our word, it isn't necessarily true, as proven by this "back road" trip through the foothills of the Hieroglyphic Mountains to Castle Hot Springs and on to Carefree.

Although there is a back-road component to this trip, much of it moves over a secondary highway only an hour north of Phoenix through terrain that is unmistakably desert, but one where visitors can swim, fish, sail, jet ski, or simply gawk at the spectacle of a desert lake impounded by a massive dam.

We begin (see Route Finder for trip details) on the western end of State Route 74 just north of Morristown, a community 10 miles southeast of the old gold-mining town of Wickenburg. Back in the days when Castle Hot Springs was an upscale resort, the train would stop at Morristown to unload celebrities, who were met by drivers from the posh health spa in the Hieroglyphic Mountains. Today Morristown functions mainly as a suburb, and the resort, which opened in 1896, now is closed. Fire gutted the resort's main building in 1976, and the property was closed to the public. But you can see it from the Castle Hot Springs Road.

The dirt road leading to Castle Hot Springs, about 23 miles from Morristown, provides a scenic trip, but in wet weather it can be soft in places. The loop road leaves State 74 heading north by northeast. Just before reaching the resort the road turns south by southeast, heading toward Lake Pleasant before returning to 74.

A little more than 2 miles before reaching the eastern junction of Castle Hot Springs Road and State 74, you'll come to an entrance to Lake Pleasant Regional Park.

The lake, created by damming the Agua Fria River, covers 10,000 acres, which may lead strangers to wonder how an arid region can accumulate so much water. Some folks regard the dam and the lake that it created as an engineering marvel, others think of it as a mere anomaly, and still others see it as a blight on the desert.

If you want to see the lake and form an opinion over lunch, it'll cost you admission at the park entrance. You can camp in the rolling desert (though campsites are primitive) or fish for largemouth bass, bluegills, crappie, catfish, and carp. You can sail, wind surf, or motorboat to many scenic bays where varieties of bird life are abundant. The lake is open year-round to all registered watercraft.

It's possible to get a good view of the lake and the surrounding countryside from another vantage, for a small fee, if you tell the ranger at the gate; he will direct you to the New Waddell Dam Scenic Overlook. From the deck at the visitors center, a good portion of the lake and dam are visible. The visitors center contains fine models of the Agua Fria watershed and the dam, as well as artifacts produced by the Hohokam, desert dwellers who inhabited the region between A.D. 700 and 1400. In the desert below the deck, visitors have seen rattlesnakes, coyotes, and entire families of javelinas. From the same perch, sparrow hawks, bald eagles, and red-tailed hawks are sometimes sighted.

Leaving the lake-park, return to Castle Hot Springs Road and head toward Interstate 17, about 15 miles east. Cross the interstate and continue east on State 74 (also called the Carefree Highway)

The desert north of
Castle Hot Springs Road
is laden with saguaro and
prickly pear cacti.

No longer a resort, Castle Hot Springs still maintains the stately appearance it presented to celebrities, politicos, and wealthy hobnobbers a century ago.

Richard K. Webb

toward Carefree, a planned resort community where fancy shops and palatial homes harmonize with the huge buff-colored boulders and steep ledges of the desert mountains. It's only 16 miles from I-17 to Carefree, and all tourist facilities are available along the way.

A couple of miles before reaching Carefree, a well-marked Cave Creek Road on the left (north) side of the highway leads to the historic community of Cave Creek, a former mining camp and ranching center settled in the 1870s. With the phenomenal growth of Phoenix to the south, Cave Creek has evolved into a suburban community. Some shopkeepers there have attempted to recapture the atmosphere of a time when the U.S. Cavalry soldiers camped along Cave Creek and sheep ranchers herded their flocks from the north to James D. Houck's shearing camp.

Returning to the Carefree Highway from Cave Creek, continue east about 2 miles to Scottsdale Road, where Carefree Highway ends. El Pedregal, an attractive shopping center that looks like New Mexico's Taos Pueblo, is directly across the road. During summer, concerts are staged in El Pedregal's amphitheater.

Turn left onto Scottsdale Road and continue a few blocks through Carefree to the intersection of Cave Creek Road. Near the intersection you can visit the K.T. Palmer sundial, billed as the largest in the Western Hemisphere; stroll through Spanish Village, a shopping center built to look like a small town in Spain; or visit the Tonto National Forest Cave Creek ranger station.

If you'd rather get away from upscale shops and restaurants, turn right (east) onto Cave Creek Road and drive a few miles to the Tonto National Forest. Approximately 2 miles from the intersection of Cave Creek and Scottsdale roads, a well-marked paved road on the right leads to Bartlett Lake and Bartlett Dam on the Verde River. From the turnoff, it's a 13-mile drive through pristine desert hills and a couple of dry washes to the lake's campgrounds and picnic areas.

Most of the year, this entire route can be driven in an ordinary passenger car. However, during the summer monsoon rains, the washes that cross the road just before Bartlett Lake will be running swiftly. The force of a flash flood can sweep your car away or pummel you with trees and brush. Under those conditions play it safe: Go back to Carefree and do something else. There'll be plenty of options.

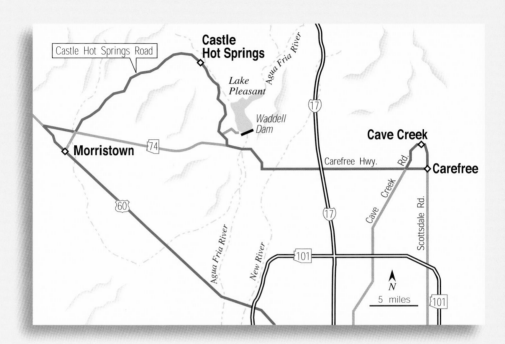

Route Finder

• Start in the western Phoenix metropolitan area and drive northwest on Grand Avenue (U.S. Route 60) to the Morristown area and State Route 74 at about Milepost 120. Note: En route to State 74 you will pass a junction marked Castle Hot Springs Road but continue past it to 74.

• Turn right (east) onto 74 and drive about a mile to the western end of the Castle Hot Springs Road loop and turn left (north by northeast).

• Continue north by northeast on Castle Hot Springs Road for 20 miles. Just after the road turns east, bear right at a fork. About a mile farther, bear right at another fork.

• Continue for 3 more miles to the closed Castle Hot Springs resort, about 23 miles from the starting point.

• From the resort, continue southeast about 9 miles to a guardhouse at a junction with a road leading to Lake Pleasant.

• Leaving Lake Pleasant, return to Castle Hot Springs Road and turn left (south) and continue about 5 miles to State 74.

• Turn left (east) onto 74 and continue for about 24 miles to Cave Creek Road. Here, you can turn left (north) to Cave Creek or continue on the Carefree Highway for a few more miles to Carefree.

Additional information: Lake Pleasant Regional Park, (928) 501-1710; www.maricopa.gov/parks/lake_pleasant. Carefree and Cave Creek, (602) 488-3381; www.carefree-caveceek.com.

The Apache Trail takes drivers past Sonoran Desert scenes punctuated with cactus and buttes. Jerry Sieve

Drive 2

Historic Apache Trail

The essence of Arizona lies along State Route 88, the Apache Trail. All of the state's essential qualities are visible here—desert, mountains, water, sky, past, present and future—between Apache Junction, east of Phoenix, and Theodore Roosevelt Dam.

The 47-mile trip from the start of the Apache Trail in Apache Junction to Roosevelt Dam and State Route 188 takes about two and a half hours due to steep mountain grades, countless curves, brief stops, and stretches of one-way traffic. The last 21 miles are unpaved but well-maintained.

The drive begins in Apache Junction at the junction of Idaho Road and State 88. Mileage references in this article begin at the border of the Tonto National Forest, which is marked with a sign a few miles after you turn onto the Apache Trail. Set your odometer to zero.

Before there was an Apache Trail, which was designated as Arizona's first historic and scenic road, there was the Salt River. Native cultures traveled the shoreline of the Salt River through the Mazatzal Mountains for a thousand years, and the fertile soil in the Salt River Valley enticed the first settlers to restore canals built by the ancient Hohokam people.

Agriculture thrived and the population grew. By 1872, a thousand families lived in the Salt River Valley.

The unpredictable hydrologic cycle of drought and flood kept the Salt uncontrollable. By 1889, the idea of reclamation gained political momentum nationally. Storing runoff for irrigation during dry times would sustain arid lands for agriculture. On June 17, 1902, President Theodore Roosevelt signed into law the National Reclamation Act.

In a narrow gorge below the confluence of Tonto Creek and the Salt River, a three-man survey team selected the site for a stone-masonry dam that would rise 280 feet above bedrock and would eventually cost $10.3 million to construct. The first 6-ton stone was laid on September 20, 1906. Its namesake, former President Roosevelt, dedicated the dam on March 18,1911.

Before the first granite block could be laid, however, a road had to be built that could bring men, equipment, materials and supplies from Mesa and Phoenix to the dam site. Road construction began in 1904, and mule teams started hauling freight wagons a year later. Apache laborers helped build the road, which was dubbed the Apache Trail.

Beginning at the unmarked Apache Gap, at mile 4.6, and going for the next 5 miles, this stretch of the Goldfield Mountains was referred to as the "Little Alps." President Roosevelt said, "The Apache Trail combines the grandeur of the Alps, the glory of the Rockies, and the magnificence of the Grand Canyon, and then adds an indefinable something that none of the others has. To me it is the most awe-inspiring and most sublimely beautiful panorama nature has ever created."

The Four Peaks to the northeast, at an elevation of 7,657 feet, are the source of a vivid purple semi-precious stone called Four Peaks amethyst. Drivers along Apache Trail will first encounter a spirit-lifting view of water at Canyon Lake Vista at mile 6.6. Retained by the completion of the Mormon Flat Dam in 1926, Canyon Lake has a surface area of 950 acres and attracts more than 250,000 visitors annually.

SPEED
25

DO NOT ENTER
WHEN FLOODED

TORTILLA FLAT
U.S. POST OFFICE

Tortilla Flat, with an
ice cream parlor, restaurant,
and a few shops, lies near
the western end of the
Apache Trail.

The wagon trip from Mesa to the dam site took three days. Tortilla Flat was the first overnight stop, 11.3 miles on the odometer. (Fish Creek was the second.) Tortilla Flat today is a friendly place. Although you won't need to stay the night, take the time to enjoy a snack on the saddle stools in the restaurant and ask about the origin of the name.

The paved road ends at 16.7 miles, and the Fish Creek Hill Scenic Vista, uphill 2 more miles, is where you can reflect on the challenges faced by teamsters who moved freight along this road.

As a rule of thumb, one horse or mule can pull 1 ton of freight. While eight- and 12-mule teams were common, 20-horse teams were also used on the Apache Trail. Mules were preferred to horses because of their stamina and their willingness to step over the long chains used to connect them to the freight wagon and water wagon. This ease with the chains was critical on Fish Creek Hill. With its tight turns and steep grade, the middle teams would have to step over the 80-foot chain and walk sideways until the road straightened.

If there's a heaven for turkey vultures, it's in the thermals above Fish Creek. There is no more graceful bird in flight.

At mile 24.5, drivers will first glimpse Apache Lake, which measures 17 miles long and was created by the completion of Horse Mesa Dam in 1927. The road follows the gorge, rising and falling with the contours of the land, sometimes as close as 15 feet from the lake's surface.

The Theodore Roosevelt Dam looms into view at mile 36.5. The masonry face of the original dam was covered with concrete and raised 77 feet in 1996 to accommodate a revised calculation of a "probable maximum flood." A bridge had to be built to divert traffic off the dam. Completed in 1990, the Roosevelt Lake Bridge is a thing of beauty, and ranks as one of the longest two-lane, single-span, steel-arch bridges in North America.

This classic Arizona road trip wouldn't be complete without a visit to the Tonto National Monument, 4 miles southeast of Roosevelt Dam on State Route 188, which leads to Miami and Globe. The visitors center displays cultural artifacts of the ancient agrarian Salado Indian culture that occupied these pueblos. To reach the lower ruins requires a moderately strenuous half-mile uphill hike. The solitude and natural beauty found there proves worth the effort.

—Tom Carpenter

From Tonto National Monument, the scene includes the Sierra Ancha Mountains and Theodore Roosevelt Lake.

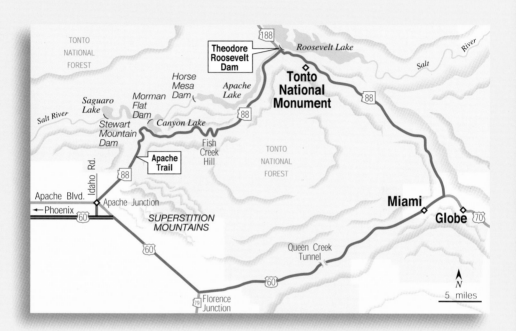

Route Finder

- *From Phoenix head east on U.S. Route 60 (the Superstition Freeway) to Exit 196 (Idaho Road) and turn left (north).*
- *Drive north about 2.2 miles to State Route 88, the Apache Trail. Turn right (northeast).*
- *Drive 47 miles on the Apache Trail to Theodore Roosevelt Dam and State Route 188. Turn right (south) on State 188*
- *Continue on 188 about 4 miles to Tonto National Monument on the right*

- *Leaving the monument, continue south on 188 for about 25 miles to U.S. Route 60 in the Globe-Miami area. Turn right (west) and drive for about 90 minutes to the eastern part of the Phoenix metropolitan area.*

Additional information: Lost Dutchman State Park, (480) 982-4485; www.azstateparks.com/Parks/parkhtml/dutchman.html. Tonto National Monument, (928) 467-224; www.nps.gov/tont. Globe-Miami, (928) 425-4495; www.globemiamichamber.com.

Desert varnish has darkened rocks
in the North Maricopa Mountains
Wilderness. Morey K. Milbradt

Drive 3

An Easy 'Stagecoach' Ride

I stood among the ghosts at the high point of Butterfield Pass running through the billion-year-old rock of the Maricopa Mountains and strained my ears against the silence. Perhaps, if I had listened long enough, I might have heard the stirrings of centuries of stragglers who trekked past this jumble of granite and saguaro cacti years ago.

A high, haunted lament braided the silence of a landscape little changed in 1,000 years of fitful human occupation that included Hohokam Indian hunters, Spanish explorers, trappers, warriors, soldiers, forty-niners, doomed settlers and now a few off-roaders and history buffs. I heard them cry out, although I knew it was only the yearning of the wind through the saguaro spines—the oldest of which may have watched Juan Bautista de Anza and his army of settlers pass through here in 1775 following a new route from Tubac to California.

"So much history," said Elissa, my wife, in a hushed voice.

We had set out from Phoenix that morning for a jaunt on the rutted dirt trail, possible with a high-clearance, two-wheel-drive vehicle. We drove south out of Phoenix on Interstate 10 and headed for the town of Maricopa (see Route Finder for details). The Bureau of Land Management marks the Butterfield road with a sign indicating access into the Sonoran Desert National Monument, which includes the wilderness area.

The road meanders along the base of mountains made of some of the oldest exposed rock in Arizona. The Gila River runs just west of the Maricopas, which accounts for the historic role of Butterfield Pass—the funnel for many centuries of human history.

Hohokam hunters chased bighorn sheep through these mountains until the Indian civilization mysteriously scattered in the 1400s. They regularly traveled the desert highway of the Gila River, which means they journeyed often through this pass to the river some 10 miles west.

In the mid-1770s, Francisco Tomas Garces, an adventurous Franciscan priest, set out from Mission San Xavier del Bac near Tucson to find a route west to missions in California. He traveled through the pass a few times. After establishing friendly relations with the Yuman Indians along the Colorado River, Garces in 1775 led Anza through the pass along with a large group of settlers intent on colonizing the remote outpost of San Francisco. The route was traveled peacefully until misunderstandings and broken promises of gifts to the Indians provoked a Yuman uprising in 1781, which resulted in the murder or enslavement of every Spaniard living along the Colorado River—including Garces.

Only hunting and trading parties of Yumans, Apaches, and Yavapais used the pass extensively for most of the next century as the Spanish Empire faltered. American trappers and trailblazers traveled warily through the pass starting in the 1820s; some sought the route to California and others went to trap beavers on the Gila River.

The 500-man Mormon Battalion labored through the pass in 1846 and camped just outside Butterfield Pass before descending to the Gila River.

The discovery of gold in California set off the flood of prospectors and settlers known as forty-niners—many of whom came through the pass. That included the family of Royce Oatman,

Low-lying clouds form a hazy blue backdrop for saguaro and prickly pear cacti in the Maricopa Mountains.

Golden, morning sunlight warms rocks and a scrubby desert patch
in the North Maricopa Mountains Wilderness.

Morey K. Milbradt

who passed this way in 1851. A few miles beyond the pass, the family was ambushed by Yavapai
Indians, who killed the adults and most of the children, but held as captives two of the teenaged
girls. One of the girls was ransomed some years later, making national headlines.

In1857, John Butterfield signed a six-year, $600,000-per-year contract with the federal
government to run a stagecoach route from St. Louis to San Francisco, right through the same
pass. His six-horse teams relied on stations every 50 miles and could make the 2,800-mile trip in
25 days, despite the constant threat of Indian raids, especially at Apache Pass in the Chiricahuas
and Butterfield Pass in the Maricopas. The stages also had to get past a 40-mile waterless stretch
that ended at the Butterfield Pass. Stage tenders built a cistern just east of the pass and hauled
water up from the Gila River.

With the onset of the Civil War, the federal government abandoned the southerly Butterfield
Stage route, and the pass lapsed into the silence of the wind in the saguaros.

Now, it offers an easy, half-day journey past ghosts and granite. The dirt road straggles
northward along the base of the mountains for some 4.2 miles until it reaches a well-marked
road junction, with a turn to the west leading up into the pass. Today the road into the pass,
which would endanger a passenger car, occasioned only two brief incidents of wheel-spinning in
my two-wheel-drive, high-clearance vehicle. The road rises to the saddle in the heart of the pass,
then drops back down on the other side of the mountains, 6.4 miles of rough travel. The road
comes to a T-intersection at that point. A left turn leads past an old corral where another left,
heading south for 1.4 miles, meets the paved Maricopa Road.

But for me, the high point of the drive was back in the heart of the pass, where I decided to
park and scramble up the steep, granite-ribbed peak for an overview. A vigorous half-hour labor
brought me to the top, with an expansive view in every direction. The peak's view would have
given any raider a good half-day advance warning to prepare for an approaching stagecoach.

I sat for a long time, staring out into the misty distance and listening to the secrets of the
wind. Then I made my way carefully down through the rattle of ancient stones to my own time.

—Peter Aleshire

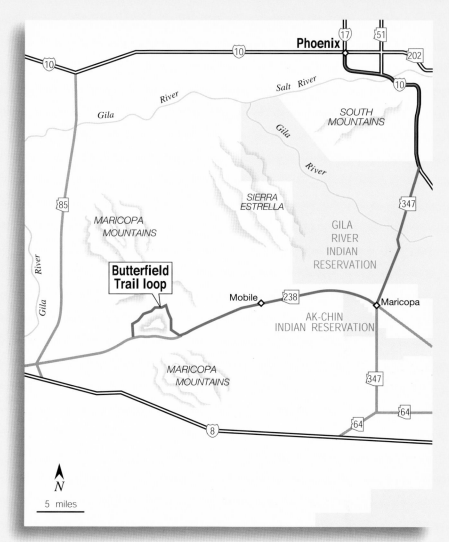

Phoenix

10 — 10 — 202

Salt River

SOUTH MOUNTAINS

River
Gila

Gila

River

85

SIERRA ESTRELLA

347

MARICOPA MOUNTAINS

GILA RIVER INDIAN RESERVATION

Butterfield Trail loop

River

Gila

Mobile — 238 — Maricopa

AK-CHIN INDIAN RESERVATION

MARICOPA MOUNTAINS

347

64

8 — 64 — 64

N

5 miles

Route Finder

• Begin on Interstate 10 south of downtown Phoenix and drive south (freeway signs will indicate you are eastbound because I-10 is an east–west road) to Exit 164, which feeds into Maricopa Road, also known as State Route 347.

• Turn right (southwest) onto Maricopa Road and drive 18 miles to the town of Maricopa at the junction of State Route 238, which also bears the name Maricopa Road. Turn right (west) onto State 238.

• Continue west on State 238 for 14 miles to the community of Mobile. From there, continue on 238 about 14 miles to the turnoff on the right to the Butterfield Trail, a dirt road. The turnoff is just less than a mile west of Milepost 18.

• The Butterfield Trail forms a loop drive for about 12 miles, returning to Maricopa Road.

• From there, turn left (east) to return to the town of Maricopa and I-10.

• Option: From the end of the Butterfield loop, turn right onto Maricopa Road and drive about 10.6 miles to State Route 85 about 3 miles east of Gila Bend and turn right (north) for a 33-mile drive to I-10 west of Phoenix at Exit 112. From there it's 30 miles to central Phoenix.

Additional information: Bureau of land Management, Phoenix Field Office, (623) 580-5500; www.blm.gov/az.

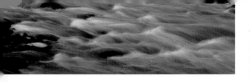

The placid Verde River spills over a rocky decline roughing up the water's mirror-like surface below the western edge of the Mazatzal Mountains. David Elms Jr.

Drive 4

Reaching the Remote Middle Verde River

I sometimes dreamed of the Verde River—especially the parts I'd never seen.

Granted, the Verde isn't famous. A modest, meandering, under-appreciated desert stream, it starts north of Prescott as mountain washes converge in the Chino Valley, and the stream winds in its deferential way east and south through mostly wild and unpopulated territory. Most of the Verde ends up in two reservoirs serving Phoenix, although a final diminished gurgle joins the Gila and Salt rivers on the outskirts of the great sprawl of the Phoenix metropolis. The confluence of these three fitful desert rivers made possible the ancient Hohokam civilization and modern-day Phoenix, which now contains more than half of the state's population.

I had spent many happy hours loafing along the Verde, usually at easily accessible spots below the Horseshoe and Bartlett reservoirs, north of Phoenix, or where it daydreams through the Verde Valley by Cottonwood and Camp Verde. Along those stretches, I'd fallen under its languid spell—its cottonwood and sycamore shadings, its opaque serenity and its wealth of birds and attendant wildlife. I'd also spent time with a fishing pole angling for bass, bluegill, sunfish, or catfish.

But I'd never visited the remote middle stretches of the Verde where an unbowed desert river remains capricious, vital, and so completely unexpected in the arid terrain. So, having no idea how daunting the final approach to the river would be, I resolved to seek access to the 41-mile-long federally designated "wild and scenic" portion of the river running from below Camp Verde to Red Creek, about 12 air miles north of 2,800-acre Horseshoe Dam, which sits at an elevation of 2,043 feet

My journey started at the three-road intersection of Cave Creek Road, Horseshoe Dam Road (sometimes identified as Barlett Dam Road) and Forest Service Road 24 (also called the Seven Springs Road). (See Route Finder for details.)

From Cave Creek Road, I turned left (north) on FR 24. The road initially is paved but quickly gives way to a well-maintained dirt road that climbs and dips through beautiful high-desert country with saguaros, agaves, sun-burnished volcanic outcroppings, and a rolling, jagged view to the far horizon. After 9 miles on FR 24, the road passes through Seven Springs—a delightful, little-known oasis shaded by more leafy cottonwoods and sycamores. Hopis have always made kachina dolls from the roots of the cottonwood, perhaps because their gnarled shapes and the green exuberance of the tree's canopy against the harsh desert seem like a prayer. Underground rock formations force water to the surface along this segment of Seven Springs Wash, nourishing gigantic trees that provide cool picnicking and camping spots in the heat of summer.

After passing Seven Springs, FR 24 narrows and develops rough patches that favor a high-clearance vehicle. At about 14 miles from the springs, the road runs along a canyon harboring an intermittent stream and more lush cottonwoods and sycamores, now joined by ash and mesquite trees. I pulled off to one side and climbed down under the trees for lunch, attended by the cheerful trickle of water.

North of Seven Springs, FR 24 encounters FR 269, which leads westward for about 20 miles to Bloody Basin and Interstate 17's Exit 259. The 24-269 intersection is 26 miles from the pavement's end.

Rising over a ridge, the sun casts a silvery glow on a small rapid and pool in the Verde River.

I turned right (east) on 269 for a slow and rugged 12-mile drive to the Verde River. The road starts down into the jagged valley the patient Verde has created, crossing beautiful little canyons with intermittent streams. This section of the route is close kin to off-road driving. It requires a high-clearance, four-wheel-drive vehicle that can do some boulder climbing—and a lot of patience. The road gets rougher and rockier as it progresses toward the river, but it offers a spectacular view of the Verde and the rows of jagged mountain ranges that surround it.

After picking my way down the road, I came at last to the Verde, an extravagant miracle in the bristling landscape. A sturdy suspension bridge spans the 40-yard-wide stream. The road ends there, but a trail continues on the other side.

Dusty, well-jounced, and hot from the long day on dirt roads, I wasted no time in peeling off my clothes and plunging into the Verde. I suspect I've been at some point in my life submerged in wetter, more refreshing water—but I can't recall the time. All I clearly remember is floating along in the Verde's gentle current around a bend, close up against a rock wall, and beneath the implausible outline of Sheep Bridge—utterly content.

I can't say exactly how long I lounged in the hot sand on the river's bank. I know it was long enough to see a bald eagle sweep overhead on a down-canyon patrol—and long enough after that to watch a summer tanager flit through the upper branches of a cottonwood, so vivid and red it nearly stopped my heart.

And so now when I dream of the Verde River, it's in color.

—Peter Aleshire

Forest Service Road 269 winds across the desert in the Tonto National Forest northeast of metropolitan Phoenix to the Verde River.

David Elms Jr.

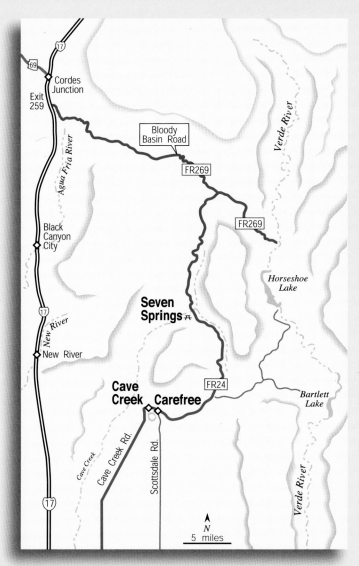

Route Finder

• From metro Phoenix, take Cave Creek Road northeast to Forest Service Road 24. Handy access to Cave Creek Road includes:

• State Loop 101's Exit 28, where you turn north onto Cave Creek Road and continue to FR 24.

• Interstate 17's Exit 223, where you turn right (east) onto the Carefree Highway and go about 14 miles to Cave Creek Road and turn left and continue to FR 24.

• Scottsdale Road or Pima Road north to Cave Creek Road, where you turn right (east) and continue to FR 24.

• At the intersection of Cave Creek Road and FR 24, turn left (north).

• After about 9 miles, you'll reach Seven Springs. Continue for 17 more miles on FR 24 to Forest Service Road 269. Turn right (east).

• Take FR 269 for 12 miles to the Verde River.

• Leaving the Verde River, backtrack on FR 269 to FR 24 and continue west on 269 (Bloody Basin Road) for 27 miles to Interstate 17 (Milepost 259). Turn left for a return to Phoenix.

Additional Information: Tonto National Forest, Cave Creek Ranger District, (480) 595-3300; www.fs.fed. us/r3/tonto/contact/districts.shtml#one.

Spiky hedgehog cactus and rose-purple owl clover, left, share space along Queen Valley Road in the spring. Jeff Snyder

Drive 5

Hunting Wildflowers in the Superstitions

I am addicted to wildflowers, especially poppies, and I have heard that in a good wildflower year, a route beginning on Queen Valley Road and winding 33.5 miles through the Superstition Mountains east of Phoenix can yield an effusion of flowers.

The Superstitions seem an unlikely setting for delicate poppies. It's a tormented landscape of hell-fired rock, fit to dumbfound Dante. But that's precisely what makes the anticipation so delicious, knowing hidden poppy seeds can nurture their luminous orange dreams of spring through decades of drought.

I cannot resist the gamble on a back road ramble to search for wildflowers, which in a dry year is like what wise men say about second marriages—the triumph of hope over experience.

So I lure Elissa, my wife, to join me, promising an easy day trip with potential flower sightings. We drive east from Phoenix on U.S. Route 60 past Florence Junction to Queen Valley Road (see Route

Forest Service Road 172 winds through rugged Hewitt Canyon, making its way up the southern slopes of the Superstition Mountains.
Morey K. Milbradt

Finder for details) and then a medley of Forest Service roads, first Hewitt Station Road (FR 357) and then FR 172, 172A and 650.

The route begins in a typical Superstition landscape, dominated by saguaro cacti. No wildflowers worth mentioning so far, just forgotten scatters of blooms.

Still, I am impressed by the riot of saguaros. They live for 200 or more years and can stash tons of water in their pleated trunks. They provide shelter for birds and food for the whole neighborhood, not to mention the mild, sweet wine made from the fruit essential to the ceremonies of several desert Indian tribes. The saguaros soon assuage my grief for the sparse wildflowers.

When we turned left from Hewitt Station Road onto clearly marked FR 172, a sign directed us to Woodbury (11 miles) and Roger's Trough (12 miles). If we'd continued east on Hewitt Station Road, we would have gone straight back to U.S. 60.

FR 172 quickly crosses Queen Creek, which flows intermittently, and narrows and roughens, but remains no challenge for my high-clearance, two-wheel-drive vehicle. The scenery gets steadily better, a deep desert treasure barely an hour's drive from the nation's fifth largest city.

The road soon drops into a narrow, beautiful canyon, with a sculpted layer of light, fused volcanic ash running like a daydream through the iron-dark lava and basalt. In the tight throat of the canyon, at about 8.4 miles from U.S. 60, we get out to look around.

I immediately start picking up heavy mica-rich rocks, thinking of the legend of the Lost Dutchman, whose hidden gold mine made the Superstitions famous. Reportedly, several people ended up dead after following Jacob Waltz into the mountains to steal the secret of his mine. Certainly, many people have died since in fruitless searches, and the legend spurred at least one

documented shooting war between rival gangs of prospectors. So I am seriously digging these rocks in the grip of a Dutchman moment.

"Oh, look," whispers Elissa.

Perched on a sloping slab 100 feet up the canyon wall, a female desert bighorn sheep watches us dubiously. She's perfect, a molded mass of muscle. Exquisitely adapted to the desert, bighorns can go several days without water, even during the summer. Poised on shock-absorber joints, they can walk a 2-inch-wide ledge, run up a cliff at 15 mph, and clear a 20-foot horizontal jump.

Bighorns have sustained and fascinated human beings here for a millennium. Spanish explorers reported finding heaps of up to 100,000 horns left behind by ancient hunters along the Gila River, reportedly to invoke the bighorn's supernatural link to the winds that bring vital rains. But the miners hunted them, and domestic sheep and goats infected them until only scattered herds along the Colorado River survived. In the past half-century, the Arizona Game and Fish Department has used those herds' sheep to repopulate various areas, including the Superstitions.

So we sit for half an hour in rapt attention, watching this gift of the wind. Finally, she disappears into a side canyon after scrambling up a 50-foot cliff face where I can scarcely see a foothold. We climb back into the car, wobbly with wonder.

The road struggles up and out of the canyon, past a small, rare volcanic arch and on through bristles of saguaros and ocotillos. Soon, it rises past the 3,500-foot-high, frost-enforced limit of the saguaros' range and into piñon pines and juniper trees, offering sweeping views in the process.

As the road becomes narrower, steeper, and rockier, Elissa and I leave the land of the passenger car behind, and I worry that we'll soon find ourselves marooned in the rugged land of the four-wheel drive.

We come finally to an unmarked T intersection at 18.4 miles and I bear right onto Forest Service Road 650, ever so slightly rattled by the elevation gain and the tenuous road. Elissa remains cheerful, but makes note of my long pause, agitated map shuffling and the fall of the gas gauge to well below a quarter tank.

A few miles later, I smell tortured rubber. Getting out, I discover a flat tire that, while I worried about other things, I've driven past recognition. So I change the tire, nearly lost and out of gas, but still impressed with the panoramic view as the hollows fill with shadow and the long last light red shifts on its trip through the atmosphere.

Fortunately, the flat tire is the final problem of the day. We roll on down the unmarked road toward the highway. The road gets so narrow and steep we have to back up to inch around the switchbacks. Another blessing: Had I done the loop in the opposite direction, I doubt I could have gotten up this grade without four-wheel drive.

At the bottom of the hill, two jaunty roadrunners watch us pass with amused contempt. I'm happy to see them. I have a private superstition that the editor will like any story based on a trip during which I have seen a roadrunner.

Some 34 miles after our start, we end up back on U.S. 60 at the junction of Happy Camp and Hewitt Station roads, close by the entrance to the Boyce Thompson Arboretum. We're running on gas fumes, but a few miles to the east stands Superior, where we can fill up and get a cold drink.

I realize suddenly that I have forgotten all about the scattered wildflowers, what with the saguaros, the bighorn, the flat tire and the roadrunners. But giving yourself to the day is like praying: You're better off listening than asking.

— Peter Aleshire

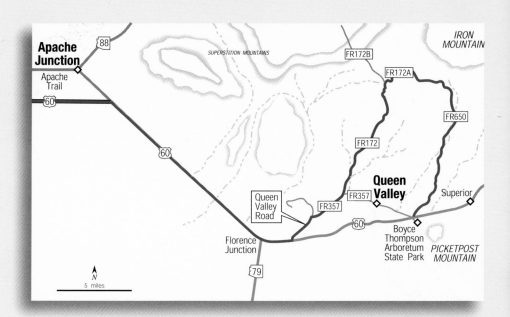

Route Finder

• Begin in Phoenix and head east on U.S. Route 60 (the Superstition Freeway) to Florence Junction, the intersection of U.S. 60 and State Route 79.

• Bear left at the junction and continue for 3 miles on U.S. 60 to the junction of Queen Valley Road and turn left (north).

• Drive 1.6 miles on Queen Valley Road; veer right onto Hewitt Station Road, also called Forest Service Road 357.

• Continue on FR 357 for 3 miles to FR 172; turn left (north). The road soon crosses Queen Creek.

• In less than a mile, bear right at an unmarked junction.

• Continue north and northeast on FR 172 for 8 miles to the junction of FR 172A. Bear right onto 172A.

• Continue on 172A for 6 miles to Forest Service Road 650, also called Happy Camp Road.

• Continue for about 15.6 miles on FR 650 to U.S. 60.

Additional information: Tonto National Forest, Mesa Ranger District, (928) 402-6200, www.fs.fed.us/r3/tonto/contact/districts.shtml#three. Boyce Thompson Arboretum State Park, (520) 689-2811; www.azstateparks.com/Parks/parkhtml/boyce.html. Superior, (520) 689-0200; www.superiorazchamber.net

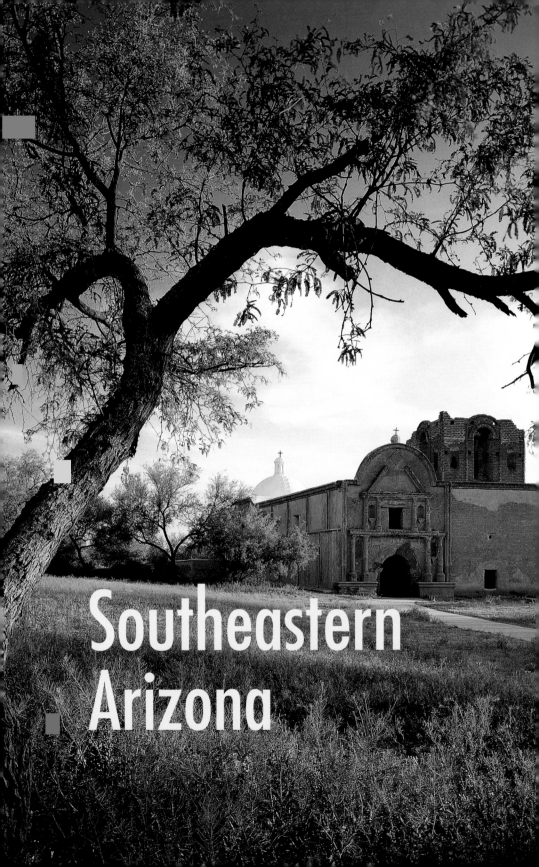

Southeastern Arizona

The Spanish padre Eusebio Francisco Kino established Mission San José de Tumacacori, far left, in 1692. Now, it's a national historical park south of Tucson. Left, visitors view food at a Spanish colonial re-enactment at Tubac Presidio State Historic Park.

Edward McCain

Traversing the High Desert

• Overview

The back roads in southeastern Arizona traverse the high desert. The routes provide good opportunities to see what the term "sky island" means. Broad mountain ranges rise dramatically above the desert floor. Kartchner Caverns State Park at Benson is a stunning limestone cave and Arizona's newest state park. Tombstone, southeast of Benson, provides a glimpse into the Arizona of 1880. The former copper mining town of Bisbee retains a turn-of-the-century ambience. Great hiking and birding areas are abundant.

• The Drives

• Towns and Sites

Tucson, Aravaipa Canyon, Benson, Bisbee, Bowie, Cochise Stronghold, Dragoon Mountains, Fort Bowie, Hot Well Dunes Recreation Area, Kartchner Caverns State Park, Klondyke, Safford, San Pedro Valley, and Tombstone.

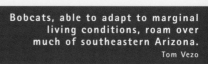

Bobcats, able to adapt to marginal living conditions, roam over much of southeastern Arizona.
Tom Vezo

In some ways, not much has changed in southeastern Arizona since J. Ross Browne dipped a toe in this terrain in 1864. Brown was a journalist from California who came to Arizona to write about the area for *Harper's Magazine*. Recalling his feelings as he crossed the Colorado River into Arizona Territory, he wrote:

"I was now on the borders of a region in which the wildest romance was strangely mingled with the most startling reality. Each day of our sojourn brought with it some fabulous story of discovery or some tragic narrative of suffering and death."

Compared to most places in the United States, southeastern Arizona remains undeveloped. In most of the many mountain ranges that rise above the Sonoran Desert, you can still hike for days or weeks without encountering another person. Browne wryly noted that this terrain had some "peculiar charms," and he listed them: "Burning deserts, dried rivers, rattlesnakes, scorpions ... Apaches." He left out black widows, kissing bugs, ticks, wolf spiders, and many other critters in the food chain.

While the character of the land is not radically different from what it was in Browne's day, there have been some significant changes. The Apaches, for example, have not been a threat to anyone's scalp since 1886, when Geronimo surrendered in Skeleton Canyon, northeast of Douglas. Browne was right about the creepy crawlies. Snakes and scorpions still call this place home, and if you're wandering the desert in the warmer months, exercise caution.

Browne might be surprised to find that the landscape around southern Arizona that he described hasn't changed much in a hundred years, but he'd undoubtedly be puzzled to learn that the cattle and mining operations that dominated the region in his day have now been overshadowed by something called ecotourism.

Ecotourism is the latest stage in the backpacking craze that swept the West in the 1970s. Many people who were frugal backpackers then are still interested in ecology, the outdoors, and nature in general, but now they carry their gear from high-priced outfitters in a $30,000 pickup truck with a $10,000 camper mounted in the bed.

Partly because of the interests of these travelers and partly because of the efforts of various federal agencies and environmental organizations, southeastern Arizona has emerged in recent decades as an enormous outdoor recreation area.

Nowadays, areas that were relatively primitive and offered little in the way of civilized accommodations even 30 years ago have evolved into comfortable and entertaining tourist destinations. As a result, a wide range of experiences—from rough and primitive, knee-wrenching backpacking trips to gentle, luxurious bird-watching resorts—are available.

The golden hue of Fremont cottonwood trees means fall is in session along the upper San Pedro River south of the Old West town of Charleston.

Tubac, some 45 miles south of Tucson, is a prime example of an area that was desiccated and vacant in Browne's day but now is a thriving art colony with expensive homes, restaurants with trendy menus, a state park, and a wonderful new trail. When Browne got to Tubac in 1864, he wrote, "There was not a living soul to be found as we approached. The old Plaza was knee-deep with weeds and grass. All around were adobe houses with the roofs fallen in and the walls crumbling to ruin."

In recent years, one of those areas knee-deep in weeds attracted the attention of a bunch of volunteers. These workers converted a strip along the Santa Cruz River to a picturesque trail linking the old Spanish presidio at Tubac with the ruins of Tumacacori Mission some 5 miles to the south.

Incorporated into as the Anza National Historic Trail, the 4.5-mile path along the grassy banks of the Santa Cruz begins directly south of the Tubac Presidio state park parking lot. It meanders through the remnants of some colonial foundations that are still being excavated, skirts a huge meadow that once was a racetrack, and crisscrosses the river several times before reaching Tumacacori.

History, a potentially boring subject, appeals a little more in southern Arizona than elsewhere because features like the Anza Trail provide physical links to the three cultures that shaped the region's character. Southern Arizona was first inhabited by Indians, later by Spaniards and Mexicans, and more recently by English-speaking settlers. Both the terrain and the architecture of the towns in the region retain the ambience created by these cultures. Tucson, the largest city in southeastern Arizona, reflects this past. The city was a Mexican town until it became part of the United States in 1854, and today, with a population of around 406,000, the city remains more than 50 percent Hispanic.

There are several other spots in southeastern Arizona, aside from major tourist destinations like Tombstone, where the past is an integral part of the present. For example, the remains of prehistoric elephants called mammoths, killed some 11,000 years ago, were found at two Paleolithic sites near Sierra Vista. Both places, Murray Springs and Lehner Mammoth Kill Site, are part of the San Pedro National Riparian Conservation Area, a giant nature preserve that straddles the San Pedro River from a point just south of St. David all the way to the Mexico border east and south of Sierra Vista. Stop at the riparian area's visitor center on State Route 90 about 10 miles east of Sierra Vista if you want to visit the archaeological sites.

There are reminders of southeastern Arizona's more recent prehistoric past along the routes described below. Some of these spots—among them small cliff dwellings and petroglyph sites in Aravaipa Canyon—are highly vulnerable to vandals because they're in remote, undeveloped, and, for the most part, unmonitored locations. As a result, specific directions to these sensitive spots have been left out of the route descriptions. Those interested in more information can inquire at the federal Bureau of Land Management's Safford District Office.

One of the most poignant and evocative sites in this end of the state is a cemetery near Klondyke where members of the Power family—nearly all of whom died unnatural deaths—are buried. Because you'll need to go through private property to get to the cemetery, it's advisable to inquire for directions at the Klondyke Store or at the BLM office when you're in the area.

Two of the men buried in that cemetery are Tom and John Power, whose fate has been the subject of at least two books and numerous newspaper and magazine articles. In 1918, when the Power brothers were in their 20s, they and their father, Jeff ("Old Man Power") were involved in a shootout with law enforcement officials at their mine in the Galiuro Mountains near Klondyke.

On the morning of February 10, 1918, four lawmen rode up to Old Man Power's cabin to arrest his sons for evading the draft. World War I could have been as remote as life on another planet, but John and Tom Power were eligible for the draft. Old Man Power didn't think his sons should have to fight in any war; he never bothered anybody in town, he figured, so no one in town should bother him. The government did not agree with that viewpoint.

A historic ranch building restored by the Friends of the San Pedro River, San Pedro House now serves as bookstore and gift shop in the San Pedro Riparian National Conservation Area.

Dave Bly

On that crisp morning in 1918, lawmen shot and killed Old Man Power in the doorway of his cabin. He did have his hands up, as his gravestone says, but lawmen thought they were up because he was reaching for a gun. When the shooting ended, three of the four lawmen, as well as Old Man Power, lay dead. John and Tom Power, guided by Tom Sisson, who lived with the family, fled their cabin site in Rattlesnake Canyon, rode south through the Chiricahua Mountains, and eventually escaped into Mexico. The law subsequently captured them in Sonora and sentenced them to life in the state prison at Florence.

Sisson died in prison in 1957. John and Tom Power each served 42 years in state prison before they were paroled in 1960. In 1969, Gov. Jack Williams signed a full and unconditional pardon for them. In 1970, when he was 77 years old, Tom Power voted for the first time in his life. The next day, on his brother's 79th birthday, Tom had a heart attack and died. In 1976, John Power was found dead in his bed in a trailer behind the Klondyke Store. He was 84 years old.

Today, all of them (except Sisson) lie buried on a hill roughly a half-mile southeast of the Klondyke Store. There are five gravestones, with the following inscriptions:

T. J. Power Sr. [Old Man Power]
"1918 — Shot Down With Hands Up in His Own Door."

T. J. Power [Tom, his son]:
"1894–1970 Poisoned in L.A., Calif., Died at Sunset, Ariz."

John Grant Power [the elder son]:
"Sept. 11, 1892–April 5, 1976 — Rest in Peace."

Roper Lake State Park near Safford provides fishing, camping, and other recreational opportunities in the Mount Graham area south of Safford.

The first permanent white settlement (1752) in what now
is Arizona, Tubac survives as an arts and crafts center with
shops such as this one featuring Mexican pottery.

Edward McCain

Off to the side is the grave of Jeff Power's mother, Martha Jane Power,
always referred to simply as "Granny," whose headstone notes that in 1915
she was "Killed by Runaway Horse and Buggy Accident." A spooked horse had
tossed her from a buckboard near the gate to her home, not far from the hill
where she is buried.

And most mysterious of all, the gravestone of Ola May Power, Old Man
Power's daughter, who died at the age of 23. Her marker says: "O.M. Power –
1917 – Poisoned by Unknown Person." The doctor who examined Ola's body
found she had some vertebrae dislocated in her neck, and that she was black
from the chest up. No one ever established the exact cause of death.

So, once again, J. Ross Browne can be admired for his prescient observations.
At the end of his 1864 journey through southeastern Arizona, Browne came to
the conclusion that this terrain was "a paradise of devils," a place populated
by "gamblers, horse thieves, murderers, and vagrant politicians." He had not
anticipated anything as bizarre as the Power Brothers tragedy, partly, perhaps,
because he was an optimist. Browne figured that if the Apaches could be subdued
and the laws of the country enforced, mines could be developed and southern
Arizona would become some sort of capitalist Mecca.

Never did he guess that birds, trees, and a few quaint buildings in decaying
mining towns would replace southeastern Arizona's silver and copper mines as
the area's chief attractions.   AH

Before dawn, a street in Tombstone, the town "too tough to die," lies in shadowy emptiness. Gunfight re-enactments later in the day will fill the street. Laurence Parent

Drive 1

Tombstone to Council Rock

Almost any place you go in southeastern Arizona, you can be confident that Apaches were there before you. The route from Tombstone to Council Rock is particularly evocative. It ends on a hill where prehistoric Indians etched symbols in the side of a giant boulder. Council Rock, as the site is known, was probably a place where Apaches also gathered for meetings. The site is within a stone's throw of the boulder-strewn clearing where the fierce and charismatic Apache leader, Cochise, finally made peace with the white men.

This excursion is particularly good for those who have a limited amount of time for exploring. The trip can easily be done in a morning and it can be combined with standard tourist fare in Tombstone, the once raucous silver mining camp that is now a national historic landmark and one of Arizona's most popular tourist attractions.

Begin your journey to Council Rock at Tombstone's City Hall, about 75 miles southeast of Tucson (see Route Finder for details).

Remember that for this trip you'll need a high-clearance vehicle, but not four-wheel drive. From City Hall, head west and north on State Route 80, as though you were going to Tucson. Within a few miles, in the distance in front of you, the sandcastle formations of the Dragoon Mountains form a jagged line against the horizon. For the first 10 or so miles, the road is wide and relatively smooth. Then the road gets narrower and rougher, and the roads become like a

Rockfellow Dome, a granite formation in the Dragoon Mountains, is a significant landmark in Cochise Stronghold, named after the famed Apache chieftain.

Tom Danielsen

Blooming soap tree yucca flourish in the desert area around Council Rock.

Granite domes, boulders, and scrub oak trees are
commonplace in the Dragoon Mountains.

Tom Danielsen

mild roller coaster in the high desert—a little up, a little down, but nothing scary. As you get closer to the crags and cliffs of the Dragoons, the vegetation turns to mesquite and oak trees and tall wild grasses.

In places a dirt road, though narrow, will appear so smooth that you may be tempted to drive faster. Resist. The route is full of surprises in the form of unexpected ruts and abrupt channels where summer rains have created deep ridges. Go slowly, and you won't have any problems. Go fast and you could end up with $500 worth of front-end repairs.

The final road you take to Council Rock is less than a mile but very narrow and badly rutted and high centered in places. It's easy to get around the roughest spots, but exercise caution. At drive's end, a foot trail leads about a quarter-mile to the top of a hill where enormous boulders lean against each other at precarious angles. Look for the sign that talks about the petroglyphs in the area. It's about 10 feet away from a boulder covered with images etched by prehistoric Indians.

It's hard to find a prettier view of the San Pedro Valley than the one from this hilltop. If it's winter, you'll take unforgettable photographs of the Huachuca Mountains, near Sierra Vista, covered in snow.

On October 12, 1872, in a clearing near the mouth of West Stronghold Canyon (slightly north of Council Rock), Cochise met with Gen. Oliver Otis Howard and agreed to make peace. In 1998, a group of Chiricahua Apaches, who now live on the Mescalero Apache Indian Reservation in New Mexico, returned to this spot for a visit arranged by friends and historians in Tucson.

Berle Kanseah, a Chiricahua Apache who had heard about the site from his ancestors but had never visited it, looked around and remarked, "If only the rocks could talk!"

You may feel the same way. The area around Council Rock and West Stronghold Canyon still has the feel of the 19th century, though the Apaches are long gone.

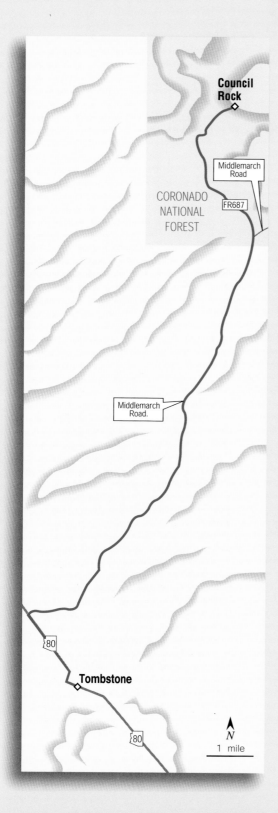

Council
Rock

Middlemarch
Road

CORONADO
NATIONAL
FOREST

FR687

Middlemarch
Road.

80

Tombstone

80

N
1 mile

Route Finder

• *Begin at Tombstone's City Hall, 315 E. Fremont St., and head west and north on State Route 80, which is Fremont Street.*

• *Go 2 miles to Middlemarch Road and turn right (east).*

• *Drive 10 miles on Middlemarch Road, then turn left (north) onto Forest Service Road 687, heading toward West Stronghold. (A sign at the junction says that Middlemarch Pass and Pearce are straight ahead.)*

• *Continue on FR 687 past several junctions with other Forest Service roads for 6.8 miles to FR 687K and turn right.*

• *In less than a mile, 687K leads to a trailhead.*

Additional information: Tombstone attractions, (520) 457-3929; www.tombstone.org. Coronado National Forest, Sierra Vista Ranger District, (520) 378-0311; www.fs.fed.us/r3/coronado/forest/contact/contact.shtml

Distinctive rock formations define the Chiricahua National Monument south of Fort Bowie. Tom Danielsen

Drive 2

Safford to Fort Bowie via Hot Well Dunes

Here's your chance to get into hot water without getting into trouble. On this obscure route from Safford to Fort Bowie, you can stop at a Bureau of Land Management Recreation Area where there is a mineral hot spring captured in two inviting hot tubs. The place is called Hot Well Dunes. You can camp there and soak until you've got more wrinkles than an old prospector.

Begin in Safford and drive through Solomon to a road that moves through a flat, desert terrain dominated by creosote bushes. After you turn off the paved highway onto a dirt road you'll see a massive, green wall off to you right. That's the Pinaleno Mountains in the Coronado National Forest. As soon as you get on the dirt road, there is a sign listing Hot Well Dunes Recreation Area as 25 miles away.

At the recreation area, which charges a daily fee, there are campsites and undeveloped camping areas, two hot tubs, and a wading area for children. If you have an ATV, there are 2,000 acres of powdery sand dunes where you can play. Or you can fish in ponds.

An oil drilling crew in 1928 discovered the thermal hot spring in the dunes. All the grinding and pumping did not produce a pint of oil, but it did bring thousands of gallons of very hot water to the surface of the parched desert.

After Hot Well Dunes, the next stop is the hamlet of Bowie. Then on to Fort Bowie National Historic Site.

In the 19th century, the route through Apache Pass would have been used frequently by the Apache warriors Geronimo, Mangas Coloradas, and his famous son-in-law, Cochise. It was also the preferred route for stagecoaches and mail carriers traveling from the San Simon Valley, in which Bowie is a dot, westward to the Sulphur Springs Valley, in which Willcox sits. For a long time, anybody who wasn't an Apache in southeastern Arizona needed protection against Indian attacks, and that explains why the Army built Fort Bowie.

Fort Bowie is reached by a beautiful 1.5-mile foot trail. If you're disabled, you can call ahead and drive in on a dirt road east of the pass, but other visitors must park at the top of the pass and hike in.

Peter Noebels

A mano and metate for grinding corn and grains sit in front of a re-created Apache wickiup.

Now a ruin, Fort Bowie was a major installation during the Apache Wars in the 1860s.

The stone foundation, foreground, of Fort Bowie's laundry
is near the remains of enlisted men's barracks.

Peter Noebels

One of the nicest things about
this walk is that anyone can now
confidently set out knowing they will
not be attacked. In the 1860s, you
couldn't be so sure.

Apache Pass was one of the
easiest places in southeastern Arizona
to get killed because it contained one
of the rarest of desert ingredients—a
reliable source of water, therefore life.
Life for the Apaches who had lived
there hundreds of years, and life for
white settlers pushing westward.

After you leave Fort Bowie,
spend some time in Willcox, which
has several attractions for Western
enthusiasts, including the Rex Allen
Cowboy Museum and Museum of the
Southwest, which has a visitors center
full of information for travelers. Allen
was born in Willcox and became one
of the silver screen's most popular
Western actors and singers more than
a half-century ago.

Peter Noebels

What's left of a 19th-century
freight wagon rests near the stone
wall of the fort's corral.

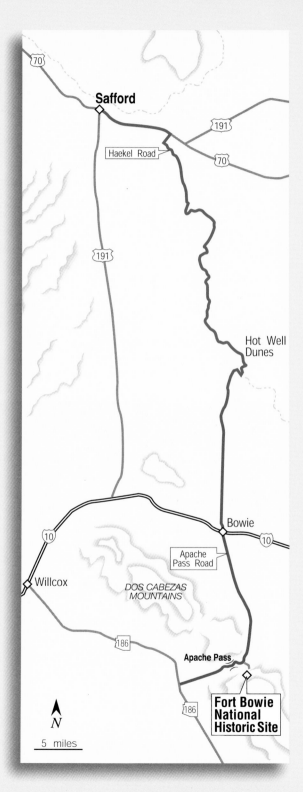

Route Finder

• *Begin in Safford on Thatcher Road at the intersection of U.S. Route 191 and U.S. Route 70.*

• *Drive about 9 miles east on the combined 191-70 through Solomon to Haekel Road and turn right (south). The turnoff is about a mile before 191 and 70 split.*

• *Continue south on Haekel Road and after a mile bear left at the fork.*

• *Continue south by southeast on Haekel Road, driving past its T-junction with Tanque Road on the right, for an additional 24 miles to the turnoff for Hot Well Dunes. Turn left for a 0.7-mile drive into the recreation area.*

• *Leaving Hot Well Dunes, turn left (south) onto Haekel Road and drive about 9 miles to the junction of Fan Road and turn right (southwest).*

• *Continue on Fan Road for 8 miles to a T-junction with Central Avenue and turn left (south).*

• *Continue on Central for 2 miles into Bowie to East Lawrence Avenue, just across the railroad tracks.*

• *Turn left onto Lawrence and go about two blocks to Apache Pass Road and turn right and follow the sign for Fort Bowie.*

• *About 12 miles south of Bowie, the pavement ends at the bottom of Apache Pass. It's an additional 1.3 miles to the parking area for Fort Bowie National Historic Site.*

• *Leaving the Fort Bowie lot, continue west 8.2 miles to State Route 186 and turn right (north by northwest).*

• *Continue north by northwest on State 186 for 22 miles to Willcox and Interstate 10.*

Additional information: Safford BLM office, (928) 348-4400; www.blm.gov/az/sfo/hot_well/hotwell.htm. Fort Bowie National Historic site, (520) 847-2500; www.nps.gov/fobo. Willcox Museum of the Southwest and visitors center, (520) 384-2272; www.willcoxchamber.com.

The San Pedro conservation area southwest of Willcox adds an incentive to a Willcox–Pima drive. Randy A. Prentice

Drive 3

Willcox to Klondyke to Pima

Don't be deceived. The beginning of the back-road drive that begins at Willcox and heads north to Klondyke and then to near the town of Pima looks uninspiring.

Initially, the landscape is covered with a scattering of rural homes, a few farms, and terrain so flat that each tree stands out as a remarkable object. But in the next 60 or so miles, this terrain will change significantly for the better. Eventually, you'll be in the vicinity of Aravaipa Canyon, one of the most pristine and dramatic natural areas in Arizona.

And then you'll drive by the site of one of Territorial Arizona's most infamous crimes, the Wham military payroll robbery, still clouded by mystery.

This trip begins (see Route Finder for detailed directions) in Willcox at Interstate 10's Exit 340, which feeds into Fort Grant Road and Rex Allen Drive. Turning right at the bottom of the exit ramp takes you into Willcox, where you can visit the Rex Allen Cowboy Museum and Willcox Cowboy Hall of Fame or perhaps the Willcox Playa, an annual gathering place for flocks of sandhill

cranes. Turn left and you're heading north on Fort Grant Road heading for Klondyke. Be aware that Fort Grant is a popular name for roads and sites in this area. There's South Fort Grant Road, Old Fort Grant Road, and North Fort Grant Road. And the fort site itself.

The fort for which the road is named no longer exists, but during the Indian Wars that ended in 1886 it was one of a string of military installations established to subdue the Apaches who dominated and terrorized southern Arizona. Cochise and Geronimo were the two of the most feared Apaches in this area who kept the cavalry troopers on their toes (and often sent them to their graves).

The first 21 miles of this route are paved. The remaining 40 miles are unpaved but generally well graded, and an ordinary sedan will have no trouble covering the distance. Unless it rains or snows, of course, in which case the road will turn slick and provide more adventure than you bargained for.

Originating in Cochise County, the route crosses into Graham County. When you start seeing large apple orchards, you're in Graham County. As you reach Ash Creek Road, note the huge assemblage of greenhouses on your left. A Dutch company named Eurofresh is using hydroponics to grow tomatoes. Millions of tomatoes, from the looks of it.

After a few miles on Ash Creek Road and another turn, the pavement abruptly ends. Soon, you'll pass Bonita School and in the next 6 or 7 miles, the scenery changes dramatically. You'll see panoramic views of the Aravaipa Valley with the Galiuro, Santa Teresa, and Pinaleno Mountains embracing the hilly, high desert terrain. When you're about 23 miles out of Bonita, you'll see a sign where Klondyke Road joins the one you're on. A sign tells you that the community of Klondyke is 7 miles straight ahead and Aravaipa is 20 miles in the same direction. Remember this location: You can take this road on the trip's final leg, but for now continue on to Klondyke.

Hikers can expect to get wet if they want to explore Aravaipa Canyon. Edward McCain

Built by and named after one of the Aravaipa Valley's earliest families, the Salazar Church sits on Aravaipa Road north of Klondyke.

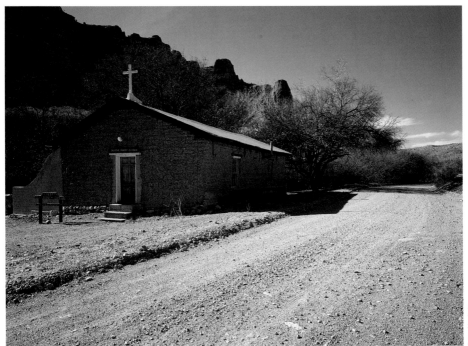

Peter Noebels

Behind the closed Klondyke Store is Horsehead Lodge, where five rooms are available. The federal Bureau of Land Management, which has jurisdiction over much of the land in the area, has an office adjacent to the store building. You can get maps and other information there. If you want to camp, go 1 mile on Fourmile Canyon Road, which is opposite the BLM office. The Fourmile Canyon Recreation Area (a fee is charged) has designated campsites, water, and rest rooms set among junipers and shrubs at the base of the Galiuro Mountains.

The road going past the store leads to a trailhead into the Aravaipa Wilderness Area, but, as of Spring 2007, the road was closed because of a right-of-way dispute.

You can return the way you came, of course, but a good alternative is to drive back toward Bonita for 7 miles and turn left (east by northeast).

About 8 miles along Klondyke Road, the landscape bears some high rocky hills on the right, and a large home sits on a hill on the left. In a cavity between the hills, on May 11, 1889, Maj. Joseph W. Wham, paymaster from nearby Fort Grant, and 12 cavalrymen were stopped by a boulder that apparently had rolled off one of the hills and blocked the path of the stagecoach they were escorting. The stage contained a chest with the military payroll.

Wham's men, members of a black Buffalo Soldiers unit, put aside their rifles and were trying to move the boulder out of the way when a barrage of gunfire rained down from the breastwork of rocks above them. Several of the soldiers were wounded, none fatally. Meanwhile, the coach was robbed. Eventually, nine men from Pima were arrested for the crime and tried. All were acquitted. The loot was never found.

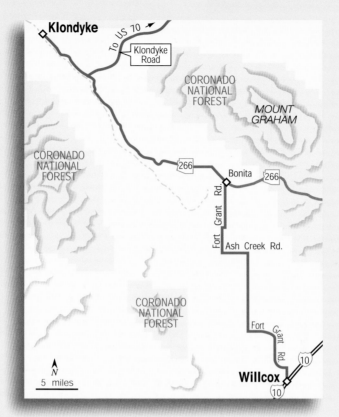

Route Finder

• Begin in Willcox at Interstate 10's Exit 340 and turn left for South Fort Grant Road.

• After about 4 miles, just past Dearing Road, the road you're on starts veering left, changing from northbound to westbound. Bear left where the road forks. Going straight puts you on Old Fort Grant Road.

• Now westbound, continue for about 4 more miles and bend 90 degrees to the right as the road turns north again.

• In about 7.5 miles the road crosses into Graham County. Just before and after this point, some maps list the road you're on as York Ranch Road or Brookerson Road.

• From the county line, continue northbound for 6 more miles and turn left (west) at the stop sign at Ash Creek Road.

• Continue on Ash Creek Road for about 3 miles and turn right (north) at a stop sign, and you're back on Fort Grant Road, the northern version. Pavement ends here.

• Drive north 8.3 miles to a T-junction, just beyond the Bonita School, and turn left. At this point you're at the western end of paved State Route 266 and the start of the Bonita-Klondyke Road (some maps list it as Aravaipa Road). Here, State 266 takes you to the old Fort Grant site (3 miles north) or to U.S. Route 191 (18 miles east). If you want to cut your trip short, go to U.S. 191 and turn right (south). In 17 miles you're back on I-10 at Exit 352, where turning right (west) takes you back to Willcox in 12 miles or Tucson in 93 miles.

• Leaving Bonita on the Bonita-Klondyke (Aravaipa) Road, travel about 23 miles to the junction of Klondyke Road. Going straight ahead brings you to the community of Klondyke in 7 miles.

• Leaving Klondyke, return to the junction listed in the line above and turn left.

• About 8 miles after turning onto Klondyke Road, you'll pass the area where the Wham robbery took place.

• Continue for 16 more miles to U.S. Route 70. Turn right for Pima and Safford and a return to I-10. Turn left for Globe and Phoenix.

Additional information: Bureau of Land Management's Klondyke Ranger Station, (928) 828-3380; www.blm.gov/az/sfo/rec/4mile.htm. For road conditions in the area, call (928) 348-4400. Willcox attractions, (520) 384-2272; www.willcoxchamber.com.

The Black Hills byway winds through sparsely vegetated, rock-strewn hills sprinkled with lava. George Stocking

Drive 4

Black Hills Back Country Byway

Nothing beats a lonesome day on a dirt track through empty hills. Throw in stops for rockhounding, hiking an oak woodland, or dallying by a desert river, and you have a trip along the Black Hills Back Country Byway.

Running for 21 miles between Safford and Clifton, the unpaved byway intersects U.S. Route 191 at both its northern and southern ends (see Route Finder for details). Though the byway itself is in good shape, a four-wheel-drive vehicle is recommended for many of its spur roads.

From the southern access the first stop comes about 3 miles along. Here, the road crests above the Twin C Ranch. It was founded in the late 1880s as a goat ranch, but the land is so dry that every few days the rancher had to herd his animals 6 miles to the Gila River to drink, then back again. The road leads past the ranch to the Black Hills Rockhound Area, popular with collectors of fire agate, a form of silica found only in desert regions of Arizona, southern California, and central Mexico. Fire agate comes in a variety of shapes and colors caused by mineral impurities. Many collectors consider these stones as beautiful as opals, but be prepared to do some digging.

Just ahead of the overlook, above the Twin C, lies a tangle of broken-down timbers—remnants of a platform from which pumice from a 1950s cinder mine was loaded onto trucks for hauling to Safford, where it was made into cinder blocks. A half-mile past the timbers lies the cinder pit, a bank of reddish earth standing in sharp contrast to the surrounding landscape.

Formed by volcanic activity 20 million years ago, the Black Hills' tall, craggy buttes sustain unusual mixtures of grass, sand, and creosote and fields of prickly pear cacti interspersed with black volcanic rock. These old lava flows, mostly andesite, rhyolite, and docite, appear in well-defined falls called talus slopes. From a distance, these look like black water running down the mountains, adding an eerie quality to the terrain that Geronimo crossed on his raids from Mexico into Arizona, and back again. The Apache war leader once said he was never lost until he and other Chiricahua prisoners were shipped to Oklahoma. In that flat Midwest terrain, he was unable to use mountain peaks as markers.

Driving the byway, one can understand what he was talking about. Above the cinder pit, there's a broad sweep of desert to tall mountains on the horizon. The Dos Cabezas Mountains—Spanish for "two heads"—jut into the sky 50 miles away. Another overlook, 3 miles beyond, offers a panorama that includes Mount Graham to the southwest, the Phelps Dodge mining operation to the northeast, and the cliffs of Eagle Creek Canyon to the north. Bring binoculars.

Between Mileposts 17 and 18, the byway crosses a portion of the Gila Box Riparian National Conservation Area, 21,000 acres of creeks and canyons popular with rafters, hikers, and photographers. You can also get there along several four-wheel-drive side roads, including one through Deadman Canyon, which earned its name when a cowboy chasing his horses there found a man's skeleton with a rope around its neck.

Dark Canyon Road, right of the byway at the 10.8-mile mark, is rough, too. But it makes a good hike. It leads into a pretty canyon bordered on the right by white oak and hackberry trees.

Desert plants and water-
loving cottonwood trees share
space along the Gila River.

A half-mile farther, perched on the hillside to the left, stands a tin miner's shed riddled with bullet holes. It looks as if one more shot will bring the whole structure rattling down. But it hangs on, full of mystery in the mountain sunlight.

Prison labor built the byway over six years beginning in 1914. The men worked with blasting powder, picks, and scrapers drawn by mules, and at night they lived in wire enclosures. Three successfully escaped, but Jesus Rodriguez did not. In December 1916, he was killed trying to flee. Two prisoners, including Rodriguez, rest in graves on the west side of the byway near its southern intersection with 191.

The remains of one of these labor camps—a small bake oven and a crumbling concrete bathhouse—stand between Mileposts 16 and 17. From

George Stocking

Prickly pear cacti, barbed-wire fencing, and a weathered sign along the byway "welcome" passersby to Allred's Ranch.

the same headquarters, between 1935 and 1937, Civilian Conservation Corps workers built the stone breastworks that still line hillsides in the area. These spreader dikes were designed to hold back runoff and reduce erosion.

Along the last half of the byway, the startling sight of Phelps Dodge's open-pit copper mine at Morenci dominates the northern horizon, stretching almost 2 miles from rim to rim of the northern horizon.

While chasing Indians in 1865, a Union cavalry troop discovered the first copper traces there. In 1881, Morenci mine owner William Church convinced East Coast merchant Anson Phelps and his sons-in-law, William Dodge and Daniel James, to invest. Their decision paid off in 1884, when demand for copper surged after Thomas Edison's invention of electric light. The hills around Morenci and Clifton turned out to be among the most copper-rich in the world.

Another impressive sight stands at 17.2 miles—the Old Safford Bridge spanning the Gila River. The same prison labor completed this remarkable concrete structure in 1919 at a cost of more than $60,000. The bridge is listed on the National Register of Historic Places.

If you're truly adventurous and have four-wheel drive, try a dip in Gillard Hot Springs on the Gila River. The hottest natural spring in Arizona, it awaits at the end of a 4-mile-long road that begins on the left side of the byway, 2 miles beyond the bridge.

If the Gila's flow runs low enough, exposing the springs, you can scoop out a hole in the sand, mixing river water with 180-degree water from the springs, and enjoy an open-air hot tub.

Underneath the bridge, weekenders launch boats and enjoy picnics. It's also fun to hike along the river or stand on the small bluffs that line its southern bank. Listening to the music of the rushing water while watching a red-tailed hawk soar overhead makes a nice end to my day in a dry land.

—Leo W. Banks

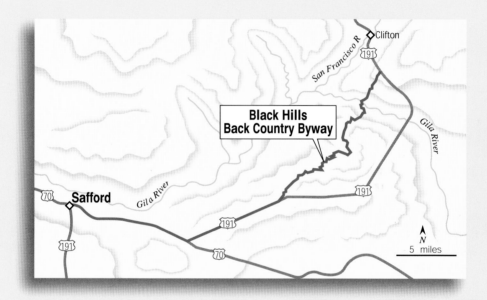

Route Finder

• Begin in Safford at the intersection of U.S. Route 70 and U.S. Route 191.

• Drive east on U.S. 70 (concurrently, you'll be northbound on U.S. 191) for about 10 miles to where the two routes split. Turn left onto 191.

• Go north on 191 for about 10 miles to the junction with Black Hills Back Country Byway on the left.

• Continue on the byway for 21 miles to its northern junction with 191. To return to Safford, turn right. Turn left for Clifton, about 4 miles away.

Additional information: A brochure on the Black Hills Back Country Byway, known as the Old Safford-Clifton Road, is available from the chambers of commerce in both Safford and Clifton, along with an audiocassette on the history and natural features of the Black Hills. Greenlee County Chamber of Commerce, Clifton (928) 865-3313; Graham County Chamber of Commerce, Safford, (928) 428-2511; Bureau of Land Management, Safford Field Office, (928) 348-4400; www.blm. gov/az/ohv/bcb.htm.

Drive 5

Tucson to Total Wreck Mine

Bonner Denton brought his rattling old Jeep to a stop and bounced to his feet next to a barrel cactus ablaze with red blossoms.

"Welcome to beautiful downtown Total Wreck," he called. "To our left you see the local brewery, up here was the butcher shop. ... Quite a place, don't you think?"

We were standing on a path that a generous person might call an unpaved road. To our left and right, the hills were covered with twisted mesquite trees, spiny catclaw bushes, and ripe yucca poles—everything dark green and glistening from the light rain that danced around us.

But the many buildings that once constituted the mining town of Total Wreck were reduced to a few stone walls scattered in the heavy vegetation of the Empire Mountains.

It is difficult to realize, once you're on the spot, that metropolitan Tucson is only some 40 miles to the northwest of this isolated and barely accessible terrain. It takes less than an hour to get from Tucson to the vicinity of Total Wreck; it takes about the same amount of time to go the last five miles on a road that carries a grudge.

It was even more difficult to get to Total Wreck in the 1880s, when the camp was in its heyday, but since there was money to be made there, and little that was much more civilized nearby, many made the journey.

Edward Vail, whose family owned the mine, was one of them. As a young man, he worked as an assayer at Total Wreck. Many years later he wrote: "The Total Wreck was a good little camp, notwithstanding its name, and a very healthy one. ... There were quite a number of prospectors in the Empire District who had located mining claims and did their trading and drinking and gambling there. All towns were wide open at that time, but it was an orderly camp, and to my knowledge no one was ever killed in a gunfight there, though there were several narrow escapes from such tragedies."

Total Wreck would be totally forgotten today were it not for its comical name. There are a couple of variations on the origin of the moniker, but both involve John T. "Jerry" Dillon, a New Mexico cowboy who came to Arizona in 1876. In 1878 he went to work for the Empire Ranch, owned by Walter Vail.

In 1879, riding over the Empire's eastern pasture with Vail and his partner, John Harvey, Dillon pointed to what appeared to be a ragged ridgeline pocked with granite and quartz deposits and said, "The whole damned hill is a total wreck."

As the three rode closer to the outcropping, they noticed that the rock appeared to contain traces of silver. Walter Vail posted location notices on three sites and named one of them Total Wreck.

Nathan Vail, Walter's wealthy uncle in California, financed most of the major development work at the silver mine. In 1880, the Vails secured complete control of the Total Wreck Mining Co. By this time, Dillon had pretty much dropped out of the picture, trading off two-thirds of his interest in the mine for legal services that he and the Vails required when their mining claims were contested. Nathan eventually bought Dillon's remaining stock.

The Total Wreck town site
rested on rolling hills in
the Empire Mountains
southeast of Tucson.

Little is known about the origin and purpose of this
Total Wreck building, which time has ravaged.

W.D. Wray

Before long Dillon was probably cursing the poverty that had forced him to sell his last portion of Total Wreck Mine, which, by the standards of the day, was a total success: from 1879 to 1887, Walter and Nathan Vail netted more than a $500,000 profit from it.

In the tunnels that snaked for miles under the dry desert hills, blasting and hauling were going on 24 hours a day. It didn't take long before the camp became the commercial and social center of the Empire Mining District.

The *Arizona Daily Star* reported on February 13, 1883, that Total Wreck Mine was producing about 70 tons of silver ore per day. "Total Wreck is a thriving village," the newspaper said, "and is daily becoming more important. ... There are five saloons, three stores, one butcher shop, four restaurants, one blacksmith shop, one shoemaker's shop, and eight or 10 Chinese washhouses." Four months later, the *Star* reported three hotels, a lumberyard, and a brewery had been added to the town's skyline.

Historians speculate that at its peak Total Wreck had a population of between 300 and 500. By 1887, however, Total Wreck was nearly abandoned, although sporadic mining operations continued until 1929.

Two things caused the demise of the camp: a diminishing supply of silver-bearing ore and steep declines in the price of silver, which dropped from $1.14 per ounce in 1882 to 94 cents per ounce in 1887, when the Vails closed their mine. Descendants of the Vails donated the abandoned mines and town site to the University of Arizona in 1985, and in 1987 the UofA decided to auction off the property.

Bonner Denton, a UofA chemistry professor who likes to crawl around in caves and old mines, bought a portion of Total Wreck. He thinks of it as a nice place to play, wandering in old mine shafts with an ultraviolet light and watching minerals fluoresce while bats flutter overhead.

Denton owns the mineshaft and knows his way around. Visitors to the area—Total Wreck town site is actually on state land abutting Denton's place—are advised to stay out of abandoned mine shafts, which are extremely dangerous.

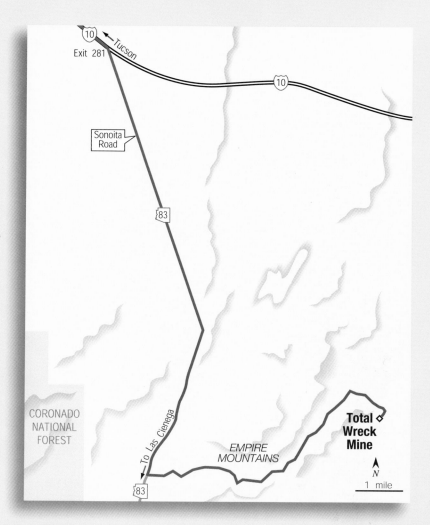

Route Finder

• Begin on Interstate 10 in Tucson and drive about 22.5 miles east to Exit 281 and turn right (south) onto State Route 83, the Sonoita Road.

• About 9 miles south of the interstate turn left onto a dirt road. The turnoff is 0.8 of mile beyond Milepost 50.

• Continue on the dirt road for 2.5 miles to the high part of a saddle. Just beyond, bear left at the fork and continue for 0.75 of a mile and bear right (northeast) at the fork.

• Continue northeast for 2.3 miles to a gate at the bottom of the canyon. Drive through the gate (leaving it open or closed, as you found it) and go 0.1 of a mile and turn right.

• Go 0.3 of a mile to another fork and pass through the gate on the right branch (southeast). In about 0.25 of a mile the foundations of the old Total Wreck stamp mill

will be on the right. At this point you are 6.2 miles from where you left pavement.

• Continue over the hill for 0.6 of a mile, and you will be in the heart of downtown Total Wreck.

• Return the way you came.

• Option: When you reach State 83, turn left and drive about 11 miles to the signed entrance to Las Cienegas Resource Conservation Area. Turn right. Situated among rolling grasslands and woodlands, the conservation is an excellent place to view wildlife, especially birds.

Additional information: Las Cienegas Resource Conservation Area, (520) 258-7200; www.blm.gov/az/nca/lascienegas/lascieneg.htm

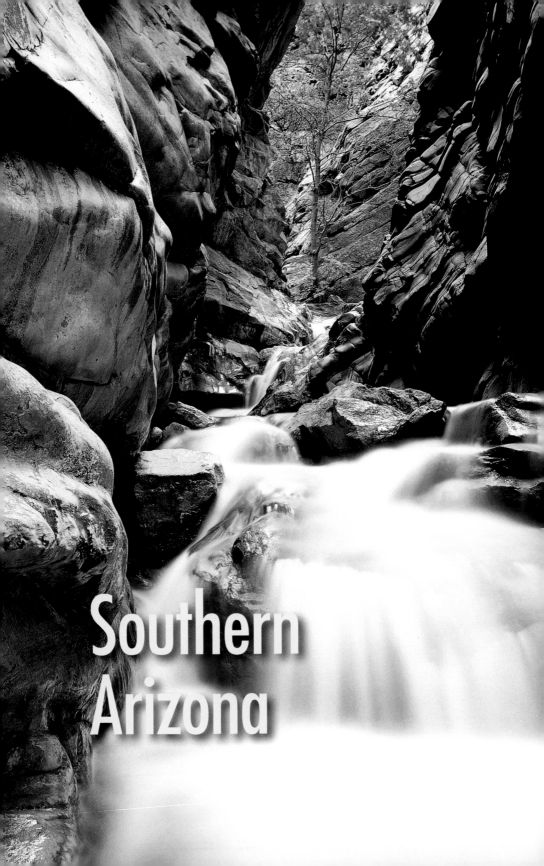

Southern
Arizona

A stream, far left, cascades down
Ramsey Canyon in the Huachuca
Mountains. Prickly pear fruit, left,
"sets fire" to a section of the
Coronado National Forest in August.

Randy A. Prentice

Rolling Desert and Volcanic Mountains

• Overview

The roads described are in the Sonoran Desert, where June
through September are very hot months, but early mornings in
the summer are excellent for bird-watching. Lush gallery forests
can be seen at the Nature Conservancy's Sonoita Creek Sanctuary.
Easy day hikes can be made along the San Pedro River east of
Sierra Vista. Steeper hikes can be made into the pines of the
Huachuca Mountains from Ramsey Canyon. Excellent trails begin
at Madera Canyon in the Santa Rita Mountains.

• The Drives

• Towns and Sites

Tucson, Arizona-Sonora Desert Museum, Green Valley, Happy
Valley, Kentucky Camp, Madera Canyon, Mission San Xavier del
Bac, Nogales, Patagonia-Sonoita Creek Sanctuary, Ramsey Canyon
Preserve, San Pedro Riparian National Conservation Area, Sierra
Vista, Titan Missile Museum, Tohono O'odham Indian Reservation,
Tubac, and Tumacacori National Historic Park.

Jack Dykinga

The mule deer is common in
the Buenos Aires National
Wildlife Refuge. G.C. Kelley

Southern Arizona is physically unlike anyplace else in the United States. It's a spacious landscape of deep shadows and enduring legends, and it's a thirsty terrain of rolling desert and volcanic mountains. It is the land of the lizard, the coyote, the javelina, and the rattlesnake. Its trees are unique and strange: There are giant saguaro cacti, lime green paloverde trees, mesquite trees, and the aptly named ironwood trees, with wood so dense you can sprain your wrists trying to chop it with an axe.

It is a place where rainfall is scarce and unpredictable. Tucson may receive about 12 inches of rainfall a year and some areas just outside the city will get a "drenching" of approximately 14.9 inches, but travel west 40 or 50 miles and that figure drops to 9.9 inches.

The landscape is remarkably deceptive. Maps show a scattering of towns ranging from bustling cities like Tucson to sleepy hamlets like Arivaca. It's easy to get the impression that civilization is never far off, but that's no guarantee of anything. Many of the desert roads and mountain ranges remain rough and in places nearly impenetrable. You can encounter adventure and danger less than 2 miles from paved roads. If you're going to travel off the beaten path, no matter what time of the year, carry a couple of gallons of water per person and be sure your vehicle and tires are in good condition. If you have a cell phone, take it along.

As you wander in this terrain, you'll see that many names reflect the influence of Tohono O'odham Indians, Apaches, Spaniards, and Anglos. The names coincide with the way history unfolded in the part of Arizona closest to the Mexican border.

A little over a hundred years ago, southern Arizona was the region that brought fame to Apache warriors like Cochise and Geronimo and to lawman Wyatt Earp, the star of Tombstone's shoot-out near the O.K. Corral. However, the most important fact of life in southern Arizona is that the region is in the heart of the 119,000-square-mile Sonoran Desert, one of the hottest, driest, and most beautiful of deserts in North America. A major chunk of this desert, a little over 3 million acres, is occupied by the Tohono O'odham Indian Reservation. You can see some of the most scenic parts of the reservation by following the route below to the village of Kaka (which doesn't mean what you think).

No one knows beyond a doubt how long the Tohono O'odham have lived in this terrain. Some scholars think they are descended from the Hohokam, desert dwellers who either left the area or were absorbed into other cultures in the 14th and 15th centuries; others think they migrated northward from Mexico. One thing is certain: They were already well-established in the area long before the Spaniards arrived in the 16th century, and they remain very much at home in a desert that many would consider hopelessly barren.

A ramada on the Mission San Xavier grounds in Tucson provides some shade around the famed "White Dove of the Desert."

Reactions to this strange landscape tend to vary widely. It is surprisingly lush and green, as deserts go, and in a wet year the spring will bring a dazzling carpet of wildflowers; but Spanish explorers, the first Europeans to come here, were looking for gold, not flowers, and they found it a harsh and inhospitable environment. The missionaries who followed them were a bit more stoical and in any case found it fertile ground for making converts. In general, the first Europeans in southern Arizona complained a lot about the hardships the desert and the natives imposed. But the Piman-speaking Indians who preceded them, and who still are there today, relate to this desert with religious depth.

The best way to familiarize yourself with the plants and animals of this landscape is to spend some time at the Arizona-Sonora Desert Museum, 15 miles west of downtown Tucson. The museum is in Tucson Mountain Park, adjacent to the Saguaro National Park's west unit.

The desert museum is part zoo, part museum, and part botanical garden. With some 300 species of animals and 1,300 kinds of plants, the museum focuses exclusively on the life of the Sonoran Desert and does it in one of the most captivating settings in the United States, a protected area where experts estimate there is an average of 15,000 to 20,000 saguaros per square mile. Since it opened in 1952, the desert museum has been dedicated to showing the interrelationship of the land, water, plants, wildlife, and people of the Sonoran Desert region. Its exhibits, packed into 12 acres, uniquely offer visitors a nearly seamless interface with animals in what appears to be their native surroundings. However, while the museum/zoo is surrounded by that habitat, most of its rocky gullies and washes, where desert bighorn sheep, javelina, mule deer, beavers, ring-tail foxes, and other creatures live, are man-made re-creations. The design, which set the standard for zoos around the world, is calculated to give spectators the feeling they are part of the animal's world, which prompted a reporter for *The New York Times* to call it "the most distinctive zoo in the United States."

Once you leave the Tucson metropolitan area, skies throughout the region are almost always clear and sunny, which explains why there are more astronomical observatories within a 50-mile radius of Tucson than anyplace else on earth. You can get a good overview of astronomy's place in the life of southern Arizona by visiting the Flandrau Planetarium at the University of Arizona in Tucson or Kitt Peak National Observatory, some 45 minutes west of the city on the Tohono O'odham reservation. If you're a shopper, at Kitt Peak you also can get good deals on Indian baskets and other folk arts at the observatory's shop or have lunch at the facility's picnic ground.

One of southern Arizona's most popular attractions is the 200-year-old Mission San Xavier del Bac, a beautifully restored architectural gem, often valued as much for the stunning art work it contains as for its religious significance. Located about 10 miles south of Tucson on the San Xavier Indian Reservation (a branch of the Tohono O'odham Indian Reservation), the mission church is often called "The White Dove of the Desert" because of its alabaster exterior and graceful design.

The architecture of San Xavier and the mission ruins at Tumacacori, some 45 miles south of Tucson in Santa Cruz County, clearly reflect the influence of Spain in southern Arizona. But southern Arizona's natural attractions have been fascinating visitors far longer than the derivative architectural designs of its man-made features.

Not often does one see snow capping saguaro cactus and dusting desert mountains.

Randy A. Prentice

An observatory housing the four-meter Mayall telescope looms
over other structures at Kitt Peak National Observatory.

Edward McCain

The landscape is a great contradiction: Its undulating deserts receive
barely enough rainfall to sustain the life of diminutive trees and shrubs, but
rising from these often barren plains you'll find numerous pine- and spruce-
covered mountain ranges sometimes referred to as "sky islands." In downtown
Tucson it may be 108 degrees in June, but at the top of the 9,000-foot-high
Santa Catalina Mountains, a one-hour drive from the center of the city, it will
likely be a comfortable 80 degrees. The same scenario is repeated throughout
the region, in the Rincon, Santa Rita, Huachuca, and Chiricahua mountains, to
name just a few.

During the latter part of the 19th century, these mountains were busy
places. For roughly 10 years after Ed Schieffelin's 1879 discovery of a
rich concentration of silver in the hills near Tombstone, that famous town
burgeoned into a bustling, raucous "metropolis" with about 8,000 residents at
its peak in the mid-1880s. The bulk of the population consisted of ignorant,
hard-working males who consumed vast amounts of alcohol and often relied
for companionship on the many prostitutes living in the Red Light District
east of Sixth Street. One report indicated there once were 110 saloons in
Tombstone, and while that figure is undoubtedly fiction, it probably is one
person's reaction to what appeared to be a main street choked with drinking
establishments, fine restaurants, stagecoaches, hotels, and crowds of people.
Wells Spicer, the lawyer who eventually led the inquest in the O.K. Corral
incident, wrote in 1880 that Tombstone had "Two dance houses, a dozen

gambling places, over 20 saloons and more than 500 gamblers," and he added, "Still there is hope, for I know of two Bibles in town."

Southern Arizona has attracted the interest of miners since the days of Spanish exploration. In modern times, mining activity south of Tucson has focused primarily on copper. Huge copper mines still operate at Green Valley and Ajo.

If you drive south of Tucson through the Santa Cruz River Valley, you'll be passing mountain ranges to your east and west that long ago proved to be sources of gold, silver, copper, lead, and zinc. South of Tucson, abandoned silver mines literally riddle the Santa Rita Mountains.

The most spectacular of these old deposits, discovered in October 1736, was found not in the Santa Ritas but a little further south, and not by a Spanish explorer but by a Yaqui Indian named Antonio Siraumea. It was called the Planchas de Plata (Sheets of Silver) and was located approximately 10 miles south and west of Nogales at an arroyo that the Indians called Arizonac.

Siraumea brought samples of the silver he had found to a Sonoran merchant, who passed the word on to others. As a result, wrote historian Odie Faulk, "Spaniards in incredible numbers rushed to the area, infected with the desire to get rich quick. Estimates of their number vary from five to 10,000. And some of them did make incredible finds. The silver strangely

George H.H. Huey

A climber takes on a face at Windy Point in the
Santa Catalina Mountains north of Tucson.

was in sheets atop the hills and gullies, and thus the strike became known as Planchas de Plata. Knowledgeable observers estimated that approximately 10,000 pounds of silver were taken from the area within a few months."

Many of those Spanish families mined the hills and creek beds of a portion of southern Arizona bordered on the west by Arivaca and on the east by the Patagonia Mountains. In the middle of the 18th century, the main population center between Arivaca and the town of Patagonia was at Tubac, about 40 miles south of Tucson. The Spaniards established a presidio (or fort) at Tubac in 1752—a reconstruction of that presidio is now a state park—so the inhabitants were marginally protected against Apache attacks, but only for brief periods.

These early Spanish miners primarily looked for gold and silver. "They worked in relatively small groups, quickly removing and processing easily accessible ore and then making a quick departure before their luck with the Apaches ran out," Wendell E. Wilson wrote in the *Mineralogical Record* in 1983.

That there was extensive mining activity, especially in the Tubac area, is evident from a report written in 1777 by Manuel Barragua, Francisco Castro, and Antonio Romero, three of the Spanish settlers there.

"There are many mines of very rich metals some 20 miles to the west in the vicinity of Arivaca," the report said. "Three of these mines are especially

David W. Lazaroff

Saguaro cacti especially like south-facing slopes like this one in the Gates Pass area of the Tucson Mountains west of the city.

A windmill pumps water for cattle in the Cerro
Colorado Mountains east of Arivaca.

Randy A. Prentice

productive. One yields eight ounces of pure silver to every 25 pounds of ore.
A second yields 45 ounces to every carga [100 pounds] of ore. The third mine
yields a little less than this.

"Ten miles east of Tubac, in the Santa Rita Mountains, two silver mines
have been worked with smelters and three more with quick silver, all with a
tolerable yield. Though these mines are common knowledge to all of the Tubac
settlers, they cannot be worked on a permanent basis because of the Apaches,
who have pastures and encampments in that vicinity ..."

From about the mid-1800's until 1886, the Apaches were a major force to
be reckoned with in southern Arizona. In 1886, Geronimo surrendered for the
last time, and he and all remaining Chiricahua Apaches were exiled to Florida.
Eventually, most of the Chiricahua Apaches were resettled on the Mescalero
Indian Reservation in New Mexico.

Today, the area once dominated by Apaches has evolved to one dominated
by outdoor enthusiasts—hikers, mountain bikers, anglers, and especially by
bird-watchers. Because of the unique combination of flora and fauna, and its
proximity to the Mexican border, southern Arizona attracts between 400 and
500 species of birds, some of them found nowhere else in the United States. The
region is regarded as among the top five bird-watching locations in the nation.

The routes described in this chapter are a tiny fraction of the places
you can explore on your own. In this end of the state, solitude is never
far away. AH

Besides harshness, the Sonoran Desert—
homeland of the Tohono O'odham Indians—
deals out colorful patches of vegetation.
Robert G. McDonald

Drive 1

The Desert, The Wind: Quijotoa to Kaka

Whether the desert has a heart, a center that pulsates and makes life possible, we have no idea. If not, maybe there is at least a place like this route through the Tohono O'odham homeland that explains the welcoming feeling many experience in this harsh landscape where volcanic mountains rise above a veil of small trees and fragrant bushes. Not much is out here in the thirsty cradle that is home to the Tohono O'odham Indians. There is the desert. There is the wind. And at day's end, there is the crimson evening.

There is also Kaka, which doesn't mean what you might think it means. Kaka is someone's attempt at spelling the Piman word for clearing, which is "gagka." Talk to any Indians in the area and they will pronounce Kaka as "GAHkah."

Kaka is a small collection of adobe and ocotillo houses and a few trailers surrounding a remarkable church in the midst of the Sonoran Desert. The village also is in the middle of the 2.8-million-acre Tohono O'odham Indian Reservation. A visit to Kaka is not like going to any off-reservation town like Casa Grande or Ajo. While the village is old and primitive, its artistically designed Church of St. Francis is the most modern church on the entire reservation.

The drive from Quijotoa to Kaka is easy—all roads are paved until you get to the village. It's also a beautiful drive through the brown palm of the Sonoran Desert, a terrain filled with saguaros, ocotillos, prickly pear, and mesquite, ironwood and paloverde trees. Wide arroyos snake between isolated volcanic mountains. In the summer months, when temperatures in this terrain pass 100 degrees, you'll encounter lots of rattlesnakes. There also are lots of coyotes and hawks and owls and mule deer, but the rattlers have a way of grabbing most of the attention.

Begin this drive in Tucson heading west on Ajo Road (see Route Finder for details) for the Gu-Achi Trading Post.

Most people driving this route are headed for Puerto Peñasco, a beach town in Mexico. Rarely does anyone leave the main road to explore the obscure routes that are the lifeline of the reservation villages. Both tourists and local Indians frequent Gu-Achi Trading Post, which means you can buy snacks, curios, or a handful of yucca to weave a basket. The O'odham are known for their artistic baskets, many of which are on sale at the trading post.

From the trading post, you'll be heading toward the feature in the landscape that gave the trading post its name. In the Piman language spoken by the O'odham, Gu-Achi means something like "big little" or "big narrow," a reference to the area where Santa Rosa Wash narrows.

All of land between this point and Kaka is open range—you've got to keep your eyes open for horses or cows that may wander into the road. When you're 11 miles north of the trading post, there's a cutoff on the right for Santa Rosa. If you drive into the village, this paved road will swing back and rejoin the road to Kaka.

In the desert near Santa Rosa there's an unusual spot called the Children's Shrine, which is not like any other shrine you've seen before. If you want to visit, ask at the tribe's district office in Santa Rosa for permission and directions. The shrine, a few miles northwest of the village, is a

At night, the Sonoran Desert takes on a solemnity below the Tohono O'odham's sacred Baboquivari Peak.

memorial to four children who, according to O'odham mythology, were sacrificed for the good of their people. The story, an allegory on the sacrifice an individual makes for the sake of his community, is a long and complicated one (see sidebar) that is held dear by many O'odham.

Leaving the village, your next stop is Kaka. The circular church there usually is locked, but if you ask around, someone may open it for you. Designed in the late 1960s by architect George Myers, who lives in Prescott, the church has a sunken nave and long bench-like pews that rise like an amphitheater above the altar. The ceiling contains vigas made from used telephone poles and is layered with ocotillo branches.

The Stations of the Cross also are unusual. Though not part of Myers' design, the 14 stations consist of large, arched alcoves with each scene represented by a painting of a Tohono O'odham basket decorated with traditional geometric designs.

Next, the tiny village of Vaya Chin, where there's a tiny trading post (you can't miss it, it's painted bright blue) and a rustic chapel with a free-standing bell tower. You can buy snacks at the store, and the proprietor says he also sells gas when he can get it.

George H.H. Huey

Tohono O'odham basket maker Ruby Thomas wove this horsehair container with decorations depicting rattlesnakes.

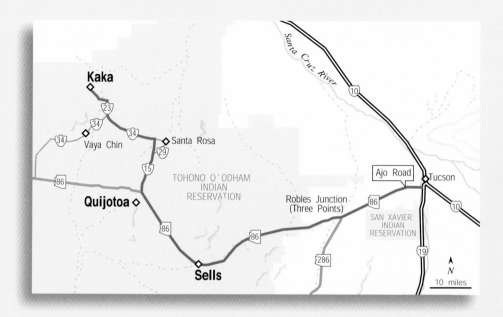

Route Finder

• Begin in Tucson heading west on Ajo Road, which becomes State Route 86.

• Travel west to Three Points (Robles Junction) at the Y-junction of State 86 and State Route 286. Bear right to stay on 86.

• Continue on 86 for 36 more miles, passing the turnoff for Kitt Peak National Observatory on the left before reaching the tribal capital of Sells, where there is a supermarket on the right.

• Continue on 86 for 22 miles until you reach Quijotoa and the Gu-Achi Trading Post.

• From the trading post, drive north on Indian Route 15 for 11 miles to a Y junction with Indian Route 29, a road that loops about 3.5 miles into the village of Santa Rosa and back to Indian 15. Bear right onto Indian 29 for Santa Rosa, or bear left if you want to bypass the village.

• About 2 miles beyond the Y junction, Indian 15 intersects with Indian Route 34. Turn left onto Indian 34. If you looped into Santa Rosa, you'll come out on Indian 15 less than a mile south of the intersection of 15 and 34. Turn right onto 15 and left onto 34.

• Continue on Indian 34 for 9 miles to its Y-junction with Indian Route 23. Bear right. Kaka is 10 miles away on Indian 23.

• Leaving Kaka, return on Indian 23 to the Y-junction with Indian 34. Bear right onto 34 and drive about 7 miles to the trading post at Vaya Chin.

• From Vaya Chin, continue west and south on 34 to State Route 86. Turn left for the return to Tucson.

Additional information: Tohono O'odham tribal office, (520) 383-2028; www.itcaonline.com/tribes_tohono.html.

Drive 1

The Children's Shrine

The Children's Shrine near Santa Rosa Village on the Tohono O'odham reservation commemorates an event from tribal mythology. The story behind the shrine varies slightly from one individual to another, but the broad outline is the same. This is an abbreviated version told by Danny Lopez, a Tohono O'odham who lives at Big Fields. The full story, told in the Papago language, would probably take two hours to tell. Here is Danny Lopez' version:

"A young man came out here hunting, and he saw water coming out of a hole in the ground. He ran to the village to tell the people. This sort of thing doesn't happen in the desert, so the people thought he had lost his mind, and most of them ignored him. But someone came and looked and saw that it was true. Then the medicine people came out to look to see if maybe the spirits had been offended or something.

"The water kept coming out the hole, and it was threatening to flood the village. At one of the gatherings, the people decided to ask I'itoi, the Creator, for help. So they sent a runner out to Baboquivari [a mountain] to ask I'itoi what to do. The runner came back and said I'itoi said the people should make an offering of whatever is most valuable to them. But what is that? the people asked. Nobody knew.

"Some thought he meant a big willow basket which they had. They got their best basket and offered that but the water kept coming. Then they thought maybe he means our best olla [a vessel for carrying water] with all the pretty designs. They offered that, but nothing happened. The people were getting desperate. Finally, they asked an old man. He said, 'Well, what is most valuable to us is our children.'

"So it was decided by the medicine people that they would offer four children and they would seek children who had special gifts, such as a boy who was an excellent hunter, a girl with long hair down to her waist, etc. The word got out in the community and the mother of a boy who was the best hunter hid her son in a mat, rolled him up in it and told him not to move. Another lady knew they would take her daughter, so she hid her under some vines.

"When the medicine people went for the boy, his mother told them he was off in the mountains. When they went for the girl, the mother said she was visiting her grandmother a long way off. So, they got four other children. They

A Tohono O'odham looks out onto the sacred
Baboquivari Mountains from his home. In Tohono
O'odham mythology, I'itoi, the creator, lives there.

Edward McCain

took them and kept them all night in the round house, singing, and then they put shell necklaces on them and got them so they wouldn't be afraid. They brought them here in the morning and lowered the children down into the hole where the water was coming out, and when they looked, the water started to slow down and then it stopped.

"Afterwards, the mother went to get her son who was rolled up in the mat, but when she opened the mat he was not there. Instead she found foam, like the foam you see on the water when the washes are running. And after that whenever the wash was running she would go out and call for her son. And the mother who had hidden her daughter, when she went to look for her under the vines, she was not there. Instead there were yellow blossoms from the squash, so when the squash comes out it reminds the people of what happened.

"From that point on, the people say every time it rains you will hear the voices of the children singing because they are happy."

Shy, white-faced pronghorns bound across a tree-dotted grassland at the Buenos Aires National Wildlife Refuge in southern Arizona. Jack Dykinga

Tucson to Buenos Aires and Arivaca

Wildlife viewing is excellent along portions of this loop drive through the desert southwest of Tucson. You're likely to see pronghorn antelope in the rolling grasslands at Buenos Aires National Wildlife Refuge. Along Arivaca Creek you may encounter deer or javelina. If you're a bird-watcher, and you make this drive in the summer months, you can plan on seeing gray hawks and Harris hawks.

You can make this 160-mile loop any time of the year, but the area is most attractive between spring and fall. Winter temperatures are mild, but all the mesquite and cottonwood trees are bare and Arivaca Creek will slow to a trickle. In the spring and summer, the giant cottonwoods and dense mesquites are green and lush and the creek is alive with activity—some 300 species of birds inhabit the area.

To begin from Tucson, drive west to Robles Junction, known locally as Three Points (see Route Finder for details). As you cross Kinney Road in Tucson, Cat Mountain is visible off to the right. You're passing the southern end of the Tucson Mountains. If you look directly ahead, meaning west, you can see some small rounded structures on a ridge some 50 miles away. The white domes house the telescopes of Kitt Peak National Observatory.

You'll find a gas station and general store at Three Points. The next services won't be available until the tiny Mexican-border community of Sasabe, 46 miles to the south.

Between Three Points and the refuge visitors center, you'll be in the Altar Valley, a wide expanse of mesquite forests laced with labyrinths of washes. The landscape is dominated by the Quinlan Mountains and especially 7,730-foot Baboquivari Peak, which you can see off to your right. Home of I'itoi, the Creator in traditional Tohono O'odham teachings, the peak figures prominently in the spiritual beliefs of the Indians, who are native to the area.

The highway enters the refuge a little more than 20 miles south of Three Points, but the turnoff to the visitors center is about 15 miles farther. You'll pass the road to Arivaca about 5 miles before coming to the refuge visitors center turnoff and will backtrack to it.

The government established Buenos Aires refuge in 1985 to preserve habitat for an endangered species, the masked bobwhite quail. The bird disappeared from southern Arizona at the end of the 1800s, but has been reintroduced at the refuge by the U.S. Fish and Wildlife Service. Today, the more than 115,000 wooded and grassy acres in the national refuge is considered to be the only location in the United States where the quail survives, along with more than 230 other bird species that have been spotted in the flowing grasslands that straddle the Mexican border.

Migratory waterfowl are attracted to the refuge's 150 lakes (most of them small basins) beginning in September and peaking in the first two weeks of October. The lakes, including the 100-acre Aguirre Lake near the refuge headquarters, are filled by monsoon rains that fall from July through mid-September.

At the refuge headquarters ask about the 10-mile loop drive to Sasabe. Most of the year, the one-lane dirt road is easily driven in an ordinary sedan, but after a heavy rain it can get badly rutted and muddy in low spots at the bottom of washes.

Poppies blanket a field
soaked with monsoon
rain in the Buenos Aires
National Wildlife Refuge.

Although it's tiny, Arivaca Creek supports much
life, and pools like this one draw wildlife.

Jack Dykinga

Leaving the refuge, return to State 286, turn right, and drive to the historic community of
Arivaca. Paved Arivaca Road meanders between the low hills of the Las Guijas Mountains on the
left and Arivaca Creek on the right. About 10 miles after turning onto Arivaca Road, watch on
the right for a parking lot and wildlife viewing area. There's a flat trail meandering along Arivaca
Creek. You'll find a park bench facing the creek about a half-mile down the trail, a great place
for bird-watching.

Two more miles of driving brings you to Arivaca. When the Heintzelman (or Cerro Colorado)
silver mine, some 8 miles north of Arivaca, was in operation in the 1800s, its ore was smelted
at Arivaca and the bullion was then hauled to the Gulf of California (Sea of Cortes) port at
Guaymas, Mexico, and shipped to San Francisco. However, the Arivaca area was inhabited long
before miners arrived.

Like much of southern Arizona, it was first populated by Pima and Tohono O'odham
Indians (formerly called Papagos). In the 1700s, Spaniards were attracted to the Arivaca region
because of its abundant water and grazing and mining potential. Known in the early days as
a ranch called "La Aribac," it was abandoned after an Indian uprising in 1751. In 1812, before
the Gadsden Purchase made the area a part of the United States, Augustin Ortiz bought the
ranch from the Spanish colonial government. The original spread included the land now on the
Rancho de la Osa guest ranch at Sasabe. Heintzelman's mining company purchased all of the
Ortiz rights in 1856. The ranch changed hands two more times until 1915, when the residents
petitioned the U.S. General Land Office for a patent to the town site. President Woodrow Wilson
signed the township deed in 1916.

Commercial enterprises in "downtown" Arivaca now include a general store with a gas
pump, a restaurant and bar, a gift shop, and U.S. Post Office. Take a left at the dirt road next
to the store and visit the town's historic schoolhouse and adjacent cemetery.

As you drive through Arivaca, watch for a plank walkway along Arivaca Creek that's a
delight to visit any time of year.

Finish this loop drive by heading for Arivaca Junction, Amado, Interstate 19, and Tucson.
As you approach Tucson, consider a visit to Mission San Xavier del Bac, founded around 1700 by
Padre Francisco Kino.

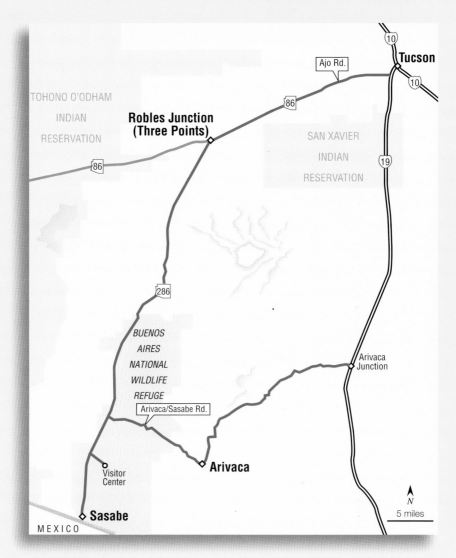

Route Finder

• *Begin at Exit 99 on Interstate 19 in Tucson. Drive west on Ajo Road, which becomes State Route 86, also known as the Ajo Highway.*

• *Drive 21 miles to Robles Junction (Three Points) and turn left (south) onto State Route 286.*

• *Continue south on State 286 for 38 miles to the turnoff to the Buenos Aires refuge. Turn left (east).*

• *Drive about 2 miles on an unpaved road to the visitors center.*

• *Leaving the refuge, turn right (north) onto State 286 and drive 5 miles to Arivaca Road.*

• *Turn right (east). In about 10 miles look for a wildlife viewing area on the right.*

• *Continue on Arivaca Road for 2 miles to Arivaca.*

• *Leaving Arivaca, drive northeast on Arivaca Road for about 23 miles to Arivaca Junction and Amado and I-19.*

Additional information: Buenos Aires refuge: (520) 823-4251, ext. 116; www.fws.gov/southwest/ refuges/arizona/buenosaires. Arivaca, www.arivaca. net. San Xavier del Bac Mission, (520) 294-2624; www.sanxaviermission.org. Amado, (520) 287-3685; www.nogaleschamber.com.

Plants and grasses huddle around the few water sources in the southern Arizona desert. Tom Danielsen

Drive 3

Tucson to Kentucky Camp

A hundred years ago, many of Arizona's mountain ranges were like intricate beehives riddled with gold and silver mines. As a result, today there are an estimated 500 to 1,000 ghost towns in various stages of decomposition, places where dried-out doors flap and squeak on their twisted hinges and corrugated tin roofs rattle in the wind. Many of these old mines were also small communities, but today most of them exist only in postal records or as items in newspapers long out of print. Many of these places are inaccessible because they're on private property or located in terrain where even burros fear to tread.

But there are exceptions, and Kentucky Camp—a mere 45 miles southeast of Tucson in the Santa Rita Mountains—is a good one. All but the last 5 miles of this drive (see Route Finder for details) are on pavement. The dirt portion can be driven with an ordinary sedan if you exercise caution. And you can rent a cabin there.

Kentucky Camp was established—with considerable fanfare—as a gold-mining operation in 1904 on the fringe of the Greaterville gold mining district, which had produced a bonanza in placer gold (gold found in the surface of creek beds) around 1880. By roughly 1885, the placer gold had played out at Greaterville and most of the estimated 400 people involved in that operation moved away.

Around 1900, an East Coast millionaire named George B. McAneny bought many claims in the area (some reports say 2,000). A placer claim is typically 20 acres. McAneny's theory was that his claims could still yield more gold if a different technology were applied to the placers. The basis of McAneny's new technology was water. He was going to impound the rain and snow melt in a series of dams and install a gravity-fed pipeline that would run water through the gold-laden silt in the creek bed.

The *Arizona Daily Star* reported on January 17, 1904:

"James B. Stetson [the mine's superintendent] ... has 40 men employed in the preliminary work of opening a ditch of six foot width and five miles length in the Greaterville, Pima County, placer mining district. Three miles of 24-inch pipe is being installed and a reservoir of several million gallons capacity will be constructed on the east slope of the Santa Ritas. Fully $200,000 will be expended before actual work in working the ground is begun."

Nowadays, the experts speculate that McAneny's operation failed because of a miscalculation. Some would call it a problem with the cost-benefit ratio. McAneny died around 1906. Jim McDonald, archaeologist for the Coronado National Forest, said McAneny's heirs probably concluded that it would simply take too much money to build a system that was going to produce very little gold.

The Kentucky Camp operation lasted two years, coming to an abrupt halt when its other misfortunes were compounded by the untimely death of the mine superintendent, James B. Stetson. Stetson had been seen sitting on the ledge of his third-floor window in the Santa Rita Hotel in Tucson shortly before he fell to his death.

A Forest Service road meanders through gentle hills in the area surrounding historic Kentucky Camp.

Kentucky Camp soon afterward was purchased by a rancher and remained in private hands until the property—four or five buildings in relatively good shape—became a part of the national forest system. In 1992, restoration of the old buildings began with the help of volunteers and a federal program called Passport in Time, which provides an opportunity for people to join Forest Service crews rebuilding and stabilizing historic structures.

Kentucky Camp has survived in fairly good shape mainly because it never made it into the ghost town books. Being on private property, it was not accessible to treasure hunters and had not been picked clean by the time it was turned over to the Coronado National Forest.

While visitors aren't permitted to pan for gold due to privately owned mining rights, the Forest Service welcomes hikers and mountain bikers to try out the portion of the Arizona Trail that follows much of the historic Santa Rita Mining and Water Mining System. When completed, the Arizona Trail will be a 780-mile route stretching from Utah to Sonora, Mexico.

The Forest Service rents a rustic adobe cabin in Kentucky Camp as a part of its "rooms with a view program." The cabin can accommodate up to four people, and it includes four twin-size bunks, an easy chair and rocking chairs, lamps, microwave and toaster ovens, some dishes, an outside picnic table and grill, and an outside vault toilet. (See "additional information" in the Route Finder.)

Randy A. Prentice

Mount Wrightson (9,357 feet), upper left, dominates the landscape south of Tucson, but its brother, Mount Hopkins, has an observatory atop it.

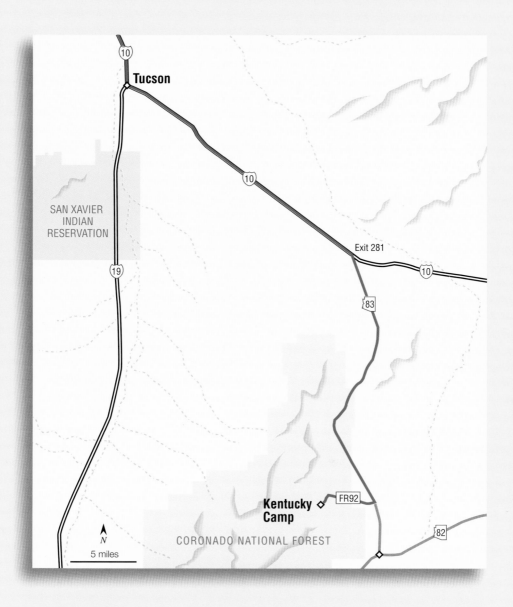

Route Finder

• From Phoenix or Tucson, drive east on Interstate 10 to Exit 281, which serves State Route 83 (the road to Sonoita).

• Go south on state 83 for 21 miles to Gardner Canyon Road (Forest Service Road 92).

• Turn right (west) onto Gardner Canyon Road and follow the signs for Kentucky Camp, about 5 miles away. Park at the gate and walk down the hill and 0.25 miles to the camp.

Additional information: Cabin rental, Coronado National Forest, Nogales Ranger Station, (520) 281-2296; www.fs.fed.us/r3/coronado (scroll to bottom of page).

Juice from agave is used to make an alcoholic drink called mescal, the name chosen for the road that leads into Happy Valley. Tom Danielsen

Drive 4

Happy Valley: Wilderness Just Around a Tucson Corner

On a cool spring morning, Mahlon MacKenzie was in his corral with a bruised pony. The 5-month-old paint had wandered into thick brush near Happy Valley, tangled itself in a fence, and ended up with nasty gashes up and down its rickety legs.

MacKenzie held the filly with a blue bridle while a Mexican vaquero peeled open the thick skin of an aloe and gently smeared the mucus-like pulp onto the pony's raw wounds.

"It's an old-fashioned remedy," MacKenzie said, "but it works."

Then he pressed his fingers on the filly's lower lip to force its mouth open so he could give it a squirt of an antibiotic. That would prevent infection.

This episode was played out a few feet from the unpaved road that leads to Happy Valley on the east side of the Rincon Mountains. It's a place that, from the ground, appears wild and scenic, a jumble of granite boulders, winding creeks, and huge oak, ash, and cottonwood trees below Mica Mountain and Rincon Peak.

Seen from the air, however, Happy Valley is so close to Tucson that the uninitiated might think of it as a suburb. If you're heading to this area, resist such thoughts and proceed as though you are entering a distant wilderness.

Mescal Road, the back road leading to Happy Valley (see Route Finder for details), is easy enough to traverse with a high-clearance vehicle, but in some ways it can be misleading because Tucson, a city of more than a half-million people, seems just around the corner. In terms of miles and time, that may be true, but Happy Valley is still a nearly unpopulated spot in an isolated canyon. If your car bottoms out in one of the many spots where the road crosses Ash or Paige creeks, you might be there longer than expected.

About a mile after Mescal Road crosses the Southern Pacific Railroad tracks, you can see the small re-creation of an Old West town in the distance. Some of the final episodes of *Bonanza,* the television series, were filmed at the set. The place is not open to the public.

Mescal is the Spanish word for the yucca plant, which grows in abundance between the movie set and the interstate highway. However, 2 miles beyond the film location, small hills appear, and gnarled mesquite trees gradually replace the yuccas.

In another mile and a half, you will encounter the first and best crossing of Ash Creek. The road has been raised slightly above the creek bed and is paved.

In late spring, the creek is likely to be dry. During summer rains, or early spring when snow melts off the higher elevations in the Rincons, water will course across the road.

Less than a mile north of the creek, the cutoff for Ash Canyon Ranch, a working cattle operation, is on the left. Continue straight. In the next 0.1 mile, the road crosses the creek twice, and the first of several primitive campsites appears on the right, adjacent to Ash Creek. At this point, the stunted desert scrub has given way to giant cottonwoods and sycamores.

A combination of flowing water and tannic acid from decaying plant life creates patterns of swirling foam where Paige Creek tumbles over a rocky slope into a small pool in Happy Valley.

A thicket of ferns and manzanitas prospers at the edge
of Miller Creek (not shown) near Happy Valley.

Jack Dykinga

The road narrows as you pass the campsites. In places, the cottonwood, oak, ash, black walnut, and Arizona sycamore recede toward the base of the mountains. The road is bordered by red-barked manzanita bushes which, in late February and March, are covered with tiny pink blossoms.

About 5 miles north of the campsites area, the road climbs a small hill that separates the Ash and Paige canyon drainages. From the crest, the grassy terrain of Happy Valley can be seen to the left (northwest). To the right, the small domes of the Little Rincon Mountains appear. The tall ridge straight ahead is the craggy outline of the Galiuro Mountains. In the fall, the cottonwood trees below blaze red and orange.

At the bottom of the hill, a cement stock tank sits on the right side of the road. Soon after, the road cuts through the middle of a wide pasture and some ranch buildings.

One-tenth of a mile beyond the pasture, a large sign appears on the left side of a road that leads to the Miller Creek Trailhead in the Coronado National Forest's Santa Catalina Ranger District. The trail, a part of the Arizona Trail system, winds after 1.5 miles to the eastern boundary of the Saguaro National Park.

From the trailhead, it is a steep 5-mile walk to Happy Valley Saddle and 8 miles to Rincon Peak (elevation 8,482 feet).

If you hike to Happy Valley Saddle, keep in mind that while you may find some water in the creek near the bottom of the trail, there usually is none at the saddle or at Rincon Peak (though you might encounter some snowmelt).

After hiking, if you do, a good place to end your excursion and have lunch in the shade of the thick walnut and sycamore trees along a stream is near the end of Mescal Road (see Route Finder for details).

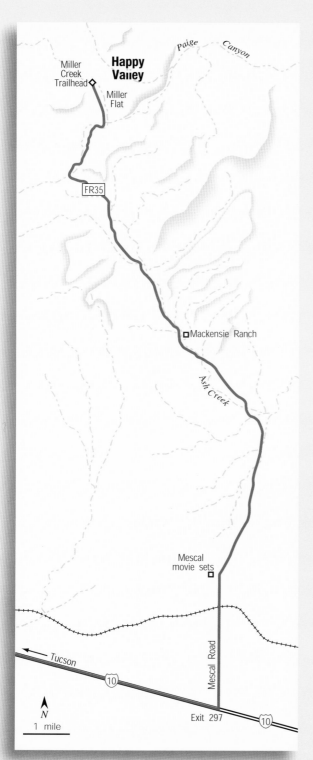

Paige Canyon

Miller Creek Trailhead

Happy Valley

Miller Flat

FR35

☐ Mackensie Ranch

Ash Creek

Mescal movie sets ☐

Mescal Road

Tucson

10

Exit 297   10

N
1 mile

Route Finder

- *From Tucson drive east on Interstate 10 and take Exit 297 for Mescal Road.*
- *Turn left (north) onto Mescal Road and the start of a 16-mile drive to a trailhead in the Coronado National Forest.*
- *Cross railroad tracks in 2.4 miles.*
- *Continue for 5.5 miles to the Ash Canyon Ranch turnoff and continue on Mescal Road.*
- *Continue 8 more miles to a sign directing travelers to the Miller Creek Trail No. 28.*
- *Turn left at the sign and drive 0.2 mile to the trailhead. Mescal Road ends a few miles beyond the sign. Taking it past the trailhead turnoff leads to a fine picnic spot.*

Additional information: Miller Creek Trail, (520) 749-8700; www.fs.fed.us/ r3/coronado/forest/recreation/trails/ miller_cr.shtml

West-Central
Arizona

Formed by the mighty Hoover Dam, Lake Mead, far left, backs up to the end of the Grand Canyon. Alamo Lake, left, is part of a state park and is popular with fisherman. The lake's outflow marks the start of the Bill Williams River.

Les David Manevitz

The Colorado River and Dry Desert

• Overview

Opportunities for water-based recreation abound along the lower Colorado River. When you're not on the river, you're in very dry desert terrain, a transition zone for the Mohave and Sonoran deserts. Summer temperatures in the area may rise to 120 degrees F. and higher, but the river is always refreshing.

• The Drives

• Towns and Sites

Ahakhav Tribal Park, Bill Williams River National Wildlife Refuge, Bouse, Dolan Springs, Grand Canyon West, Havasu National Wildlife Refuge, Hualapai Mountain Park, Kingman, Lake Havasu City, Lake Havasu State Park, Lake Mead National Recreation Area, Meadview, Parker, Swansea Townsite, Wikieup, and Wild Cow Springs Recreation Site.

George H.H. Huey

The Western bluebird thrives in the woodlands, primarily in higher elevations, of this region.
Neil Weidner

The west-central portion of Arizona mostly consists of an arid terrain of sand castle bluffs and dramatic mesas sculpted by wind and the cutting force of the Colorado River. At a glance, the terrain will seem strange and barren to many visitors, yet it is full of surprises for those who are patient and adventurous.

Mohave County, which dominates most of the region, ranks as the second-largest county in the state. Most of the county's 13,479 square miles is classified as desert, but 186 square miles are water. Contradictions appear to be everywhere, according to statistics compiled by county officials: Clearly, the landscape ranks as desert, but the county boasts 1,000 miles of shoreline—mostly Colorado River lakes—and is a great area for water-based recreation. The federal Bureau of Land Management and the U.S. Forest Service control 55.2 percent of Mohave County's land; the state of Arizona controls another 6.6 percent; and Indian reservations own 6.7 percent. Much of the land is open for public use.

In the hills and plains surrounding Kingman, one of the few populous towns in the region, three major landscape features come together. The Colorado Plateau sweeps down from the northeast and ends in the same vicinity where the Mohave and Sonoran deserts join hands. This means that, using Kingman as a starting point, you can easily visit the western portion of the Grand Canyon (the most famous feature on the Colorado Plateau), and you can also see one of the most peculiar trees known to man, the Joshua tree, which grows only in the Mohave Desert. Because west-central Arizona is a transition zone between the Mohave and Sonoran deserts, you'll occasionally see both the giant saguaros and Joshua trees in the same area.

The area has been inhabited for a long time, first by nomadic peoples from the north hunting sloths and mammoths at the end of the last Ice Age, according to accounts published by the Mohave County Historical Society. From about 5000 B.C. through the time of Christ, other groups followed the older trails but began trading and eventually settling into a more sedentary life of farming and fishing on the Colorado River. Sometime after 1100 A.D. the area that is now Mohave County became home to Indians known as the Cerbat People. Experts think those Indians may have been the ancestors of today's Hualapai and Mojave Indians.

Remnants of Indian communities that existed from 700 to 1200 A.D. have been found at the historic Crozier Ranch, some 35 miles east of Kingman, but no detailed studies or excavations of these stone-masonry ruins has ever been done. Most of what is known—that the area once was used by Indians who lived in caves and stone buildings, that it was a major trade route for the

A beavertail prickly pear fits comfortably among a pile of boulders. The Hualapai Mountains lie in the distance.

Hualapai and Hopi Indians, among others—is based mainly on scant evidence or the observations of early travelers.

Referring to the pass that today accommodates old Route 66 and snakes through Crozier Ranch and leads through the middle of Kingman, former Bureau of Land Management archaeologist Don Simonis noted, "The journals of almost every early traveler describe this unique pass and how it literally saved many of them. In the history of the West this trail was every bit as important as the Oregon Trail."

Among the first of these early travelers to leave a written report was a Franciscan friar named Francisco Garces. Garces, once pastor of San Xavier Mission in Tucson, wandered far and wide among Arizona's Indian population and eventually was killed by Indians at Yuma. In 1776, however, he found himself in the vicinity of Truxton Canyon, the place that eventually became Crozier Ranch.

Garces ended up stopping in the vicinity of Crozier for the same reason that prehistoric Indians and later settlers had: reliable water. In a part of the world that is lucky to see 11 inches of rainfall a year, the presence of reliable springs becomes a seductive and essential oasis for animals and humans alike.

Randy A. Prentice

Those who take the Kingman to Pearce Ferry drive described in this chapter will see scenes like this in the western end of the Grand Canyon.

David Muench

Spring flowers decorate a slope off a bay of
Lake Mead north of Kingman.

In 1829, a trapping party led by Ewing Young came through the same area
and gathered at Peach Springs, now the headquarters for the Hualapai Indian
Reservation about 20 miles east of Crozier. Among those in Young's party was
a young man who later became famous as an Indian fighter. His name was
Christopher "Kit" Carson.

The Beale Wagon Road, the first federally funded interstate highway, was
constructed between 1857 and 1883, partly with the help of camels brought
in from the Middle East. West-central Arizona, which may look sparsely
populated to many people today, was a vast no-man's-land in those days.
Mohave County—Kingman is the county seat—wasn't created until 1864.
According to the late Roman Malach, who was the county historian, there was
no record of any ranches in the area in 1864. In 1866, two were listed on the
tax records, and by 1876, there were 28 more. Sheep far outnumbered cattle in
1876. The tax records listed 8,350 sheep and only 1,267 head of cattle.

Ranching and mining became the principal activities of the arriving white
settlers, and for a number of years there were bloody conflicts with the native
Indians, whose custom it was to travel from one watering hole to another.
White settlers wanted the same water. Eventually, many of the Hualapai and
Mojave Indians in the area ended up working on ranches and in the silver and
gold mines that cropped up.

Crozier Ranch, still a cattle operation today, began life in 1872 when W. F.
"Bud" Grounds and John and Jim Cureton drove the first herd of cattle into

Mohave County. Crozier has always been a major cattle operation, and in the 1920s it also became a major tourist attraction with a restaurant, motel cabins, and a 9-foot-deep swimming pool. The place was so popular in the 1930s that the railroad used to run a special car from Needles to Crozier for people who wanted to spend the day picnicking and return in the evening.

Crozier's swimming pool, built in 1923, was a big draw for people from Kingman. Among the visitors at Crozier's pool in the 1920s was one who was destined to become famous as a Hollywood actor. His name was Andy Devine and he was attending high school in nearby Kingman. Even then, Andy was an extra large, and it seems he had a peculiar affection for breaking diving boards. Evidently it pleased him no end to stroll to the end of the board, leap straight into the air and give it all he had, which was ample.

Were he still alive, Andy Devine would not recognize western Arizona today. While much of it remains undeveloped, much also has changed. Major resort-type facilities have developed along the Colorado River, and every winter those seeking relief from ice and snow settle at places like Lake Havasu City, Parker, or Quartzite, or at state parks and other campgrounds not far from these towns.

The Indians, too, are providing tourist and entertainment for visitors. If you head east of Kingman to Peach Springs, you'll find that the Hualapai Indians have built an excellent motel where you can get a good meal and

Edward McCain

The Bill Williams River ends its short stretch (less than 50 air miles) between Alamo Lake and the Colorado River, just south of Lake Havasu City.

The Cerbat Mountains (Windy Point is shown) form the western edge of Hualapai Valley, the start of a drive from Kingman to Pearce Ferry.

George Stocking

arrange to take a day-long raft trip down the Colorado River from Diamond Creek to Pearce Ferry.

If you take the excursion to the ghost town of Swansea (described later in this chapter) you can visit the Ahakhav Tribal Preserve on the Colorado River Indian Tribes Reservation at Parker. The preserve includes a park with about four acres and is a wilderness with about 1,200. You can picnic or rent a canoe for an hour, a day or even an overnight trip. Also, the park is a great spot for bird-watching or meandering along the Colorado River. Touring information is available at www.critonline.com/crit_contents/tourism or by calling (928) 669-6757.

To find the preserve from Parker, drive about 2 miles west on Mohave Road from State Route 95. Turn north on Rodeo Road where there is a large sign that says PIRA (Parker Indian Rodeo Association). Drive a half-mile (you'll pass the rodeo grounds) and watch for a small sign on the left to Ahakhav Tribal Preserve.

At Parker, you'll also find that the Mojaves have built a huge, Las Vegas-style resort hotel and casino. If you're not interested in gambling, you can at least be assured of a good meal in the casino's restaurant.

The back roads described below provide only a glimpse of the variety to be found in Mohave and La Paz counties in west-central Arizona. Study a map and you'll find that, sprinkled along routes near the ones presented here, there are several excellent state parks and a couple of national wildlife refuges. The area is extremely hot in summer, but many visitors find they don't mind the heat as long as they can take a dip in the refreshing waters of the Colorado River. 𝐀𝐇

Drive 1

Wikieup to Kingman—The Exotic Way

Using most of the popular routes into Kingman, the development makes it hard to realize the city is surrounded by the Mohave Desert. But drive to Kingman on this back road from Wikieup, and you will have no doubts about where you are. It's a wonderfully exotic route where you can see the Mohave and Sonoran deserts join hands in the hills of west-central Arizona.

There are 300 miles between Phoenix and Las Vegas, Nevada, and only three towns along the most popular route: Wickenburg, Wikieup, and Kingman. Wikieup, where this back-road adventure begins, is 78 miles northwest of Wickenburg on U.S. Route 93—roughly midway between Phoenix and Las Vegas—in the Big Sandy Valley. The Big Sandy River trickles through the valley north to south, seldom carrying much water. To the east of Wikieup you can see the dry hills of the Aquarius Mountains, and to the west and north, the Hualapai Mountains (described later in this chapter).

Hidden in all of these hills are old abandoned mines. In the 1800s, Mohave County was extensively mined for gold, silver, lead, zinc, copper, and other minerals, though little evidence of the mines can be seen along this route.

Begin this drive (see Route Finder for details) in Wikieup by turning from U.S. Route 93 onto Chicken Springs Road (County Road 131) at the Arizona Department of Transportation yard. The road is paved for the equivalent of a couple of blocks and then becomes washboard dirt. Though the road is sometimes bumpy, it can be driven in an ordinary sedan. The road climbs through a pass directly north of Aubrey Peak.

After you've driven 4 miles, a road takes off on the left. This is one of several roads to ignore. As the main dirt road winds up and over the mountain, the desert vegetation thickens. The first Joshua trees appear before the top of the pass and get larger as you descend the other side.

The presence of these strange-looking trees is proof that you've entered the Mohave Desert. Most of the Mohave Desert stretches through eastern California and Nevada, but portions of it extend like stubby fingers into Arizona and form a transition zone with the Sonoran Desert to the south. The Joshua tree is the emblem of the Mohave Desert just as the giant saguaro is the emblem of the Sonoran Desert. As you drive over the mountain, you'll see both saguaros and Joshua trees—the two deserts are overlapping.

If you're never seen a Joshua tree, you're in for either a surprise or a shock. The tree at first glance looks like a large person with short hair who has been hit by a high voltage electrical line. Capt. John C. Frémont, an explorer and a Territorial governor of Arizona, passed through the Mohave Desert in 1844 and characterized the Joshua as "the most repulsive tree in the vegetable kingdom." Another traveler called them dagger trees. Mormon pioneers, however, gave them the name that stuck. Evidently the shape of the tree reminded these Bible-reading settlers of the bearded Old Testament leader beckoning them to the Promised Land.

Rather than accept Frémont's description, you'd do well to get out of your car along the route and look more closely at these peculiar trees with their hollow trunks and spiny clusters. Hard to believe, but the Joshua tree, being a tree-sized yucca, is a part of the lily family.

As it backs up to the
Grand Canyon, Lake Mead
exhibits a serene mood,
reflecting cliffs at sunset.

Mormon settlers gave the Joshua tree its name. Although the Joshua is called a tree, it's a member of the lily family.

George Stocking

Many animals use the Joshua tree, but perhaps none more intimately than the yucca moth, which uses it to create new life. The female yucca moth gathers pollen from Joshua tree blossoms, moves to another blossom, lays her eggs, then moves up the plant's female portion, the pistil, and deposits some of the gathered pollen it was carrying under its neck into the flower's stigma, thus fertilizing the flower, which can then produce seeds. Thus, the moth creates its own offspring while simultaneously pollinating and facilitating the growth of new Joshua trees.

Another creature that likes to live in the Joshua tree is the desert (or yucca) night lizard. This critter is less than 2 inches long and may be brown or yellow with black speckling. It often lives under the fallen debris under the Joshua tree. If you detect something darting under the tree, it's probably a night lizard. It could also be a rattlesnake, but you're not likely to confuse the two.

Probably the most surprising tenant in the Joshua tree apartment house is Scott's oriole, a beautiful bird that most people have seen in very different habitats. The male, about 7 inches high, has a black head and throat, a bright yellow body and black wings striped with white. The female is a faded greenish-yellow. Scott's orioles nest in the Joshua tree, although most people are accustomed to seeing them around oaks and junipers.

When you've driven 15 miles west of Wikieup, Chicken Springs Road meets Alamo Road (shown on some maps as Alamo Crossing Road). Turn right. You'll find yourself on a wide, smooth dirt road for the next 25 miles to the outskirts of Yucca. As you drive, watch the mountains on the right. You'll be following the foothills of the Hualapai Mountains. After 25 miles, you're back on pavement for the rest of the day.

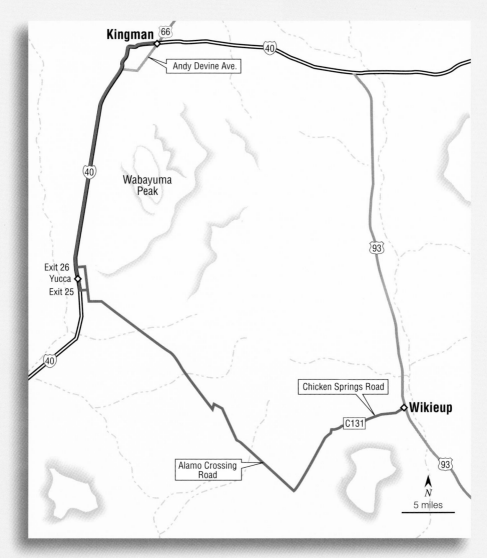

Route Finder

• Begin on U.S. Route 93 between mileposts 123 and 124 in Wikieup, about midway between Phoenix and Las Vegas, Nevada.
• Turn west onto Chicken Springs Road (County Route 131) at the Arizona Department of Transportation yard.
• Continue on Chicken Springs Road in a west-southwesterly direction for 15 miles to its T-junction with Alamo Crossing Road (some maps list it is Alamo Road). Turn right (northwest).
• Continue on Alamo Crossing Road 25 miles to a Y-junction with Boriana Mine Road and bear left (west).
• Just before reaching the junction, the dirt road turns to pavement.

• Continue for a mile on Alamo Road and it turns north. In the next few miles you'll come to junctions (Exit 25 and Exit 26) with Interstate 40. The latter is next to the Ford Motor Company Arizona Proving Ground.
• Turn right (north) onto I-40. The Beale Street Exit to Kingman is 22 miles away.

Additional information: Joshua trees, www.nps.gov/jotr/naturescience/jtrees.htm. Kingman area attractions, (866) 427-7806; www.kingmantourism.org.

A setting sun silhouettes the Black Mountains just off old Route 66 after it has passed through Kingman heading west.
George Stocking

Drive 2

Kingman to Pearce Ferry

The terrain outside of Kingman has been stimulating people's imaginations for years. Some people claim to have seen flying saucers, alien creatures, and a rock that kills on contact. The back-road route from Kingman to Pearce Ferry roams over such an unusual terrain—barren, spooky, and in some ways strangely beautiful—you may wonder which planet you've landed on. If nothing else, you'll understand why the landscape is such a fertile breeding ground for legends and extraterrestrials.

Begin this 155-mile loop drive, which takes you to Lake Mead and Grand Canyon West on the Hualapai Indian Reservation, at Interstate 40 and Stockton Hill Road in Kingman (see Route

Finder for details). As the paved (it becomes dirt later) road heads north and west, you'll venture into more sparsely inhabited areas. The dirt roads on this drive can be handled with an ordinary two-wheel-drive vehicle.

As you head out Stockton Hill Road, you'll find yourself traveling along one side of a wide valley. In the distance to your right, the Grand Wash Cliffs stand like a giant bookend holding the valley together. Later you'll see the cliffs again where the Colorado River forms Lake Mead. On your left lie the Cerbat Mountains.

The Cerbats are very dry and covered with granite outcroppings and diminutive desert scrub. In addition to bighorn sheep, the steep hills and deep canyons of the range are home to a herd of about 100 wild horses. And someplace in a narrow gorge, there is reportedly a big rock that emits an inviting pale blue light. This rock is known as "the Death Trap" and also as "the Rock That Kills."

The gist of the legend connected to this mysterious gorge is that any living creature that steps on the rock dies immediately. In 1966, a writer for *True West* Magazine said that some hunters pursuing a bighorn sheep watched it race into a narrow gorge and then, to their amazement, fall dead as its hooves hit the rocky outcrop. Seeing the strange death of the bighorn, the hunters started walking toward the rock to investigate. Suddenly an old Hualapai Indian jumped out of the brush and, with hand signs and animated speech, warned them off.

Undaunted by the terrain, a hiker ventures over the Grand Wash Cliffs east of Pearce Ferry. Tom Bean

**Although the face of the Grand Wash Cliffs is craggy,
the top nourishes a rolling grassland.**

Tom Bean

"He said the sheep had stepped upon the Death Trap, and if we followed after it, we would die even as the sheep. He pointed out the number of whitening bones that had fallen from the rock into the gorge," the article said.

The legend of the Rock That Kills has been attributed to the Hualapai Indians who live in the area, but an anthropologist who worked with the tribe for many years said he never once heard it. Others, seeking a rational explanation for the alleged power of this rock, claim that it is uranium and highly radioactive. Many rock formations across northern Arizona are naturally radioactive, but geologists dismiss the notion of one that is so hot that it kills on contact. Such facts do not convince everyone, and you can still find people in the vicinity of Kingman, Chloride, and Dolan Springs who have no doubt that such a lethal rock exists somewhere in the Cerbats.

Less mysterious and more obvious as you continue northwest along this road is a large, dry lake bed west of the Grand Wash Cliffs. This is Red Lake, one of three dry lakes in Arizona with the same name, and it's colored by the soils in the area.

A few miles beyond Red Lake and past 3,696-foot Table Mountain, the pavement resumes even though you're nowhere near civilization. Four miles later you come to Pearce Ferry Road, which is also designated County Road 25.

The spiny Joshua trees with their twisted limbs grow abundantly in this area, a clear indication that you are in the Mohave Desert. You'll notice that nothing grows very tall in this desert. The Joshua tree, which may grow as tall as 40 feet, are giants compared to most plants. (See a more detailed description of the Joshua in the preceding Wikieup to Kingman drive.)

Pearce Ferry Road leads to South Cove and Pearce Ferry in the Lake Mead National Recreation Area. En route, you'll pass a turnoff for Meadview, a tiny community where there is a motel and restaurant. There's a boat-launch ramp at South Cove.

At Grand Canyon West, the Hualapais have developed ground and air tours, view points and other recreational facilities. Parking is free; there's a fee, which includes a meal, for entry.

Route Finder _____

• *Begin in Kingman at Interstate 40 Exit 52 and drive north on Stockton Hill Road (Mohave County Route 20; some maps list portions of this road as Stockton Road).*

• *Continue on Stockton Hill Road for 21 miles to a Y-junction with paved Pearce (some maps spell it Pierce) Ferry Road (County Route 25).*

• *Bear right (northeast) onto Pearce Ferry Road and continue for 7 miles to the Y-Junction with unpaved Diamond Bar Road. At this point Pearce Ferry Road veers left from northeast to north.*

• *Continue north on Pearce Ferry Road for about 14 miles to the edge of Lake Mead.*

• *Approaching the lake, Pearce Ferry Road turns (left) west while a dirt road goes off to the right, leading in about 5 miles to Pearce Ferry. Staying on the paved road leads to Lake Mead's South Cove, also about 5 miles away.*

• *Leaving Lake Mead, return on Pearce Ferry Road to Diamond Bar Road. Turn left.*

• *Continue on Diamond Bar Road for 21 miles. The road ends at the only entrance to Grand Canyon West. The first 14 miles are dirt, but the final 7 are paved.*

• *Leaving Grand Canyon West, return via Diamond Bar Road to Pearce Ferry Road, turn left, and drive about 26 miles to U.S. Route 93.*

• *Turn left onto U.S. 93 and drive about 30 miles into Kingman.*

Additional information: Lake Mead National Recreation Area, (702) 293-8990 or 293-8906; www.nps.gov/lame. Grand Canyon West, (877) 716-9378 or (702)-878-(9378) or (928) 769-2219; www.destinationgrandcanyon.com.

Drive 3

Kingman to Hualapai Mountain Park and Wild Cow Springs Recreation Site

Every desert community deserves an oasis. Kingman, located near the eastern edge of the Mohave Desert, has a refreshing one right over its shoulder in the cool green Hualapai Mountains, a place that is simple to get to but virtually unknown outside of Mohave County.

The Hualapai Mountains, named for the Indians who used to inhabit them, form a bulky wall along the southeastern edge of Kingman. Hualapai, in the language of the natives, means "people of the tall pines." The accuracy of the name will be confirmed as you take the scenic drive from to Hualapai Mountain Park and a Bureau of Land Management recreation site and campground called Wild Cow Springs at the top of the mountains.

The trip is one of the most civilized back-country excursions you can take in a state where mountain roads often are unpaved and dangerous. With the exception of a very short stretch, this route into the Hualapais is a breeze. From Kingman, the entire one-way route to Wild Cow Springs is 16 miles, and 12 are paved. Furthermore, the paved road goes right through the heart of Mohave County's 2,300-acre Hualapai Mountain Park, where you can rent a cabin or a room in a lodge, camp, picnic, and hike any one of a dozen trails.

Begin this trip on Hualapai Mountain Road in Kingman (see Route Finder for details). The road quickly climbs Sawmill Canyon to the park entrance. One minute you're in tumbleweed country at the edge of a subdivision, and the next you're rolling through hills covered with piñon pines (once a major food source for the Hualapai Indians) and junipers. Subdivisions are gradually inching their way up the mountain, but not enough to obscure the passage from desert to pine forests. Within minutes the road passes from high desert to hills covered with spruce and aspens and dramatic outcroppings of lichen-speckled granite. In less than an hour the habitat of the Gila monster and desert tortoise gives way to a habitat for mountain lions, elk, deer, the tufted-eared Abert's squirrel, and the more elusive Hualapai vole, a mouse-like creature that is threatened with extinction.

The road begins at an elevation of about 3,300 feet and reaches 8,200 feet at Hualapai Mountain Park, about an 11-mile drive. En route, the road bisects Sawmill Canyon, named for a sawmill that operated near the mountaintop around the early 1900s. In addition to the sawmill, the Hualapai Mountains were the site of extensive gold and silver mining. In the 1870s, numerous prospectors poured into the range from California and Nevada.

At park headquarters you can get information about the facilities and hiking trails in the area. The county parks department maintains 16 cabins, four of which are rustic stone structures, within the park. If you want to make a reservation (a good idea in the summer), call the parks department (see Route Finder for details).

Now, onto the Wild Cow Springs Recreation Area, maintained by the federal Bureau of Land Management. (See Route Finder for details; the BLM recommends you have a high-clearance vehicle and a trailer no longer than 20 feet).

Hikers who make it to
the end of Hayden Trail
in Hualapai Mountain
Park have this view
from Dinosaur Rock
Overlook as a reward.

One of Kingman's local in-spots is Rosie's Den at Milepost 28
on U.S. Route 93. Rose Larsen, the owner, cooks items like
barbecued pork steak and home fried potatoes from scratch.

David Zickl

When you are about 2 miles from Wild Cow Springs, you'll pass a sign identifying the historic Flag Mine, one of the big producers in the area a hundred years ago. Iron bars now seal the adit (or mine passage), but in its day, the Flag Mine was one of the major sources of high-grade silver in Mohave County. Its ore was packed on mules from the mine to a point that used to be called Devil's Dip, where it was loaded on ore wagons and taken to Hardyville, a community on the Colorado River located near the site of present-day Bullhead City. From Hardyville it was taken south by boat to Yuma, loaded on a windjammer, and shipped to a smelter in Wales (the one in Great Britain). In those days Yuma was a seaport on the Sea of Cortes at the mouth of the Colorado River.

At Wild Cow Springs, there are camping sites, rest rooms, drinking water, and picnic tables (see Route Finder for details). Overlooking the desert below, the site is located amidst oak and large ponderosa pines at 6,200 feet elevation. Most visitors to the Hualapai Mountains stop at Hualapai Mountain Park, so Wild Cow Springs is not heavily used, and usually it's a good spot to find peace and quiet.

If you want more adventure, and have a four-wheel-drive vehicle, travel down the mountain from Wild Cow Springs for about 35 miles to Yucca, a community along Interstate 40 south of Kingman. Otherwise, return to Hualapai Mountain Park and the paved drive down the mountain.

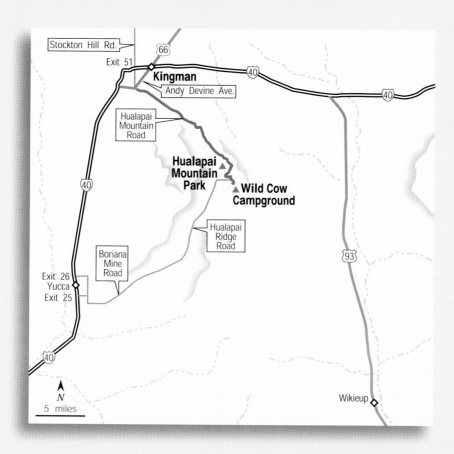

Route Finder

• Begin in Kingman at Exit 51 on Interstate 40 and go south on Stockton Hill Road, which turns into Hualapai Mountain Road.

• Drive 11 miles on Hualapai Mountain Road to the Hualapai Mountain Park headquarters/ranger station/visitors center.

• Leaving from the ranger station for Wild Cow Springs, drive south on Hualapai Mountain Road for about 1 mile (go past the fire station) to a fork. Bear right onto Flag Mine Road.

• Follow signs on Flag Mine Road for about 5 miles to the turnoff for Wild Cow Springs.

• Continue through the community of Pine Lake to its fire station. Across from it is a sign saying Wild Cow Springs is 4 miles away. Turn right onto the one-lane dirt road.

• Continue for about 3.2 miles to a junction where a sign says Wild Cow Springs is 0.4 mile to the left.

• To reach Yucca, take the right fork in the direction immediately above (Remember, a four-wheel-drive vehicle is recommended.)

• The road to Yucca is listed as Hualapai Ridge Road on some maps, and it leads into Boriana Mine Road, which leads to Interstate 40 at exits 25 and 26. Go right (north) for a return to Kingman.

Additional Information: Hualapai Mountain Park, (928) 681-5700; www.mcparks.com. Wild Cow Springs, (928) 718-3700; www.blm.gov/az/kfo/wcs.htm

Drive 4

Parker to Swansea and Bouse

A hundred years ago, many of Arizona's mountain ranges were like intricate beehives honeycombed with gold, silver, and copper mines. Many of these mines also were small communities, but today most of them exist only in postal records or as items in newspapers long out of print. As a result, there are an estimated 500 to 1,000 ghost towns in various stages of decomposition, places where dried-out doors flap and squeak on their twisted hinges and corrugated metal roofs rattle in the wind.

Swansea, named for the town in Wales where a lot of the ore ended up, is different from most other ghost towns. It is on public land controlled by the federal Bureau of Land Management, which encourages people to go out and have a look. There are still standing buildings, or portions of them, and mining equipment scattered about the desert.

Along the way to Swansea, and then to Bouse, you'll encounter one of the hottest and driest of the North American deserts. This was the terrain that Gen. George Patton chose as a training ground for his tank battalions during World War II.

The roads to Swansea and Bouse are easy to follow and surprisingly smooth. Begin in Parker (see Route Finder for details). The first 13 miles are on a paved road but drive cautiously on it because there are many potholes.

In that first 13 miles, the terrain is so parched that even the creosotes seem to have difficulty growing, and yet some saguaros and paloverde trees are sprinkled in the hills. The road climbs

David Muench

Beavertail cactus thrive in both the Mohave and Sonoran deserts and bloom from March to June.

The flowers of purple
mat, evening primrose,
and ocotillo enliven
the desert from late
February to mid-April.

gradually until it meets a dirt road on the right and a BLM sign that says "Swansea Ghost Town 17 miles."

About 10 minutes later, you'll cross an aqueduct of the Central Arizona Project, a federal project that siphons water from the Colorado River and delivers it to Phoenix and Tucson, among other places.

Remarkably, when you're 7 miles beyond the CAP canal, you come to a four-way stop sign in the middle of nowhere. To get to Swansea, continue straight and on your return trip you'll be turning left toward Bouse when you reach this junction.

Once you leave the four-way stop, the road narrows and winds through some steep terrain until you drop down on the north side of a pass into Swansea. The BLM recommends that you use a high-clearance vehicle—a four-wheel-drive vehicle is not necessary.

Like most ghost towns, Swansea is a forlorn and evocative place. The first silver claims in the area were recorded in 1886. Copper was also discovered, but in the early years there was no market for it. When copper prices jumped, in the 1890s, there was renewed interest in Swansea. It operated as a copper mine from 1908 to 1937. There was a smelter, hospital, and many homes at Swansea during its heyday, when it recorded about 750 residents. Now there are extensive ruins, mineshafts

A memorial at Bouse is dedicated to Gen. George Patton's tank troops who trained for combat in the desert near the town.

David H. Smith

surrounded by fences, abandoned vehicles, and mining equipment. The camp is basically an industrial bone yard surrounded by a desert wilderness. Swansea's geology—a lot of fractured rock riddled with hematite—proved too unstable for an extensive underground mine, and the operation folded a few years prior to the United States' entry into World War II.

When you leave Swansea, return to the four-way stop sign and turn left for Bouse, heading through a BLM preserve called the East Cactus Plain Wilderness. En route, you'll come to a sign directing you to a spot called Midway. The bulletin board at Midway says, "Not far from here the military under Gen. Patton trained for the invasion of North Africa during World War II." Some people who have roamed the area say tank tracks can still be found in the remote reaches of this desert.

You'll learn more about Patton and his tank battalions when you reach the pavement at Bouse, 12 miles south of the Midway sign. There's a tiny museum in an old assay office at Bouse, and at the town's main intersection on State Route 72 you'll see tanks and a few other military relics, as well as plaques detailing the role that Camp Bouse played in World War II.

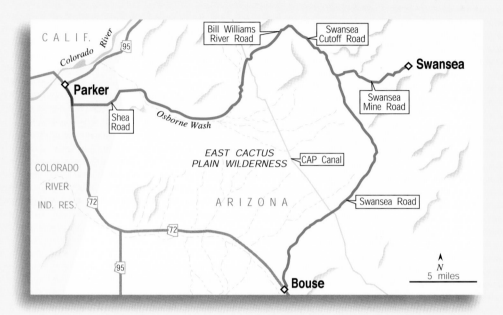

Route Finder

• *Begin in the southern end of Parker, about a quarter-mile south of the railroad tracks, at the intersection of State Route 95 and Shea Road. Turn east onto paved Shea Road.*

• *Continue on Shea Road for approximately 13 miles as it starts in an eastward direction, bears northward, eastward again, southward, and then eastward again. Turn right onto a dirt road identified on some maps as Parker-Swansea Road. A BLM sign at the junction says Swansea is 17 miles away.*

• *Continue on the dirt road for about 4 miles, crossing the Central Arizona Project aqueduct.*

• *Continue for 7 more miles on the road to a four-way stop sign. Note this location, for you will backtrack to it to reach Bouse. To reach Swansea, go straight for 6 miles.*

• *Leaving Swansea, backtrack to the four-way stop sign and turn left (southward).*

• *Continue for 20 miles (going past a sign marking Midway) to Bouse. At about Midway , the road veers from a south-southeasterly direction to southwesterly.*

• *Bouse is located on State Route 72. Turning right (westward) returns you to Parker in about 30 miles. Turning left takes you to U.S. Route 60 in about 22 miles.*

Additional information: Swansea, BLM, (928) 505-1200 or (888)213-2582; www.blm.gov/az/rec/swansea.htm. Parker, (928) 669-6511 or (928) 669-2174; www.parkertourism.com or www.parkerareachamberofcommerce.com. Bouse, (928) 851-2174; www.bouseazchamber.com.

A visitor cautiously peers into the opening of an abandoned mine in Black Rock Gulch, off Red Cloud Mine Road. David Elms Jr.

Drive 5

Martinez Lake to Imperial National Wildlife Refuge on Red Cloud Mine Road

The former manager of the Imperial National Wildlife Refuge, north of Yuma, tried to prepare me for what to expect on Red Cloud Mine Road. In a couple of phone conversations, Mitch Ellis called it a treat for the backcountry enthusiast. The location is remote, the road challenging but not impossible for a high-clearance vehicle up to a point. The scenery often reminds visitors of an alien landing site in a really bad movie.

"There are some old mines out there, and there's a good chance of seeing bighorn sheep," Ellis added. "Anyone planning to camp should be prepared for the wild burros. There are a lot of them, and they bray all night. We call them desert canaries."

To photographer David Elms and me, it sounded perfect. After turning onto Red Cloud Mine Road (see Route Finder for detailed directions) we stopped at the U.S. Fish and Wildlife Service visitors center. There we learned there are four pullouts along Red Cloud Mine Road where visitors can scan the riparian landscape of the lower Colorado River: Paloverde, Mesquite, Ironwood, and Smoke Tree. Between the Mesquite and Ironwood points lies the short Painted Desert Trail. Beyond the trailhead, a four-wheel-drive vehicle is recommended for travel on Red Cloud Mine Road.

Now approaching four-wheel-drive terrain, we continued past the trailhead to Ironwood Point, our first stop of the day. The point overlooks a backwater lake bordered by giant cane grass, with stretches of the Colorado River visible a few hundred yards beyond.

The first thing we noticed was the moisture in the desert air and the sweet smell. The morning shadows still hung in the creases of the aptly named Chocolate Mountains flanking the Colorado on the California side.

The lake hummed with exuberant life this day. Hundreds of tiny swallows were lighting on the mesquite snags jutting from the water. With their fervent twittering, the nasal honking of the American coots, and the assorted cheeps and whistles of numerous other birds, it sounded like we'd stumbled into a party.

We spent about 40 minutes enjoying the shoreline before getting back on the road. It curled over rock hills, and, in a couple of spots, the surface was marked by deep depressions that had to be negotiated at slow speed.

Within 4 miles after leaving the visitors center, we'd gone from water and grassland to the stark Trigo Mountains and the thrilling sight of three desert bighorns. We'd just parked and hiked the crest of a hill when Elms spotted the animals hoofing down a ridge. They were too far away to photograph with his zoom lens, but close enough to examine with binoculars.

While I had one ram in my sights, he caught the sound of our voices and turned to look—right into my eyes. What a treat to see these creatures up close as they ballet-stepped over this hard terrain like four-legged Nureyevs.

California's Chocolate
Mountains rise like mounds
of fudge near Butler
Lake, a backwater pond
on the Colorado River.

Just then, three sand rail-style buggies buzzed past, the occupants waving as they went. We got into our truck and caught up with them at Black Rock Mine, about 2.5 miles down the road and around the next bend. We found these high-spirited outdoorsmen were retirees from Oregon on a daylong adventure.

All but two were experienced explorers, and their sand rails were packed with gear, including CB radios to communicate while driving. We'd chatted for only three minutes when they invited us to eat lunch with them.

But first we had fun inspecting Black Rock Wash, less than a quarter-mile up the road. We saw, carved into its high banks, the dugouts that miners once used as homes. One still had a smoke pipe coming out the top of the hill, a crude ventilation system for the wood-burning stove that some enterprising miner had hauled into his hole.

The Trigos are full of old mines and markers, usually rock cairns, noting the location of modern-day claims. If you're like me, you wonder what combination of hope and desperation could make someone see these mountains as his ticket.

David Elms Jr.

The Imperial refuge provides an ideal habitat for the Western diamondback rattlesnake, which has heat-sensitive pits on its head to guide its strikes at prey.

They're a place of horrible beauty. The hills are strewn with black volcanic boulders that trace your footsteps down the slope, avalanche-style, when you hike up. The ground is dry as a lizard's belly and supports almost no vegetation. Maybe a paloverde tree here, an ironwood tree there, but they're gnarled and twisted for lack of moisture.

When it does rain, the monsoon water slashes over the ground, carving cracks and arroyos with 20-foot walls. The occasional *ka-boom* of military ordnance from the U.S. Army's Yuma Proving Ground, directly east, adds to the otherworldly atmosphere.

At about 12 miles from the visitors center, we reached the Red Cloud Mine. First worked for silver and lead in the 1870s, it was named for the brilliant red-orange wulfenite crystals found there.

Less than a half-mile beyond the mine, we turned left down an arroyo, followed it to another fork at the head of Red Cloud Wash and turned right. Then we followed that road another 6 miles to a place nicknamed "the falls." Here, the road drops several feet in a hurry and hangs up quite a few travelers.

Visitors without four-wheel drive wouldn't get that far anyway. Beyond the Red Cloud Mine, even finding a route becomes challenging in the maze of tracks and washes that look like roads. Then you have to turn around and drive out the same way. Those with sturdy four-wheel drives can continue past the falls to the Cibola National Wildlife Refuge, 6 miles up.

Elms and I had parked our truck and rode with the snowbird brigade in the sand rails, which easily negotiated the trail. At a wide spot, they stopped and prepared a meal of tortillas and sausages cooked over a big fire, with pickles, salami, beer, even mussels out of a can.

Late in the day, Elms and I drove back to the Painted Desert Trail. This enjoyable, self-guided hike runs 1.3 miles and passes bizarre volcanic rock formations, drops into a shady wash decorated with purple and red boulders, and climbs dunelike mountains.

From these peaks, we looked west and saw the Colorado River again, blessedly wet. It appeared as a ribbon of sparkling blue under the setting sun, which seemed the perfect close to a day of unusual fun in an unusual land.

—Leo W. Banks

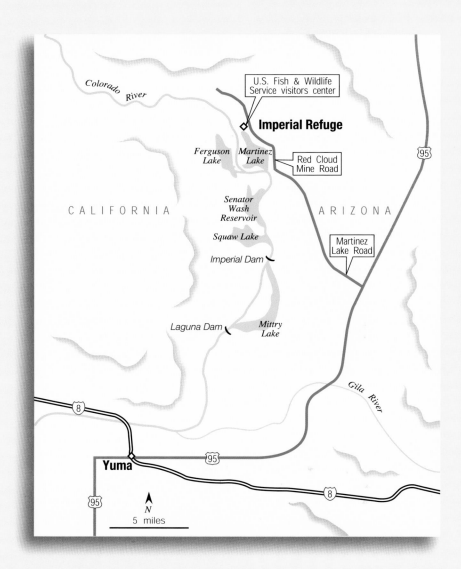

Route Finder

• Begin on U.S. Route 95 in Yuma and drive north. About 8 miles after crossing the Gila River turn left (west) onto Martinez Lake Road. The turnoff is between mileposts 46 and 47.

• Continue northwesterly on Martinez Lake Road for about 10 miles to Red Cloud Mine Road and turn right (north)

• Take Red Cloud Mine Road for about 3.5 miles to the marked turnoff on the left for the U.S. Fish & Wildlife Service visitors center. The center is just off Red Cloud Mine Road.

• Return to Red Cloud Mine Road and turn left. It's about 2.3 miles to a short nature-hike trail and 3.4 miles to Smoke Tree vista, the farthest north of 4 pullouts on the road. Travel beyond this point on Red Cloud Road probably will require a four-wheel-drive vehicle.

Additional information: Visitors center, (928)-783-3371; www.fws.gov/southwest/refuges/arizona/imperial.html

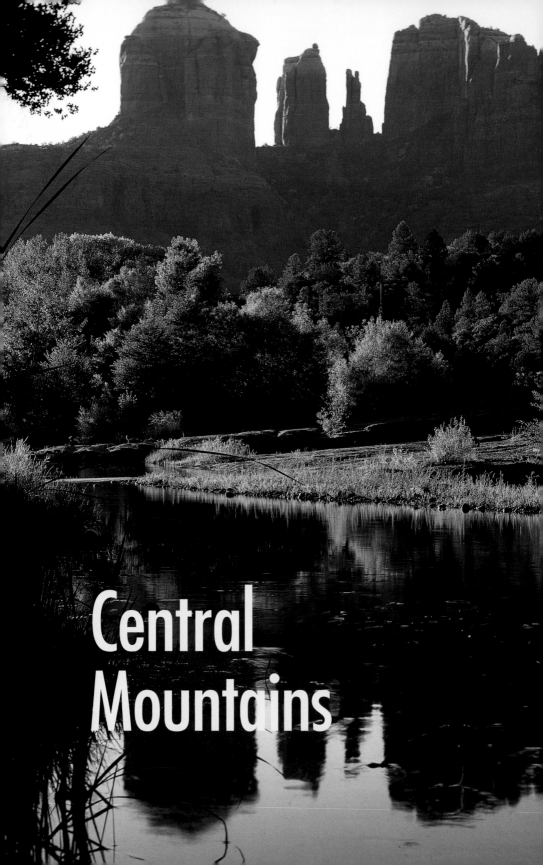

Central
Mountains

Oak Creek, far left, reflects Cathedral Rock, one of the most famous red rock formations in Sedona, located between Prescott and Flagstaff. Beaver Creek, left, meanders through the Verde Valley near the town of Camp Verde.

George H.H. Huey

Prescott, Verde Valley and Mogollon Rim

• Overview

The routes described here are easy to reach from either Prescott or Camp Verde. Montezuma Castle, a Sinagua cliff dwelling, is at Camp Verde. The charm of a restored ghost town can be seen at Jerome. At Dead Horse Ranch State Park, you can camp and go fishing and boating in the Verde River. In Sedona, dramatic red cliffs frame the town, where you will also find upscale restaurants and art galleries.

• The Drives

• Towns and Sites

Apache Maid Mountain, Camp Verde, Camp Wood, Cottonwood, Heber, Jerome, Mogollon Rim, Payson, Prescott, Sedona, Skull Valley, Stanton, Stoneman Lake, and Yarnell.

David Muench

The hardy, adaptable coyote makes a living in most parts of Arizona and many other parts of North America.
George H.H. Huey

Some 90 miles north of Phoenix on Interstate 17, a long steep hill descends into the Verde Valley. When you're nearly to the bottom of the hill, and assuming you could take your eyes off the road without getting killed, a panorama of rose-colored cliffs appears north and west of the highway. At the very bottom of the hill, you'll see the Verde River, or rather the tall cottonwood trees that line the river. You can't actually see the water until you're practically on top of it.

But the water is there, a near-miracle in an arid landscape where rainfall is scarce and sunshine abundant. The river is the bottom of a wall of mountains to the north, however, and is fed by a number of big streams—Wet Beaver, Dry Beaver and Beaver Creek among others, which you can explore on the Stoneman Lake back road described later.

The town of Camp Verde, some 100 miles north of Phoenix, is a good place to stop and take stock of the surrounding terrain. If you could take an elevator a few thousand feet into the sky above the town, you would see that in every direction mountains cascade like a fountain of lava that rises and falls, forming pine- and spruce-covered peaks eastward to the Mogollon Rim and White Mountains, dipping into deep canyons, and fording clear streams all the way to Mount Baldy and Escudilla near the New Mexico line. To the people who live on the Colorado Plateau to the north and to those living in the vast deserts south of the escarpment called the Mogollon Rim, these mountains are a special gift, a haven from searing summers when temperatures in the lower elevations will often exceed 100 degrees.

Scattered among these densely forested mountains are some of Arizona's most popular smaller communities. From your perch in the sky, look to the northwest and you can see the dramatic red cliffs of Sedona rising above Oak Creek Canyon. Look southwest toward Mingus Mountain and you can see Jerome, a copper-mining town that was saved from oblivion by a handful of artists and artisans who adopted it in the 1960s. Look across the top of Mingus Mountain and you'll drop down in Prescott, a small, attractive city surrounded by the Prescott National Forest and mountains where a fortune was made in gold. Nowadays, these towns are the jewels of central Arizona.

One of the most productive gold-mining regions in the state was southwest of Prescott, in the Weaver Mining district (see the Prescott to Stanton drive). At a place appropriately named Rich Hill, prospectors in 1863 found gold nuggets the size of potatoes. Placer gold (gold found in the surface sands in creek beds) was found in Weaver and Antelope creeks and precipitated the settlement of Octave, Weaver, and Stanton, places now vacant and silent in the valley south of Yarnell. A sign at Stanton, which boasted a population of 3,500 in 1868, says $100 million in gold, garnets,

Bear Wallow Canyon lies along scenic but rugged Schnebly Hill Road, which links Sedona and Interstate 17.

and gems were recovered in the area before most of the gold was depleted in the early 1900s.

You can easily get into that gold-mining region by using Prescott as a base. If you have not yet visited Prescott, you can expect a pleasant surprise. Around Arizona, people seem to have a special affection for Prescott because of its agreeable climate and friendly hometown atmosphere. The town was Arizona's first Territorial capitol, and it lies in the state's geographic center. It looks and feels like a small New England city, though the residents are generally more outgoing than people in the Northeast. The town, in fact, was designed by New Englanders dispatched by President Lincoln to the Wild West to establish the Territorial government. Situated at an elevation of 5,000 feet, Prescott offers an ideal climate. Summer days are warm but not searing, and the nights are cool. Trees lining streets of story-book Victorian homes put on a colorful display in the fall, and winters usually see enough snow to give the place a Norman Rockwell cast but not enough to make driving dangerous. Prescott likes to think of itself as "Everybody's Home Town," an artifact of the 1950s where Ozzie and Harriet might still be comfortable. The city has the cozy, inviting feel of a kitchen filled with the fragrance of freshly baked bread.

Sedona, on the other hand, is not so much cozy as it is dramatic, a place of such bold colors and shapes that, once seen, it is never forgotten. The town lies

David H. Smith

The corner of Gurley and Montezuma streets forms one edge of Prescott's notorious Whiskey Row. The saloons are gone, but the name survives.

Jerome maintains the look of a frontier mining town, but
its streets now are lined with shops and restaurants.

George H.H. Huey

in a bowl at the edge of Oak Creek Canyon, about 120 miles north of Phoenix.
Although the main streets are lined with art galleries, gift shops, and tourist
facilities, Sedona's chief attraction is its natural beauty. While the inhabited
part of the town is only 4,400 feet high, striking red buttes, pinnacles, spires,
and domes rise above it like a sanctuary for mythical gods, although in reality
it has long been a haven not for gods but for artists and writers and retirees. In
the 1920s, Zane Grey made the place famous with his book, *Call of the Canyon,*
which became a movie shot amid the rose- and pink-colored cliffs. These
sandstone cliffs and rugged formations—with names like Snoopy, Bell Rock,
Slide Rock—are not red as in apple red, but change colors throughout the day,
from pink to magenta to purple.

Jerome, on the other hand, has a rustic charm but nothing as glamorous as
the upscale shops and restaurants of Sedona. In 1903 a reporter for the *New York
Sun* visited Jerome, southwest of Sedona, and went home in a state of shock.

"Jerome," he wrote, "is the wickedest town in America." About four years
earlier, in the aftermath of one of the town's devastating fires, a representative
of the Salvation Army had stood in the middle of what remained of Main
Street and offered her prayers for "the Sodom and Gomorrah of Arizona." God,
declared the Salvation Army's Mrs. Thomas, had burned Jerome to purify it.

The prehistoric Sinagua ("without water") people built what's now known as Tuzigoot National Monument on a knoll with a commanding view of the Verde Valley and Verde River.

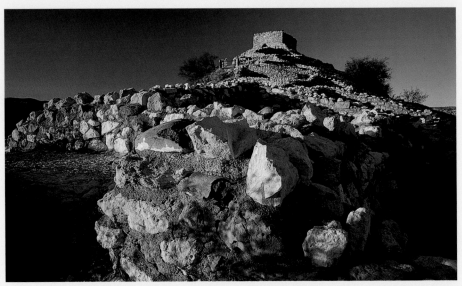

Tom Danielsen

Things couldn't help but get better after that.

When artists and craftsman discovered Jerome in the 1960s, the former copper-mining town was nearly abandoned. Now the town on Mingus Mountain is a quaint art colony where you can park your car and walk the hilly streets to several galleries and coffeehouses. Built on rock terraces along the side of Cleopatra Hill, Jerome annually attracts a million visitors with its charmingly narrow streets and turn-of-the-century architecture. In its heyday in the 1890s, the town had 15,000 residents. Today a few hundred, most of them artists, call the place home.

Ever since its incorporation in 1899, it seems, Jerome has been getting a bad press. And yet, for the last 20 years, tourists have been coming in ever-increasing numbers. Some of them have heard that it was a ghost town, the remnant of one of the richest ore-producing mines in the United States. Still others have heard that Jerome is a colorful and casual art colony. While Jerome is not, strictly speaking, a ghost town today, in the mid-1960s it came pretty close. In 1964, the town had about 20 voters. The water system had collapsed; the sewer system was just about gone. The Town Hall even collapsed. Mrs. Thomas would have been delighted.

But Jerome has a history of bouncing back from adversity. Some of the earliest mining entrepreneurs had been skeptical of the prospects there because the ore bodies were so distant from a railroad line. Hence, soon after the United Verde Mine was organized, in 1883, it built its own railroad. Two major fires, one in 1898 and another in 1899, nearly destroyed the entire community, including the town jail. The town revived. The police department even improvised by taking its feisty prisoners and handcuffing them with their arms around telegraph poles.

The era of the United Verde Mine ended in 1935 when it was sold for $20.8 million to the Phelps Dodge Corp. Between 1916 and 1937, when it finally ended all operations, the United Verde had produced $150 million in gold, silver, and copper. Some no doubt thought the end had come with the demise of the United Verde, but Phelps Dodge continued to mine the hills until 1953.

Today, the Verde Valley and central Arizona has become an easy get-away destination, especially for people from Phoenix who only have a two- or three-hour drive to reach scenic locations and good fishing and canoeing spots along the Verde River.   ᴀʜ

George Stocking

The town of Cottonwood spreads in the Verde Valley below Mingus
Mountain, the photographer's vantage point here.

Drive 1

Prescott to Stanton:
Gentle Drive in the Hills

The back road from Prescott to Stanton takes you to a place where that silly line about gold "in them thar hills" is actually accurate. Evidently some of the gold is still there to be found. In March 2000, a recreational prospector at Stanton had found a fist-sized chunk of gold. Not fool's gold. This was the real thing.

Most of this loop drive is paved (see Route Finder for detailed directions). The route takes you through the granite boulders and juniper-covered hills of Yavapai County. You can comfortably drive this route any time of the year except on those few days when there is snow. The entire route can be driven in a leisurely morning or afternoon. There are antique and curio shops and restaurants scattered along the way, especially in Yarnell.

Along the loop you'll pass through Skull Valley, Kirkland and Kirkland Junction, Peeples Valley, Yarnell and the St. Joseph's of the Mountain Shrine, Stanton, and Wilhoit.

Skull Valley, the first community along the way, was named for the many bleached skulls found there by the first non-Indian settlers. The skulls were reportedly the end result of a fierce battle between Maricopa and Apache Indians. The Skull Valley General Store is worth a stop, if only to browse. Leaving there, you pass through Kirkland, Kirkland Junction, Peeples Valley, and Yarnell en route to Stanton.

As you move through Peeples Valley, the road leads between green pastures and climbs a small hill into the community of Yarnell, where you'll find gas, restaurants, and gift shops. Yarnell is 22.5 miles south of Skull Valley.

In Yarnell, directional signs will direct you to St. Joseph of the Mountain Shrine, located about a quarter-mile off the highway. The park-like place is set at the base of a rocky hill amid a desert bouquet consisting of small oak and pungent juniper trees, red-barked manzanita, native grasses, prickly pear cactus, lichen, and a little fern. The shrine includes a statue of St. Joseph holding the Christ child and the 14 Stations of the Cross cast in concrete along a loop trail leading up the hill.

From Yarnell the highway narrows as it twists its way for 6 miles to the bottom of Yarnell Hill. About halfway down the hill there's a scenic pullout. The cows you can see in the distance are part of a dairy which you will pass as you drive in to Stanton.

Stanton is named for Charlie Stanton, a real person until 1886, when his various misdeeds caught up with him, and he became indisputably a very dead person. Before his death, he was known to many as an opportunist who feigned piety while directing a gang of thieves and murderers. His worst mistake, however, was to make a vulgar remark about a teenage Mexican girl. For that bit of insensitivity, the girl's brothers turned Stanton into Swiss cheese.

Members of the Lost Dutchman Mining Association, a prospector's club which now owns the Stanton town site, re-enact the shooting of Charlie Stanton every New Year's Eve in the

Besides serenity, Prescott's Watson Lake and park in the Granite Dells offer boating and fishing, picnic facilities, hiking trails, and camping (with showers).

Once a depot for the Santa Fe Railroad, this building now houses a museum. The name? Supposedly, early settlers found many skulls in the area.

David H. Smith

original saloon/opera house adjacent to the stagecoach stop where Stanton was killed on November 13, 1886.

Anyone can visit Stanton. The club members, who are recreational prospectors, happily will show you around the stage station, the dilapidated remains of an 11-room hotel, and the saloon. Free tours are available any day between 8 A.M. and 5 P.M.

Stanton is about 40 miles southwest of Prescott at the base of 5,200-feet-high Rich Hill, so-named because prospectors in 1863 made a fortune digging baseball-sized gold nuggets from its surface soils.

Nowadays, the area may be more abundant in lore than ore, but between 1863 and 1894, the gold discoveries in the Weaver Mining District, which included Stanton, attracted droves of prospectors from California. One historian reported that Abraham Harlow Peeples (you'll drive through the valley named for him), who headed the first group of California prospectors, "picked up $7,000 worth of gold before breakfast." Both gold mining and violence dominated life in the area until the 1930s, but fires, scarcity of water, and declining productivity all took their toll.

The area was largely forgotten until 1959, when the *Saturday Evening Post* purchased 10 acres of Stanton. At that time there were only two people living in the town that once boasted a population of about 2,000. The magazine changed Stanton's name to Ulcer Gulch (which never stuck). It said it would award Ulcer Gulch—a nickname for the Madison Avenue advertising district in Manhattan—to the person who provided the best last line of a promotional jingle.

What the jingle was all about, we couldn't say, but newspapers from 1959 did record that Mrs. Anne Foster, a 30-year-old employee at the New York advertising agency of J. Walter Thompson, had won herself a ghost town out in Arizona. She moved to Stanton with her pet monkey, but after about two years both she and the monkey had moved on.

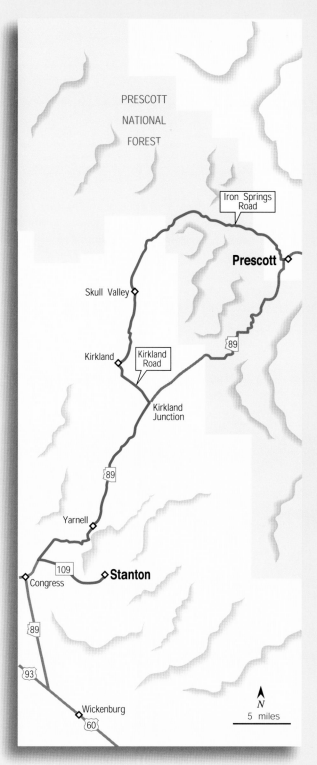

PRESCOTT

NATIONAL

FOREST

Iron Springs
Road

Prescott

Skull Valley

89

Kirkland
Road

Kirkland

Kirkland
Junction

89

Yarnell

109   ◇**Stanton**

Congress

89

93

N
5 miles

Wickenburg

60

Route Finder _____

• *Begin in Prescott at the northwest corner of the plaza in the center of town and drive west on Gurley Street about five blocks to Miller Valley Road. Turn right.*

• *Continue on Miller Valley Road to its junction with Whipple Street, Willow Creek Road, and Iron Springs Road. Bear left (northwest) onto Iron Springs Road.*

• *Continue on Iron Springs Road (also marked as County Route 10) for about 20 miles to Skull Valley.*

• *Continue south on Iron Springs Road for about 7 miles to the Kirkland Post Office. Turn left (southeasterly) onto Kirkland Road.*

• *Continue on Kirkland Road for 4 miles to Kirkland Junction. Turn right (south) onto State Route 89, also known as White Spar Road.*

• *Continue south on State 89/White Spar Road for 22 miles through Peeples Valley to Yarnell.*

• *Continue south on State 89/White Spar Road for 8 miles past the junction of State Road and Shrine Street in Yarnell to County Route 109, also the Stanton Road. Turn left.*

• *Continue for 6.5 miles to Stanton.*

• *Leaving Stanton, backtrack to State 89. Turn right (north).*

• *Continue north for about 38 miles to Prescott.*

Additional information: Prescott, (928) 445-2000; www.prescott.org. St. Joseph's Shrine, (928) 778-5229; www.st.joseph-shrine.org.

Drive 2

Prescott to Camp Wood, A Territorial Cavalry Post

There are many reasons to like Prescott. For one thing, the town is a mile above sea level, so its climate is moderate. It actually has four distinct seasons. With its big trees and gingerbread architecture, Prescott seems to remind most people of someplace else—usually the small town in the Midwest or New England where they grew up. It's also a gateway to some of the

Hikers make their way up Granite Mountain in the Prescott National Forest near Prescott. George H.H. Huey

most beautiful undeveloped country in central Arizona. If you like mountains, tall trees, open prairies, and wildlife, you won't be disappointed on this easy drive from the center of Prescott to Camp Wood.

Camp Wood was a minor substation of Camp Hualpai, a cavalry post established in 1869 on a mesa above Walnut Creek, some 11 miles north of Camp Wood. Hualpai was originally called Camp Toll Gate (the name changed in 1870). Both Hualpai and Wood served the same purpose, which was to protect travelers from Indian raids along the so-called Hardyville Toll Road. The toll road was one of Arizona's early stagecoach routes that connected Hardyville on the Colorado River (where Bullhead City is today) with Prescott and Fort Whipple. Several smaller stagecoach lines operated between Prescott and Williams to the north in the days when the railroad was being built across northern Arizona, and the excursion described here crosses the same terrain those little wagons followed.

However, you won't get jostled as badly as travelers did at the end of the 19th century. The first 23 miles from Iron Springs Road to the turnoff for Camp Wood are paved.

Start at the courthouse plaza in the center of Prescott (see Route Finder for detailed directions) and work your way of town heading north and northwest. After reaching Williamson Valley Road,

you can see Granite Peak, a Prescott landmark, to the west (left). From there the next 23 miles are a smooth, paved ribbon through open grasslands dotted here and there with clumps of juniper and oak trees. When the summer rain arrives, the valley turns to an emerald green carpet.

After 23 miles, turn left onto Forest Service Road 21, an unpaved Prescott National Forest road. The road is narrow in places but easily driven in an ordinary two-wheel-drive vehicle. The area called Camp Wood is 16 miles away.

There is nothing left of Camp Wood except a clearing that the Forest Service refers to as a dispersed camping area. Years ago it was a camp for the Civilian Conservation Corps, but the buildings from that era have been removed. What remains are tall stands of ponderosa pines and refreshing shade.

If you are driving a high-clearance vehicle, you can turn right when you get to Camp Wood and follow the signs for 11 miles to Walnut Creek. Some low creek crossings along that road make it not advisable to try this route in a family sedan. The Forest Service has a ranger station at Walnut Creek and if it happens to be open, someone may be able to point you to the mesa where Camp Hualpai was located (although the site is now privately owned). From the Walnut Creek ranger station, drive east and return to Williamson Valley Road. As you approach Prescott from the north, watch on the right (west) side of the road for the Granite Mountain Recreation Area, a part of the Prescott National Forest. You can reach a hiking trail into the Granite Mountain Wilderness by turning right onto Iron Springs Road and then turning right on Granite Basin Road. The trailhead is 3.2 miles west of the turn-off from FR 374 for Granite Basin Lake. If you don't want to hike, turn left when Williamson Valley Road reaches Iron Springs Road and return to Prescott.

George H.H. Huey

The horseman in front of the Yavapai County courthouse depicts local hero Buckey O'Neill, a frontier lawman and member of the Rough Riders in the Spanish-American War.

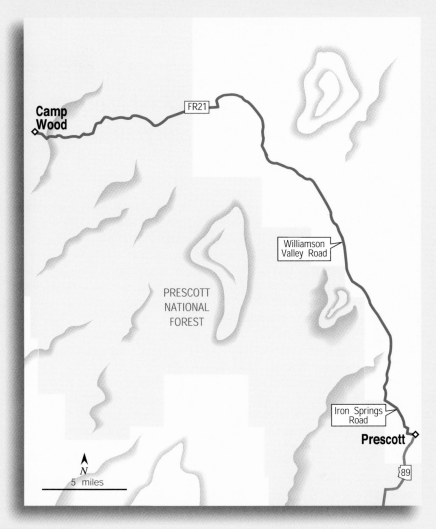

Route Finder

- Start at the northwest corner of the plaza in the center of Prescott.
- Drive west on Gurley Street a few blocks to Miller Valley Road. Turn right.
- Continue on Miller Valley Road for a few blocks to Iron Springs Road. Bear left (northerly).
- Continue 1 mile on Iron Springs Road to Williamson Valley Road. Turn right (north).
- Continue for 23 miles on Williamson Valley Road (also known as County Route 5) when it enters the Prescott National Forest to Forest Service Road 21, also known as Behm Mesa Road. Turn left.
- Continue on FR 21 for 16 miles to the Camp Wood site.
- Option: You can retrace your route to return to Prescott, or continue to Walnut Creek if you are driving

a high-clearance vehicle. A sign at Camp Wood directs you to Walnut Creek, 11 miles away via Forest Service Road 95.
- Leaving Walnut Creek, continue northeast on FR 95 about 4 miles to FR 6. Turn right onto FR 6 (it leads into Williamson Valley Road) for a 40-mile return to Prescott.

Additional information: Recreation in Prescott National Forest, Bradshaw Ranger District, (928) 443-8000; www.fs.fed.us/r3/prescott/recreation/trails/index.shtml. Chino Valley Ranger District, (928) 777-2200.

The Verde River provides the basis for recreational opportunities at Dead Horse Ranch State Park near Cottonwood.
George H.H. Huey

Drive 3

Stoneman Lake to Apache Maid Mountain: Tracing an Old Spanish Explorers Route

The back road from Stoneman Lake through a ponderosa pine forest to the base of Apache Maid Mountain more or less traces a route once used by Spanish explorers, the U.S. cavalry, and stage coach companies. In some places, it still looks like an old wagon road, but evidently it's not quite as intimidating as it was when Martha Summerhayes came through in 1875.

Martha was the wife of a cavalry officer named Jack Summerhayes. Nowadays nobody remembers Jack, but Martha immortalized herself with her engaging memoir of Army life in Territorial Arizona. Her book, *Vanished Arizona,* provides a vivid portrait of the state in the 1870s and tells of her all-too-human reactions to the privations of life on the frontier. Traveling with her husband and a newborn baby through a portion of what is now the 1.8-million-acre Coconino National Forest to his posting at Camp Apache, she was terrified by the dangerous descent from the Mogollon Rim down into the Verde Valley at Beaver Creek.

Al Doyle, a Flagstaff pioneer and a guide for Zane Grey, notes in his memoirs that, before the arrival of the railroad in northern Arizona, "travel east and west was all by way of the old Star Route stage line, which ran from Santa Fe, N.M. to Prescott ... mail and passengers were brought across the Mogollon mountains by way of Sunset Pass and Chavez Pass, Stoneman Lake, Beaver Head , Camp Verde and into Prescott."

Martha Summerhayes and her husband traveled that route on their way to the General Crook Trail, a military wagon road that connected Fort Verde to Camp Apache (which became Fort Apache in 1879).

Many years later she recalled the beginning of that descent off the Rim: "... we soon found that the road (if road it could be called) was worse than any we had encountered. The ambulance [a coach drawn by mules] was pitched and jerked from rock to rock and we were thumped against the iron framework in a most dangerous manner. So we got out and picked our way over the great sharp boulders ... Little by little we gave up hope of reaching Verde that day. At four o'clock we crossed the 'divide' [the Mogollon Rim], and clattered down a road so near the edge of a precipice that I was frightened beyond everything: my senses nearly left me. Down and around, this way and that, near the edge, then back again, swaying, swerving, pitching, the gravel clattering over the precipice, the six mules trotting their fastest, we reached the bottom and the driver pulled up his team. 'Beaver Springs!' said he, impressively, loosening up the brakes."

Afterwards she asked the driver why he had gone at "such a break-neck pace!" To which he replied, "Had to, ma'am, or we'd a'gone over the edge."

Not to worry. The drive through this terrain today is not nearly as intimidating, although it remains fairly isolated.

To see this area, take Interstate 17 north from Camp Verde to Stoneman Lake Road at Exit 306 (see Route Finder for directions).

Forest Service Road 229 seems to say "come drive me" and wander into the Coconino National Forest.

Below Apache Maid Mountain, juniper and ponderosa
pine tress dot an alpine meadow.

Charles Lawsen

When you reach the lake, the road splits. The left leg leads around the lake's northern side, where there are a parking area, picnic tables, and an outhouse in a 6,900-foot setting of ponderosa pine and Gambel oak trees and several privately-owned cabins. In recent times the lake's level has been falling.

Leaving Stoneman Lake, continue eastward on Forest Service Road 213. If you want to camp, you'll find plenty of dispersed campsites—meaning flat clearings among the trees.

Now you are about 15 miles from Apache Maid Mountain. The road meanders between some refreshing green meadows ringed with ponderosa pines. The road gets narrower and a little rougher than 213, but any high-clearance vehicle will make it in dry weather without difficulty.

Apache Maid Mountain, elevation 7,302 feet, looms over the headwaters of West Beaver Creek. The trees open up a bit in that area and the fire lookout on the mountain is clearly visible and you are in the midst of history.

Charles Lawsen

Evening primroses flourish
naturally in Arizona, which
counts about 20 species of
the wildflower.

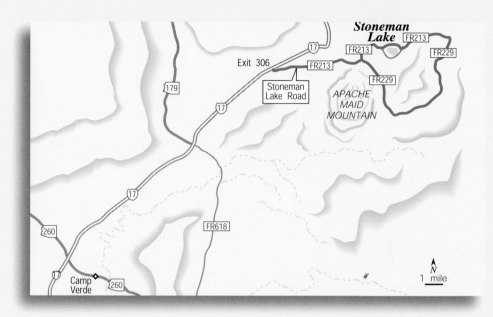

Route Finder

• Start at Exit 306 on Interstate 17, about 19 miles north of Camp Verde. Turn right (east) at the end of the exit ramp onto Stoneman Lake Road, also Forest Service Road 213.

• Continue east and northeast on Stoneman Lake Road. In the first 1.5 miles the road comes to junctions with a dirt roads on the right. Continue straight on the paved road.

• About 8.5 miles after leaving the interstate, FR 213 comes to a junction with Forest Service Road 229 and the pavement ends. Bear left, staying on 213.

• Continue on 213 for a little more than 2 miles. As 213 approaches the lake it splits, 213A going left to a day-use area, and 213 going right.

• Leaving Stoneman Lake day-use area, return to the 213-213A junction and turn left. In the next 6 miles, 213 bears southeast, east, northeast, and east before reaching a junction with Forest Service Road 230. Turn right (south).

• In about 8 miles FR 230 comes to a junction with FR 229. Continue on 230, bearing left. The road (230) climbs switchbacks up the mountain for about 3.5 more miles. About halfway up, Forest Service Road 620E leads to the left for less than a mile to the eastern trailhead of Apache Maid Trail.

• Return to the junction of 230 and 229. Turn left onto 229 (north).

• Continue on 229 about 5 miles to Stoneman Lake Road (FR 213). Turn left and return to Interstate 17.

Additional information: Stoneman Lake, Coconino National Forest, Red Rock Ranger District, (928) 282-4119; www.fs.fed.us/r3/coconino/recreation/red_rock/stoneman-boat.shtml. Apache Maid Trail, www.fs.fed.us/r3/coconino/recreation/red_rock/apache-maid.shtml.

The three men buried here were victims of an Old West lynch mob during the Pleasant Valley feud between two families and their allies. George Stocking

Drive 4

Heber to Mogollon Rim: Lynchings and More

First take three lynchings, one deadly ranch war, two historic trails, and a desperately crooked deputy sheriff. Then throw in a ranch full of beautiful women and the world's most famous UFO abduction.

This might sound like a new fiction category: Sci-Fi Western Romance. But up on the Mogollon Rim, such plot lines form the basis of history books and a great backcountry trek in the April-November period.

One historic example: In mid-August 1888, a cowboy on the Rim found three grisly bodies hanging from a pine tree. The victims—Jamie Stott, Jim Scott, and Billy (or Jeff) Wilson—had been lynched. Some accuse Deputy Sheriff J.D. Houck, who coveted Stott's land.

Another example: In November 1975, a tree-thinning crew decided to investigate a strange light emanating from near the edge of the Rim. Their search supposedly led to a disk-shaped spacecraft hovering at treetop level. One crew member, Travis Walton, inexplicably ran toward the ship, but he was stopped cold by a bolt of blue light. By the time his buddies had recovered their senses, Walton and the spacecraft were gone, the young man not turning up until five days later, confused and dehydrated, relating fantastic tales of his tour aboard a flying saucer.

If you're interested in a more conventional, terrestrial tour of the Mogollon Rim's most scenic and spooky sites, consider a loop route along those two historic trails—one a famous 1870s military road, the other a cattle route dating from the 1880s.

Begin in Heber and head south into the Sitgreaves National Forest (see Route Finder for detailed directions). You'll soon break out toward the Mogollon Rim on Forest Service Road 86. One hundred years ago, you might have passed a stagecoach or a cattle drive plodding along this road. Today you're as likely to see elk as traffic.

As you progress south by southwest up the canyon, you'll find yourself surrounded by cliffs and rock formations. Hidden among them are red-painted pictographs perhaps 900 years old. Nearer the road, you'll see pockmarked limestone boulders cropping up like half-buried skulls.

Six miles from the highway, at Wilford, the road crosses a low bridge. This abandoned community thrived in the early 1880s. Beyond it 2.5 miles lies historic Black Canyon Ranch, the property occupied by Deputy Sheriff Houck on the day that Stott, Scott, and Wilson were murdered.

Another 1.5 miles brings you to lovely Baca Meadows, named for Juan and Damasia Baca, who began homesteading this area in 1889. Their ranch soon became the most celebrated stop on the entire cattle trail—partly because of Damasia's legendary hospitality, but mostly because her seven pretty daughters represented the best concentration of young womanhood almost anywhere in the Territory. A family cemetery ringed by aspens and blanketed with wildflowers lies nearby on the left side of the road.

Within 15 minutes you'll be at the turnoff for Black Canyon Lake, situated at about 7,600 feet elevation. It'll take just a few minutes to drive to the lake and back to FR 86; or you can use the lake's camping and picnic facilities, including water and vault toilets.

Bluestem pricklepoppies
commandeer a patch of land in
an area of the Mogollon Rim
otherwise dominated by trees.

Your next waypoint is a primitive track called Spur No. 9. With a high-clearance vehicle, you can follow this track back into the forest 1.5 miles to a small rail-fenced enclosure protecting the somber gravesites of Stott, Scott, and Wilson. The tombstones, curiously, are etched with the date "August 4, 1888," seven days before the true date of their demise.

Returning to Black Canyon Road, turn left onto Forest Service Road 300, which is commonly called the Mogollon Rim Road, and also known as General Crook Trail, a tactical military supply road surveyed by the famed commander in 1871 during his campaign against the Apaches. Along here you'll start to find official Crook Trail markers—small white Vs tacked to tree trunks.

Two miles east, stop at Gentry Lookout, a Forest Service fire tower. If invited, climb the stairs and enjoy the view. To the north is the sinuous green body of Black Canyon Lake; west is Baker Butte, highest point on the Rim; southwest you can see Four Peaks, guardian of the Phoenix metropolitan area; south lies the vast White Mountain Apache Indian Reservation, and beyond it the summit spire of Mount Turnbull on the San Carlos Apache Indian Reservation.

From Gentry head east for 4 miles along the edge of the Mogollon Rim and you will pass Forest Service Road 87 at Turkey Springs Canyon, the vicinity of Travis Walton's purported harrowing encounter with space aliens. Stop a moment and feel the mystery.

The road continues east along the edge of the Rim, continually playing tag with Crook's historic route. About 6 miles beyond FR 87, the General Crook Trail takes off northeasterly; but don't follow. Instead, turn left, and travel north 2 miles to Phoenix Park.

Pause awhile at Phoenix Park and imagine its long grassy pasture filled with cavalry horses and blue-clad soldiers. The spot's grasses also attracted several cattle growers. One of the first was James Stinson, an absentee rancher whose foreman inadvertently touched off the Pleasant Valley War in the 1880s when he accosted local Tewksbury clan members about some stolen horses. Bad idea. Tewksbury six-shooters erupted, the foreman and his cousin caught lead, and by the end of a decade-long killing spree, up to 50 men were dead.

While at Phoenix Park, look north for a sandstone chimney marking the foundations of two ranch buildings. These originally belonged to pioneer Sarah Holcomb, whose parents acquired the property after Stinson. They died when she was only 14. Orphaned and alone, brave young Sarah carried on at the ranch.

From Phoenix Park, the road climbs north and makes connections returning you to State 260. This is journey's end, only 10 miles east of Heber. Crook Trail, meanwhile, has already branched off to the east. In a few miles it, too, seems to end, disappearing ghostlike in the shade of distant pines.

—Rick Heffernon

George Stocking

Cool summer temperatures, picturesque scenery, and rainbow trout
lure vacationers to Black Canyon Lake on the Mogollon Rim.

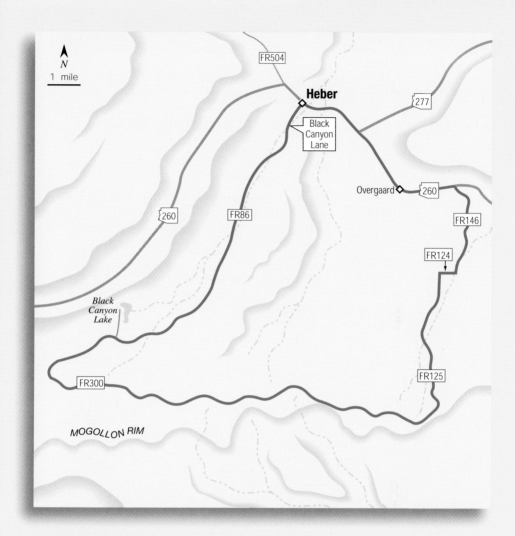

Route Finder

• Start on State Route 260 in Heber just west of Milepost 304.

• Turn south onto Black Canyon Lane, which eventually feeds into Forest Service Road 86. Follow it through a small residential area and you will break out toward the Mogollon Rim.

• About 13 miles after turning onto Black Canyon Lane, you'll come to the signed turnoff on the right for Black Canyon Lake, a short distance off FR 86.

• Leaving the lake, continue west-southwesterly on 86 for about 2 miles (if you reach Forest Service Road 300, you've driven too far) and the junction with a primitive road called Spur No. 9 and a brief side trip.

• Back on 86, continue a short distance to the junction with FR 300. Turn left (east).

• About 12 miles from the 86-300 junction turn left (north) onto Forest Service Road 125 and continue for about 5 miles through Phoenix Park and onto Forest Service Road 124.

• Turn right (east) on FR 124 and go 3.75 miles to Forest Service Road 146. Turn left (north) and go 3 miles to State 260 about 10 miles east of Heber.

Additional information: Black Mesa Ranger District, (928) 535-4481. Apache-Sitgreaves National Forests, (928) 333-4301; www.fs.fed.us/r3/asnf.

Vegetation in the Little Harquahala
Mountains seems limited to the hardy,
dry-climate plants, like the prickly pear
seen here. Randy A. Prentice

Drive 5

You'll Find Bird's-eye Views,
Old Observatory Atop Harquahala Peak

Harquahala Peak loomed just over the next hill or maybe just around the next hairpin curve, where the deeply incised road seemed to vanish against a jumble of sedimentary rocks.

Cheryl Blanchard knew our route exactly, but this peak near Wickenburg involved terrain new to me. Blanchard, an archaeologist with the Bureau of Land Management, agreed to guide me to an unusual ruin on the summit.

Most of the ruins in Arizona are remnants of prehistoric Indian communities or the skeletal remains of desiccated mining towns. Not so the ruin at Harquahala. This recent relic of scientific exploration is called the Harquahala Peak Smithsonian Observatory.

From photos, I knew this structure with the lofty title was a tin-clad building similar to sheds I'd sometimes found at abandoned railroad sidings. It didn't look like any observatory I'd ever seen. The structure's story intrigued me more than the building itself, and, frankly, a chance to spend a day in that barren no-man's-land around Harquahala Peak seemed even more appealing.

We left Wickenburg on a chilly morning and drove west on U.S. Route 60 to Aguila (see Route Finder for detailed directions). As we got to Harquahala Mountain Road, a sign recommended a four-wheel-drive vehicle and pointed across the highway to the unpaved road that winds 10.5 miles up to Harquahala Peak. We turned right. The road looked smooth at first, but before long it became the sort of terrain where even javelinas must have second thoughts. In some sections, it became so rocky and rutted that we tossed like a couple of stones inside a lapidary tumbler. Four-wheel drive shouldn't be recommended for this trek—it should be required.

Blanchard dropped into four-wheel drive, and we proceeded at a walking pace. In that isolated landscape, temptation to get sidetracked emerged everywhere: A narrow wash disappearing into a puzzle of boulders where the Earth had convulsed eons ago looked inviting; lichen-coated limestone and chunks of rose quartz begged for closer examination; the muted colors of every plant and rock, deepened by the mixture of rain and snow that had preceded my visit by a day or two, could have lured me off the track for hours. When the desert blooms in the spring, the saguaro forest, intermixed with ocotillos, ironwoods, chollas, paloverdes, mesquites, and creosotes, dominates the views on both sides of the road.

Inch by inch, we made our way to the 5,681-foot summit of Harquahala Peak, where the road ended. Harquahala lies in the upper Sonoran Desert, a water-scarce place where many plants don't grow much taller than an average human being. In summer, temperatures exceed 100 degrees; the thought of snow would challenge the imagination.

But this was winter and the strange scene before us had prickly pear cacti, ocotillos and jojoba bushes standing in an ankle-deep carpet of snow.

This saguaro cactus probably was growing already when an observatory was built atop Harquahala Peak.

Harquahala is an anglicized translation of a Mojave Indian expression, *Aha qua hala,* which means "water there is, high up," probably a reference to a spring (now dry) about a mile below the summit.

The tallest vegetation consisted of very old ironwood trees, saguaro cacti, and a scattering of arthritic mesquites trees. Treacherous veins of Christmas cacti were barely visible between the tiny leaves of the creosote bushes and the hair-thin tines of the ubiquitous cholla cacti.

A small group of scientists had settled on this remote summit in 1920 to conduct an esoteric experiment in long-range weather forecasting. "How do people find such places and what do they do there?" I wondered.

In this case, Blanchard said, the nature of the Smithsonian's project determined the location to be used. Samuel Pierpont Langley established what is known today as the Smithsonian Astrophysical Observatory in 1890. Langley was an inventor, among other things. His main invention was a device called the bolometer, which detected heat emitted from any warm object as infrared radiation. When Langley aimed this instrument at the sun, he was able to map the entire infrared spectrum known at the time, but then he stumbled onto something new. As he later wrote, "[I] found, suddenly and unexpectedly, a new [part of the infrared] spectrum of great extent, wholly unknown to science."

Langley's research led him to believe that further study of what he called "the solar constant," the amount of heat reaching the Earth from the sun, might vastly improve the science of weather prediction.

Langley's premise, still debated in scientific journals, got its first test on Mount Whitney in California. Later a permanent facility for long-range observing was established at Mount Wilson near Los Angeles, which proved imperfect because of its proximity to the smoke and dust of the city. There weren't enough clear days for collecting data.

Charles G. Abbot, a Langley protégé and pioneer in solar research, was dispatched to find other locations for observatories in places with low humidity and clear skies. The weather bureau office in Phoenix voted for Harquahala Peak, some 70 miles northwest of the city and roughly midway between Wickenburg and Quartzsite.

Abbot went to see the spot and was impressed, he said, because "the prevalence of dwarfed vegetation in the desert and upon Mount Harqua Hala [the spelling in use at that time] would tend to keep down dust," a factor that would contribute to the accuracy of the data collected.

The observatory's original adobe structure, which later was clad with sheet metal to protect it from the winds that tear across Harquahala Peak much of the year, is all that remains on the mountaintop the Smithsonian used from 1920 to 1925. The observatory located behind a barbed-wire fence is off-limits to visitors, but you may sign the summit book located in front of the historic site and read the experiences of fellow Harquahala adventurers.

The observatory remains a memorial to American science and provides a good excuse for exploring and climbing to the top of an isolated peak in the Sonoran Desert.

Randy A. Prentice

Corrugated metal covers the original adobe structure used for an observatory.

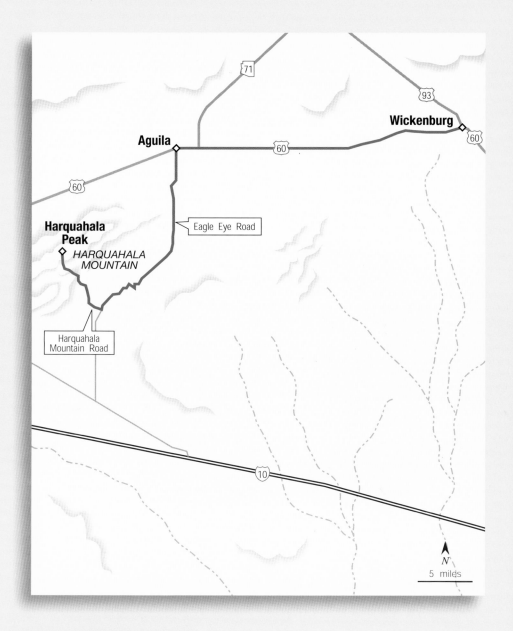

Route Finder

• Start in Wickenburg at the intersection of U.S. Route 60 and U.S. Route 93.

• Drive west on U.S. 60 for 25 miles to Eagle Eye Road in Aguila. Turn left (south) onto Eagle Eye Road.

• Continue 18.5 miles south and then southwest on Eagle Eye Road to Harquahala Mountain Road. Turn right about a half-mile past Milepost 9.

• Continue 10.5 miles to Harquahala Peak.

Additional information: Bureau of Land Management, (623) 580-5500; www.blm.gov/az/ohv/harq.htm.

The White Mountains

Edward McCain

McKay Reservoir, far left, ranks as the largest pond in the Apache National Forest's Sipe Wildlife Area, located near Eagar and known especially for birds that nest there. Skiers pass a log cabin at Hannagan Meadow Lodge on their way to a cross-country trek.

A Recreational Paradise

• Overview

The drives in this chapter are located on the White Mountain Apache Indian Reservation and the Apache-Sitgreaves National Forests and pass through unpopulated and densely forested regions with aspen, spruce, and ponderosa pine trees. The area is a outdoors paradise with ample opportunities for hiking, hunting, fishing, hiking, bird-watching, or nature photography. Remember, tribal permits are necessary if you enter the backcountry of the White Mountain reservation.

• The Drives

• Towns and Sites

Alpine, Blue, Chevelon Canyon, Escudilla Mountain, Fort Apache, Greer, Hannagan Meadow, Heber, Homolovi Ruins State Park, Lakeside, Payson, Pinetop, Show Low, Springerville, Sunrise, Terry Flat, White Mountains, Whiteriver, and Winslow.

Bernadette Heath

The colorful American kestrel makes its home near Escudilla Mountain in the White Mountains.
Marty Cordano

There's something mysterious about the fall. Often the air is still before the first frost arrives. The trunks of aspens soften to gray, and downed logs of yellow pines, soaked from summer rains, lie dark on the soft ground in a nest of dying ferns. Underfoot, a mosaic of orange and red leaves, mostly aspen but mixed here and there with oaks and maples in the transition zones, fill the air with a fragrance that suggests a small fire in crisp air. Many who come to Arizona thinking only of deserts, grieve for those gifts of the fall, the shower of changing leaves, the days redolent in the speckled light of the deep woods.

But how can you live in the desert and still enjoy the luxury of a Midwestern or New England fall?

The answer is on the Arizona map: It is a large, diagonal swath of green. There is a geological feature near the upper portion that is called the Mogollon Rim; the area straddling the Rim contains a broken string of mountains known collectively as the White Mountains. In the summer, the whole range, which includes the small towns of Payson, Show Low, Lakeside, and Pinetop in the west to Alpine in the east, is usually at least 30 degrees cooler than Phoenix or Tucson, Arizona's two major desert cities.

From late September through about the middle of October, anyone hungry for a taste of fall can find it on any of the back roads in the White Mountains described later. However, persons with respiratory ailments or pacemakers should keep in mind that the area we are talking about ranges in elevation from 5,000 to 11,500 feet and may not be a wise retreat, no matter what time of year it is.

For others, the White Mountains is an ideal escape from the hubbub of the big city. Driving at normal speeds, you can get to the Show Low, Lakeside, Pinetop, Greer, and Alpine in four to six hours—just two hours if you're only going from Phoenix to the vicinity of Payson.

The White Mountains have evolved into one of Arizona's most popular outdoor recreation areas, filled with tall pines, large grassy meadows, campgrounds, and good lakes and streams for trout fishing.

Bands of Western Apaches, who now live on the 1.6 million acre White Mountain Apache Indian Reservation, originally populated the area. Permit fees for camping, hunting, fishing and backcountry travel (See Sunrise to Whiteriver description later) form a major source of income for the tribe. Mormons followed the Apaches into the White Mountains and founded several communities in the late 1800s.

Since World War II, these ranching and logging communities have attracted a more diverse population of retirees and vacation homeowners. When temperatures in Tucson and Phoenix reach 100 plus, many head for their cabins in the White Mountains.

The golden leaves signal
autumn season in the White
Mountains. For current
reports on fall color and
road conditions, check
www.wmonline.com/sitedir.htm.

Show Low was one of the first Mormon communities in the range. It got its name as the result of a card game. The participants in the card game were Corydon E. Cooley and Marion Clark. Long before the present town was in existence, they decided their neck of the woods was too crowded for their two ranches, so one would have to move. They agreed to play a card game called "Seven Up," where the low card wins. The loser would move and give the other man more room. So Clark supposedly said to Cooley, as he dealt the cards, "If you can show low, you win." Cooley then turned up the deuce of clubs and announced, "Show low it is!" Even today, whenever there is a runoff for mayor, the political opponents settle the issue with a deck of cards. The first to draw the deuce of clubs becomes the new mayor. And the main street through town is named the Deuce of Clubs.

At the southeastern end of the Show Low-Pinetop area, State Route 260 takes off to the east alongside the Apaches' gambling casino at Hon-dah. The road goes through the old timbering town of McNary and for the next 50 miles it gently bends through a forest filled with pines, aspens, and spruce trees, separated here and there by wide valleys that roll away to the north and south.

Sunrise, 32 miles east of McNary, is a ski resort on the White Mountain Apache Indian Reservation. It is both a summer and winter resort with an indoor swimming pool and two Jacuzzis: In the summer, its 9,200-foot

Randy A. Prentice

Colorful names—drive 2 in this chapter takes you to the cobble-filled Blue River, where it crosses Red Hill Road in the green Apache National Forest.

A cloud haze throws a gauzelike cover over ridges in
the Blue Range in the Apache National Forest.

George H.H. Huey

elevation guarantees comfortable days and nights cool enough for a sweater.
There's also good fishing in the lake adjacent to the lodge. Located on State
Route 273, 4 miles south of State 260, the lodge faces aspen- and spruce-
covered hills dotted with some 25 lakes and numerous streams where the
fishing is excellent (the resort sells tribal fishing permits). Cross-country
and downhill skiing, as well as snowmobiling and other winter sports,
are available during the winter months. If you bypass the turn for Sunrise
and stay on State 260, you will soon come to the cut-off for Greer, another
popular mountain retreat offering numerous campgrounds and lodges. The
Little Colorado River flows through the edge of town and tempts fishermen
as a good place to find native trout.

Most of the White Mountain area lies within the Apache-Sitgreaves
National Forests, which is interspersed with state parks, campgrounds, lakes,
and rolling hills covered with ponderosa pine, aspen, and spruce trees.

The farther east you go, the deeper you get into the "Apache" portion of
the Apache-Sitgreaves National Forests. Also, the farther east you go, the
fewer humans you will encounter. Where Arizona meets New Mexico, the
population dwindles to a small number of ranchers and relatively few other
inhabitants. This is country so quiet you can often hear the beat of a crow's or
an eagle's wings. The isolated and scenic terrain south of Nutrioso and Alpine
is so vast and unpopulated that the U.S. Fish and Wildlife Service in recent

Stately and sturdy as they are, ponderosa pine trees
do not infringe on grassy mountain meadows.

Larry Ulrich

years reintroduced a pack of Mexican gray wolves to see if they would survive and replace their predecessors, who were hunted to extinction in this terrain early in the last century.

Until 1935, the steep canyons at the eastern extremity of the White Mountains were also grizzly country. Aldo Leopold, a forest ranger, writer, and one of the nation's earliest advocates for wilderness areas, talked about Escudilla and the grizzlies in his book of essays, *Sand County Almanac,* which was published in 1949. Broad-shouldered Escudilla at 10,877 feet is the third tallest mountain peak in Arizona. It rises about 10 miles north of Alpine.

In his book, Leopold told a story about a grizzly the rangers called Bigfoot. Leopold thought that when Bigfoot was killed he was the last remaining grizzly in Arizona, but Game and Fish Department records indicate the last one was later killed at Strayhorse 40 to 50 miles south of Escudilla, in 1935. Bigfoot's demise is told in more detail, in the description of the road from Alpine to Terry Flat, but for now suffice it to say there are no longer grizzlies in Arizona.

There are, however, many black bears (which happen to be cinnamon-colored) and they are numerous in the rough canyons of eastern Arizona, especially along the 24-mile stretch of the Blue River. The area also runs wild with elk and deer, which was one of the reasons the wolves were reintroduced. Visitors rarely see bears because they shy away from humans (garbage bears are not a problem in the rough mountains of eastern Arizona), but deer and elk are almost always seen, especially in the forests between Beaverhead and KP Cienega south of Alpine. Don't be surprised if you see elk and cows grazing in the same meadow. Take a walk on the Steeple, Foote Creek, or Butterfly Cienega trails from Hannagan Meadow, and you'll almost certainly see elk, especially in the fall when the bulls are gathering their harems.

The main road through this eastern portion of the White Mountains is U.S. Route 191, usually referred to as the Coronado Trail, a scenic and sometimes perilous drive which begins at Springerville and heads south through Alpine and Hannagan Meadow and ends in the copper-mining town of Morenci. If you get vertigo on steep and winding roads, cut short your trip down the Trail at Blue Vista, a lookout point south of Hannagan Meadow.

There are four rivers—the Black, the Little Colorado, the Blue, and the San Francisco—in the Apache-Sitgreaves National Forests, as well as 24 lakes and reservoirs and an estimated 680 miles of clear trout streams. Except for the dead of winter, it's an ideal area for hiking or camping or getting a taste of fresh air.

The routes described are generally passable with an ordinary high-clearance vehicle. If you go in the winter, however, you will need four-wheel drive or chains. The Coronado Trail from Alpine south is often closed during periods of heavy snow.   ✠

This section of the Mount Baldy Wilderness in the Apache National Forest features domed granite rocks and spruce and aspen trees.

Robert G. McDonald

Blue grama grass raises its curled "flags" among the shrubbery of a meadow in Brookbank Canyon. Jerry Sieve

Drive 1

Winslow to Heber
via Chevelon Canyon

Ever notice how many people assume that all rivers run from north to south and that trees are bigger in the north than they are in the south? If you're one of those people, the back road from Winslow to Heber via Chevelon Canyon is going to seem upside down. The only river in the area flows northeastward (when it flows at all), and to reach the tall pines from Winslow you have to head south, not north.

Winslow is a small railroad town about an hour east of Flagstaff. For centuries before the arrival of the white man, this area was populated by Hopi Indians and their ancestors, the Ancestral Puebloans. The ruins of 13th- and 14th-century pueblos can be seen at Homolovi Ruins State Park, just a few miles from Winslow. You can also learn more about Winslow and the area you'll be exploring by stopping at Winslow's Old Trails Museum on Kinsley Avenue.

Once you've familiarized yourself with the history of the area, follow State Route 87 south across the railroad tracks, drive 2 miles to a fork, and you're on your way to Heber (see Route Finder for detailed directions) in a treeless plain interrupted here and there by an occasional jumble of sandstone boulders. To the east, still out of sight, Chevelon Creek is inching its way northward to the Little Colorado River, but at this point neither the creek nor the canyon is visible.

When you're 7 miles south of the interstate, the road dips into a little ravine and crosses Clear Creek, another tributary of the Little Colorado. At this point, Clear Creek is the centerpiece of McHood Park, a good place to fish or picnic.

As you leave the park and continue south, the vegetation begins to change. Small clumps of shagbark juniper appear on either side of the road and there are more hills in the distance. Keep your eyes open for pronghorn antelope throughout this area. Experts estimate there are some 8,000 in Arizona.

In the spring, you may encounter people on all-terrain vehicles in these plains collecting elk antlers. Dealers will buy the elk racks for $10 a pound. The antlers are ground into a powdery substance which supposedly acts as an aphrodisiac. Evidently the end product sells well in East Asian countries.

Most of the year, there's nothing in the area to block the view of an enormous sky. However, from the middle of December through January, there's a thick layer of fog that settles in the broad basin south of the Little Colorado River. During that period, temperatures will drop to 15 or 20 degrees. But, most of the year, visibility is excellent.

Six miles after crossing Clear Creek, the valley widens and visibility is perfect for 50 miles or more in every direction. Chevelon Butte, a prominent landmark, is clearly visible to the southwest. The locals say a trapper named Chevelon died there in the 1800s, reportedly from eating poisonous parsnips, and was buried at the base of the butte that bears his name. When you're 18 miles south of I-10, a sign says you've come to the end of State Route 99; you have also

Cottonwood trees thrive in water-rich areas like this one along Chevelon Creek (not shown) near Mormon Crossing.

come to the end of the pavement, but the road continues as Forest Service Road 34. About 10 miles later, FR 34 veers southwest and Forest Service Road 504 heads southeast (or left) toward Mormon Crossing and Chevelon Canyon. Take the left fork and cross the boundary into Apache-Sitgreaves National Forests.

Heber is only about 23 miles southeast of that forest boundary, but it is going to be slow going on a hard-packed rocky road through Chevelon. As FR 504 twists and bends and begins dropping, sometimes steeply, to Mormon Crossing, it seems clear that this is an easy place to get yourself killed. Go slow and don't get distracted by the dramatic scenery.

Mormon Crossing is a historic spot in northern Arizona, and one of two places where it is possible to drive across Chevelon Creek (the other is Territorial Road, just south of McHood Park). Around 1879, Mormons from Brigham City and Sunset, two communities that no longer exist, graded a road through Chevelon and homesteaded near the spot now called Mormon Crossing. However, they eventually abandoned those homesteads because the creek didn't provide enough water to make farming feasible. Today, wild mulberry and tall stands of black walnut trees grow in abundance at the crossing.

Two miles beyond Mormon Crossing, there's a cutoff for Chevelon Lake, one of a string of isolated lakes that dot the Mogollon Rim between Winslow and Payson. The sign announcing the lake also says you're 20 miles from Heber and 35 miles south of Winslow. The main part of Chevelon Canyon is just 2 miles ahead at the bottom of a series of steep switchbacks best negotiated at speeds of no more than 10 to 15 miles an hour. At the low end of the switchbacks, the road passes a forest campground and then begins the gradual ascent on the other side of the canyon. As you get higher on the rim, small meadows appear at irregular intervals. In the spring and summer, these little parks are bright with wildflowers.

About 7 miles south of the Chevelon Campground, the road begins crossing a series of side canyons—Wildcat, Daze, and Wiltbank, for example—that are roughly a mile apart. The road gets choppy but never bad enough to require four-wheel drive. Still you should think twice before driving it in an ordinary sedan.

A mere 54 miles after leaving Winslow, you're back on the pavement on the outskirts of Heber. The blacktop is State Route 260 and Heber is only 1 mile to the left (east), a good place for a snack and a rest before heading back.

Named for an early trapper and scout, Chevelon Creek
wends through its namesake canyon.

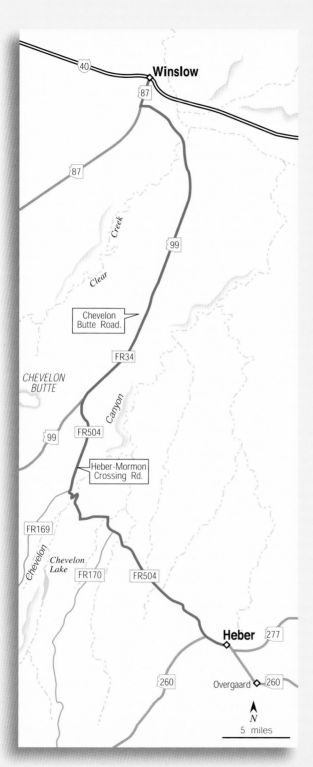

Route Finder _____

• *Begin in Winslow, located along Interstate 40 about 50 miles east of Flagstaff.*

• *From Exit 253, drive south on State Route 87 for 2 miles to a junction with State Route 99. Turn left (east) onto State 99.*

• *After 18 miles State 99 becomes Forest Service Road 34.*

• *Continue on FR 34 for another 10 miles to a Y-junction with Forest Service Road 504. Bear left onto FR 504.*

• *Continue on FR 504 for 23 miles to a junction with State Route 260. Turn left and you're in Heber in a few miles.*

Additional information: Winslow Old Trails Museum, (928) 289-5861; www.winslowarizona.org. Homolovi Ruins State Park, take Exit 257 from I-40; (928)289-4106; www.pr.state. az.us/Parks/parkhtml/homolovi.html.

A downed tree—it's called a snag—in a White Mountains lake makes excellent cover for trout. Randy A. Prentice

Drive 2

Beaverhead to Alpine via Isolated Blue River

If you're spending a weekend in the vicinity of Alpine or Hannagan Meadow in east-central Arizona, you can make this scenic excursion into the isolated Blue River country in a leisurely morning's drive.

"Leisurely," in fact, is the only way to drive this route. There are several hairpin curves on the dirt road that drops off U.S. Route 191 to reach the Blue River. As the driver, you probably won't have much opportunity to take your eyes off the road, but your passengers will be treated to a visual feast consisting of the densely forested mountains in the Blue Range Primitive Area and the folds of the Gila Mountains lying a few miles to the east in New Mexico. Throughout this terrain, elk, black bear, deer, and mountain lions are abundant.

The landscape remains largely unpopulated, which is one reason the U.S. Fish and Wildlife Service chose it as a place to reintroduce a pack of Mexican gray wolves in the 1990s. There's only a slim chance you'll see any of them because there are so few wolves in such a large and rugged region. If you do see one, it likely will be wearing a transmitter collar, which puts out a signal enabling biologists to keep track of where the wolves are wandering.

Begin this trip at either Alpine or Hannagan Meadow on U.S. 191, which is also known as the Coronado Trail (see Route Finder for detailed directions).

The point where you turn off the Coronado Trail is called Beaverhead; years ago there was a lodge and gas pump there; now those buildings have been removed. Keep in mind that at the bottom of this road at Blue Crossing you'll have to drive through the river, which flows most of the year. The river crossing is firm and as long as the river isn't in flood stage, most vehicles will have no trouble getting across. A vehicle with high clearance is recommended.

The Red Hill Road is the shortest route (about 13 miles) down to Blue Crossing. It is also the steepest and, if the road is wet, it can be slippery. Memorize the word "slow" and respect it. The area you're heading into is remote, and assistance is not readily available.

The "community" in Blue Country consists of widely scattered ranches, a one-room schoolhouse, a fish hatchery, and a post office. Most of the area is part of the Apache-Sitgreaves National Forests, a 2-million-acre collection of forests, streams and lakes, and hiking trails. From Blue, the nearest community is Alpine, 24 miles to the north. The nearest community to the south is Morenci, roughly 70 miles away. Reserve, New Mexico, is about 30 miles to the east. If you had a good pair of wings and headed directly west of Blue, you wouldn't hit anything resembling a city until you saw the outskirts of Phoenix. There are more people in any hospital in Tucson or Phoenix than there are along the entire Blue River. Do not look for restaurants, stores, or gas stations on the Blue River.

In the first mile after you turn east off U.S. 191, look for a meadow through the trees on the right. Occasionally, you'll see elk grazing in the same pasture as cows. After a few miles, the road

There are no boundary fences
here, but the ridges in the
distance lie in New Mexico
along a route leading out of
the Blue River area.

Wildflowers and a rustic log fence line the Coronado Trail
(U.S. Route 191) near Hannagan Meadow.

Randy A. Prentice

comes out of the forest, and there are panoramic views into the Gila Wilderness area to the east and the southern reaches of the Blue River.

When you reach the river, look for the narrow entrance to the small (about four units) Blue Crossing Campground on the left. In the northeastern corner of the small campground, a gate leads to a petroglyph site. No one knows precisely when prehistoric Indians scraped these symbols into the rock wall or even what they mean. The campground makes an idea base if you want to fish the Blue.

After crossing the river, you can turn left and drive an excellent dirt road to Alpine, or you can turn right and see a bit more of the Blue River country.

Let's turn right onto Forest Service Road 281.

About 2 miles south of Blue Crossing, a stone building, once a lodge, appears on the left near the junction of FR 281 and FR 232, the Pueblo Park Road. Cross the river and, for a modest fee, you can fish for rainbow trout at Jim and Cassie Joy's Blue River Hatchery. The Joys are also outfitters and guides, and if you're interested in staying longer to hunt or merely explore the country, they can provide horses and meals and a guide (928-339-4404).

Further along FR 281, you come to the tiny Blue Post Office, presided over by Mona Bunnell. Mona and her husband, Bill, also preside over her family's Downs' Ranch Hideaway (928-339-4952; downsranchhideaway@frontiernet.net) and if you're looking for true isolation, they've got four cabins for rent. Bill is also a licensed hunting guide. The Downs Ranch (named for Mona's father, Herschel Downs) is 10.5 miles south of the hatchery.

There are several hiking trails along the river (see Additional Information at the end of Route Finder). FR 281 virtually ends at a trailhead.

Leaving the primitive area, you have three choices—taking a sortie along a Forest Service road to a paved road in New Mexico for a return to Alpine; returning the way you came; or taking FR 281 (the Blue River Road) north to a paved road just east of Alpine.

The mail for residents along the Blue River comes down from Alpine along FR 281, so it tends to be kept in better shape than the other routes. The road will slither through Jackson Box, an area of vertical red cliffs and giant cottonwood trees. When you're 6 miles north of Blue Crossing on 281, Upper Blue Campground appears on the left (west) side of the road. Unlike Blue Crossing, this campground contains drinking water. Most of the year you can also fish in the river, which meanders along one side of the campground.

Route Finder

• *Begin at either Alpine or Hannagan Meadow on U.S. Route 191. From Alpine drive 14 miles south to Forest Service Road 567 (Red Hill Road). From Hannagan Meadow drive 8 miles north to the same road and turn right.*

• *Continue on FR 567 for 13 miles to Blue Crossing and cross the river.*

• *Option: Turn left onto Forest Service Road 281 (Blue River Road) for a 22-mile drive to Alpine.*

• *Turn right onto FR 281 for about a 10-mile drive southward along the river during which you pass or come near to a hatchery, the Blue Post Office, and hiking trails.*

• *Leaving, there are three options.*

1) Return to the junction of FR 281 and FR 232, the Pueblo Park Road. Turn right onto 232.

Continue for about 18 miles (staying right at a fork about 3.7 miles along) to U.S. Route 180 in New Mexico. Turn left (north) onto U.S. 180.

Continue on 180 for about 35 miles to Alpine.

2) Return to the junction of FR 281 and FR 567. Turn left (west) onto 567, driving out the way you came in.

3) Return to junction of FR 281 and FR 567 and continue straight (north) on 281 for about 18 miles to U.S. 180. Turn left (west). Continue on 180 for 4 miles into Alpine.

Additional information: Apache-Sitgreaves National Forests, Alpine Ranger District, (928) 339-4384; www.fs.fed.us/r3/asnf/recreation/alpine_trails/index.shtml.

Drive 3

Alpine to Terry Flat and Escudilla: A Short Drive to High Country

If you can stand high elevations, make this short drive from Alpine to Terry Flat in the fall, when the leaves are a brilliant yellow and red, and chances are you'll never forget it. Once you reach Terry Flat—a huge meadow just off the brow of Escudilla Mountain—you'll be above 10,000 feet. You may find yourself huffing and puffing if you go for a walk, but it's worth the effort. The hiking trail up Escudilla Mountain is one of the most beautiful in Arizona, and the dense aspen forest in the first mile turns golden in the first weeks of October.

Alpine is a tiny community with a few motels and summer cabins for rent, a handful of small stores and restaurants, and one gas station. The Apache-Sitgreaves National Forests have a ranger station there where you can obtain information and maps.

To get to Terry Flat, drive north on U.S. Route 191-180 for 6 miles. Watch on the right (east) side of the highway for a sign designating Forest Service Road 56. The sign is pushed back off the road a bit and is easy to miss (see Route Finder for detailed directions). Soon after you turn onto FR 56, a road on the left heads for a short drive to Hulsey Lake, a small pond suitable for fly fishing.

Return to FR 56. The road quickly winds up the mountain to the clearing called Terry Flat. The meadow was named for Lewis K. Terry, a rancher who lived a few miles southeast of Alpine during the 1920s and had a Forest Service permit to graze his cows in the high meadow that forms a shoulder just off Escudilla, the third-tallest peak in Arizona (10,877 feet).

As you drive around the large bowl-shaped meadow, stay left when you encounter another road going right. FR 56 will make a loop around the periphery of the meadow. In late spring and early summer, you'll find wild irises and other flowers dotting the grassy fields. Before you complete the loop, you'll come to the Escudilla National Recreational Trail.

The 3-mile trail leads to a fire lookout tower, but most people stop when they get to Profanity Ridge because there's not much you can see from the lookout that you can't see from the ridge just below it. Most of the hardest part of the climb is in the first 1.5 miles as the trail switchbacks through dense thickets of aspens. Along the way, there are numerous overlooks that provide excellent views of prominent peaks across northern Arizona. On a clear day, you can see the San Francisco Peaks far off to the west in Flagstaff.

Aldo Leopold, a forest ranger and author of *A Sand County Almanac,* a collection of essays that has become a classic of environmental literature, worked around Escudilla as a young man (a wilderness area in nearby western New Mexico is named for him). In his book Leopold told of a ragged old grizzly he called Bigfoot.

Bigfoot favored the high country up around Terry Flat and Escudilla Mountain. Once a year, he'd eat a cow; the rest of the time he'd sleep or wander in a spruce- and aspen-covered paradise where—even today—he'd have plenty of privacy.

Gold and green are
the dominant colors
on Escudilla Mountain
in the Autumn.

The 3-mile Escudilla National Recreational Trail overlooks a meadow.
Even a short walk on the trail yields excellent scenery.

Marty Cordano

Bigfoot has been gone for many decades. Leopold chronicled his death in *A Sand County Almanac,* published in 1949. A federal trapper had been called in to rid the area of livestock-killing wildlife, Leopold recalled. Here's his account of what happened next:

"The trapper packed his mule and headed for Escudilla.

"In a month he was back, his mule staggering under a heavy hide. There was only one barn in town big enough to dry it on. He had tried traps, poison and all his usual wiles to no avail. Then he had erected a set-gun in a defile through which only the bear could pass, and waited. The last grizzly walked into the string and shot himself."

As far as anyone knows, there are no longer any grizzly bears in Arizona. Leopold wrote as though he thought Bigfoot was the last. But another grizzly was shot at Strayhorse, roughly 50 miles south of Escudilla, in 1935. That was the last grizzly killed in Arizona, according to records of the Arizona Game and Fish Department. But was it the last? The tracks of two grizzly cubs were detected where that one was killed, and those two were never heard from again.

Forest Service and Game and Fish officials are confident you will not encounter any grizzlies along this trail. For many hikers, that will probably be comforting news, but some may agree with the sentiments Aldo Leopold felt, when he wrote:

"Since the beginning, time had gnawed at the basaltic hulk of Escudilla, wasting, waiting and building. Time built three things on the old mountain, a venerable aspect, a community of minor animals and plants, and a grizzly.

"The government trapper who took the grizzly knew he had made Escudilla safe for cows. He did not know he had toppled the spire off an edifice a-building since the morning stars sang together."

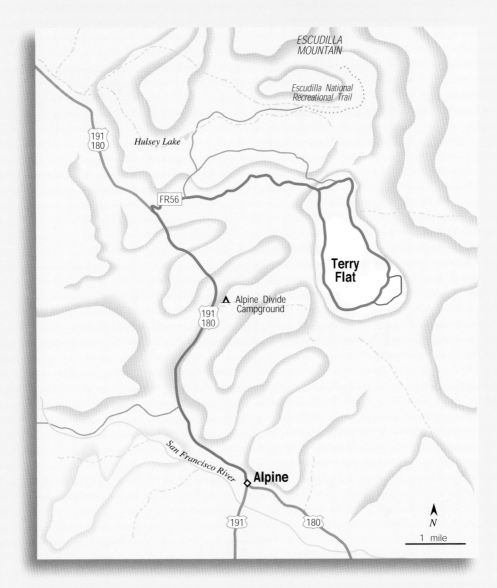

Route Finder

- Begin on U.S. Route 191-180 in Alpine and head north for 6 miles to Forest Service Road 56. Turn right (east).
- Option: About 1.2 miles along FR 56, the road forks. Bear left for Hulsey Lake, less than a mile away.
- Return to the fork. Turn left back onto FR 56.
- Continue on FR 56 to a fork in 2.9 miles. Bear right for a 6-mile loop drive around Terry Flat, staying left at upcoming forks.
- About 1 mile before reaching the start of the Terry Flat loop, you'll come to the Escudilla National

Recreational Trail, which leads up the mountain for about 3 miles.
- Leaving the trail, resume driving west on FR 56 to U.S. 191-180.

Additional information: Alpine, (928) 339-4330; www.alpinearizona.com. White Mountains, www. wmonline.com. Apache-Sitgreaves National Forests, Alpine Ranger District, (928) 339-4384; www.fs.fed. us/r3/asnf/recreation.

A great blue heron lifts off from Pacheta Lake, located on the White Mountains Apache Indian Reservation along the drive to Whiteriver. Morey K. Milbradt

Drive 4

Sunrise to Whiteriver
Past a Chain of Lakes

Beginning at Sunrise, this route meanders through alpine meadows and tall forests and past a chain of scenic, fishable lakes. The roads will take you through the backcountry of the White Mountain Apache Indian Reservation and end at Whiteriver, the seat of government for the White Mountain Apache Tribe.

Because nearly all of this route lies on the reservation, you'll need to buy a tribal permit for backcountry travel as well as a fishing license (see Route Finder for details). If you have an Arizona fishing license, you'll still need the tribal permit for reservation fishing. However, the route catches a portion of the Apache-Sitgreaves National Forests and crosses or comes close to some of its waters, including the West Fork of the Little Colorado River, White Mountain Reservoir, and Lee Valley Reservoir.

The tribe's 1,500-acre Sunrise Park Resort, located some 225 miles northeast of Phoenix and Tucson, or roughly 25 miles southeast of Pinetop, is a stunning natural playground where visitors can ski more than 60 runs on three mountains just under 11,000 feet high, fish a pristine lake bordered by hills covered with pines and aspens, or engage in numerous other recreational activities. This Apache-owned enterprise has a 100-room hotel with a small indoor pool, Jacuzzi and sauna, as well as outdoor Jacuzzis, a restaurant, and bar. The hotel faces Sunrise Lake, located at an elevation of 9,200 feet.

Conventional wisdom has it that Indian reservations are for the most part barren wastelands, usually far removed from a tribe's aboriginal homeland. The exact opposite is true of the White Mountain reservation. It covers 1.7 million acres or 2,601 square miles of their original homeland, stretching about 75 miles from the east to the west and roughly 45 miles from north to south. There are 800 miles of perennial streams and 26 lakes on the reservation, but this route will cover only a fraction of them.

Begin at the intersection of State Route 260 and State Route 73 in Hon-Dah, where there is a complex with a large casino, hotel, and restaurant; store and gas station; and an outdoors-equipment store. You can purchase a fishing license or backcountry permit at the store, and the outdoors shop is a good place to check on fishing conditions.

Travel east on State 260 through the old timber camp at McNary until you reach State Route 273, the turnoff for Sunrise (see Route Finder for detailed directions). State 273 begins as a paved route and becomes a patchwork of paved and unpaved sections until it crosses the Little Colorado River at Sheeps Crossing. After that you won't see any pavement until you get to the outskirts of Whiteriver.

Within 2 miles after passing the Sunrise ski lodge, you'll come to a convenience store where you can pick up a fishing and backcountry permit if you didn't get them at Hon-Dah. The store also sells maps of the reservation.

Just north of Whiteriver, lush vegetation lines the shimmering North Fork of the White River along Indian Route 61.

When you reach Sheeps Crossing, you'll be at one of the most beautiful spots in the White Mountains. The elevation here is 9,370 feet. You can fish in the West Fork of the Little Colorado River or hike most of the way up Mount Baldy. The 11,403-foot high summit has religious significance to traditional Apaches and is off limits to non-Indians, but visitors can still hike most of the way up.

Six miles after leaving Sheeps Crossing, watch for a right turn to Forest Service Road 116 and Reservation Lake on the White Mountain Apache Indian Reservation. You'll be heading into an area dense with aspens. The road tends to become rippled like a washboard in the first 4 miles. The road winds around for 10 miles before it reaches the lake.

There's a cutoff at the sign for the lake; you can turn right and go to the lake or continue straight. The two roads will eventually come together as Indian Route Y20.

About 1 mile beyond Reservation Lake, a sign says it is 8 miles to Pacheta Lake, but it's not a straight shot. Four miles beyond the sign, you'll first come to Drift Fence Lake, a peaceful clearing where you can camp among small aspens and pines. There is no drinking water here.

From Drift Fence Lake, it is 3 miles to the signed cutoff for isolated and beautiful Pacheta Lake. The forest near the lake is a good place to spot trophy-sized elk.

Leaving Pacheta, return to Y20 and take it to signed Y55, where it says Whiteriver is 34 miles away. There, you can turn right onto State Route 73 for a return to Hon-Dah; or turn left for U.S. 60 and Globe.

Larry Ulrich

Joe-Pye weed lines the banks of the Black River south of Fort Apache. According to legend, Joe Pye was an Indian who used the plant to reduce fever.

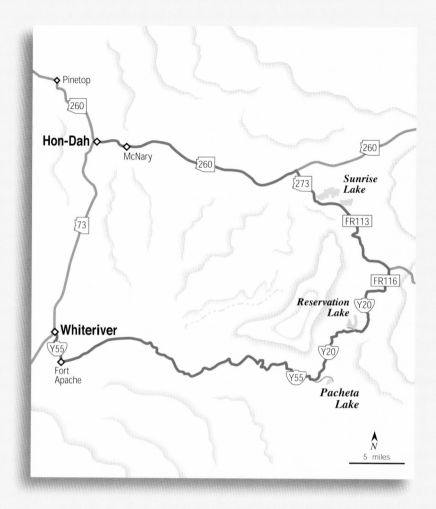

Route Finder

- *Begin in Hon-Dah at the junction of State Route 260 and State Route 73.*
- *Travel east on State 260, through McNary, for 20 miles to State Route 273. Turn right (south).*
- *Continue on State 273 for about 4 miles to turnoffs for Sunrise Park Resort.*
- *Leaving Sunrise, continue southeastward on 273 for 6 miles to Sheeps Crossing. En route you'll cross into the Apache-Sitgreaves National Forests and 273 turns to Forest Service Road 113.*
- *Leaving Sheeps Crossing, continue southward on FR 113 for about 6 miles to FR 116. Turn right onto 116 and within 10 miles you'll first cross back into the reservation and then drive by turnoff roads for*

the Reservation Lake. When FR 113 crosses into the reservation it becomes Indian Route Y20.
- *Leaving Reservation Lake, continue southward on Y20 for about 8 miles to a turnoff for Pacheta Lake, just off Y20.*
- *Leaving Pacheta Lake, return to Y20. Turn left.*
- *Continue on Y20 to Y55. Turn right for a 34-mile drive to Whiteriver.*

Additional information: White Mountain Apache Tribe, (877) 338-9628, www.wmat.nsn.us. Sunrise, (928) 735-7669 or (800) 772-7669; www. sunriseskipark.com. Apache-Sitgreaves National Forests, (928) 333-4301; www.fs.fed.us/r3/asnf.

Drive 5

Whiteriver to Reservation Lake Reveals Pristine Apache Lands

Strolling across the Fort Apache parade grounds, I anticipate my adventure and wonder why the Apache Indians fought so desperately to hang onto what remains a remote, lightly populated wilderness in east-central Arizona.

The fort's 288-acre collection of Army barracks, school buildings, and the Apache Cultural Center remains shadowed by ironies, and so offers the perfect preparation for my 90-mile drive through the heart of the White Mountain Apache Indian Reservation, the ecological equivalent of a quick drive from Mexico to Canada.

The resourceful White Mountain Apaches now have laid claim to the fort built by white men, just as visionary leaders like Chief Alchesay learned to compromise and adapt to hold tenaciously onto this spectacular, 1.7 million-acre reservation. The sprawling reservation includes the Salt River Canyon at 2,700 feet elevation and Mount Baldy at 11,403 feet, which remains one of the wettest places in Arizona. To hold onto their home, the White Mountain leaders even proved willing to serve as scouts for the Army in the terrible war with Geronimo's Chiricahua Apaches.

In part, the White Mountain Apaches served the Army because they believed their culture and morality depended on an intimate connection with the land. Here every bend of the stream had a sacred name and a story that helped parents teach children correct behavior, as so beautifully described in Keith H. Basso's *Wisdom Sits in Places: Landscape and Language Among the Western Apache.* The Apache people believe the land's spirit can impart wisdom to those who pay close attention.

Now the White Mountain reservation harbors just 12,500 people and some of the most remote, pristine, and diverse wilderness in Arizona, including a splashing tumult of streams that nurture the Apache trout—brought back from the brink of extinction through a cooperative effort of the tribe and Arizona Game and Fish Department.

My journey of discovery started with the purchase of a fishing permit at the Wildlife & Outdoor Recreation Division in Whiteriver next to the White Mountain Apache Motel and Restaurant—the only motel in 5,200-resident Whiteriver. You need a permit any time you leave the paved road on the reservation, whether or not you fish. Then I headed south to Fort Apache (see Route Finder for detailed directions).

After leaving the fort, the road leads to Indian Route Y55 and rises steadily from the juniper grasslands around Whiteriver. The road continues past scattered homes along the East Fork of the White River. Less than 100 yards after the pavement ends, the road forks. I initially explore the road's left (northern) fork that runs along Deep Creek, a soul-soothing stream too shallow to harbor hope of trout. I savor the stream, but turn back after a mile when the road climbs up from the creek toward Christmas Tree Lake, where you can catch 20-inch Apache trout on a $25-a-day fishing permit.

The narrow East Fork of the
White River originates below
Mount Baldy on the White
Mountain Indian Reservation.

Back on Y55, I drive steadily up the mountain, marveling at the riotous mix of vegetation. The forest crowds the road with oak, ash, walnut, and cottonwood trees, augmented by old-growth ponderosa pines. Soon, seductively white-trunked aspens make their appearance, hedged by brooding Douglas firs. The road climbs easily up to a ridge with stirring panoramic views and on past a succession of cheerful streams. At nearly 8,000 feet, I encounter a vibrant forest of blue spruce and corkbark firs, more like a Tolkien fantasy than an Arizona landscape. All the while, rain spatters, lightning flashes, and cloud-tumbled holes open overhead, allowing sunlight to sparkle on bejeweled ferns.

And all that before I come to Big Bonito Creek, some 40 miles after leaving Whiteriver. Big Bonito emerges from the closed area of the reservation north of the road, a sprawling wilderness centered on sacred Mount Baldy. The Apache fishery department has stocked the golden, speckled Apache trout in Big Bonito, which remains open to fishermen south of the road. Men in an Apache road crew laugh, joke, and splash as they build a fish barrier to protect the Apache trout from the downstream rainbows and browns.

I'm instantly smitten: Grabbing my fly rod, I head downstream to float my hopeful fly through the tiny pools and musical riffles. I catch nothing, since my natural aura repels fish and crashes computers. No matter: I fish so I'll have an excuse to stand in a stream as the afternoon swirls past.

Finally, I tear myself away and scud along, as leaves before the storm. Five miles later, I reach the junction of Y55 and Y20. I detour briefly to catch-and-release Pacheta Lake, then I go on to Reservation Lake, which boasts a store, campgrounds, boat rentals, and some of the best lake-fishing on the reservation.

But I can't linger long. I left Whiteriver at 11 and now it's past 5, which leaves two hours of daylight. So I return to Y20 and continue south past the junction with Y55. After puzzling out the mismatched bewilderment of the reservation's seemingly random road designations, I reach Y70. As 70 drops down the mountain, firs yield to ponderosas, then to oaks, then to junipers.

I encounter Bonito Creek, after Big and Little Bonito have merged into a lower-elevation version of Oak Creek in Sedona, with sycamores, cottonwoods, deep pools, brown trout, and lurking bass.

After that, the road descends to a grassy prairie graced by pronghorn antelope, which briefly race the jeep—completing a stirring sample of nearly every sort of Arizona terrain save low, saguaro desert.

Shortly after the junction of Y70 and Y40, I pass the inconspicuous tracery of Turkey Creek, hidden on the right side of the road in the bottom of a 15-foot-deep gash in the volcanic rock. Along this creek, the U.S. Army confined Geronimo and his Chiricahua band, as detailed in Britton Davis' *The Truth About Geronimo*. Harried into surrender by Gen. George Crook and the White Mountain Apache scouts, Geronimo's people settled here for a time. But fear, pride, rumors, and bungling finally prompted Geronimo to bolt, triggering the final, bloody, two-year phase of the Apache Wars that horrified the nation and sucked in one-quarter of the U.S. Army.

I pass the site as darkness gathers. Drunk on the day, as the shadows lengthen, I think of the gleam of the trout, the sound of the stream, the trunks of the aspen, the sway of the spruce, the luminous green of the grass, the reflections of the clouds, the call of the turkeys, the golden glow of the elk and the track of the bear. And in this one day's wander, I understand utterly why the Apaches fought so hard—even if I do not know the proper names of the places that can make me wise.

—Pete Aleshire

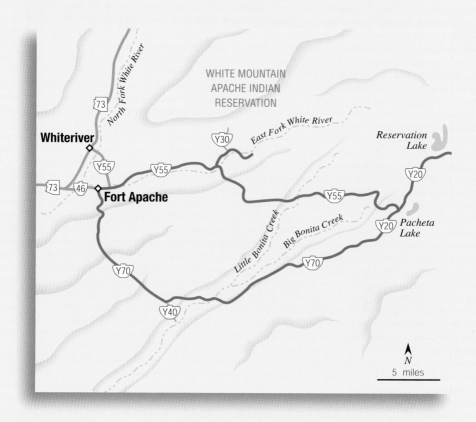

Route Finder

• Take U.S. 60 northeast from the Globe area or south from Show Low to State Route 73. Turn east onto State 73 for Whiteriver.

• Buy permit in Whiteriver at Wildlife & Outdoor Recreation Division office, northwest corner State 73 and Fatco Road.

• Returning to State 73, drive south 2.5 miles to Indian Route 46, marked by a sign to Fort Apache. Turn left.

• Pass Fort Apache turnoff at 0.7 mile.

• Continue east on Indian 46 for 3.7 more miles to a T-junction with Y55. Turn right.

• Y55 pavement ends in 7.2 miles.

• Optional: About 100 yards past pavement's end, turn left (northeast) onto R30/R60 along Deep Creek. Return to Y55. There is a cluster of directional and road signs at this junction, including one for Reservation Lake.

• Back on Y55 continue southeast and then east for 22 miles to Y20 junction. Turn left (north).

• Option: To reach Pacheta Lake, continue eastward across the Y55/Y20 intersection and follow directional signs.

• For Reservation Lake from the Y55/Y20 intersection, turn left (north) and continue for about 7 miles.

• Leaving Reservation Lake, drive south on Y20, past its junction with Y55, and continue south for about 8 miles to Y70. Turn right (west).

• Continue east on Y70 for 23.5 miles to its junction with Y40. Turn right, staying on Y70.

• Continue on 70 for 15.2 miles to the junction with Indian Route 46 (Fort Apache Road). Turn left for a return to State 73.

Additional information: White Mountain Apache Tribe, Office of Tourism, (928) 338-1230 or (877) 338-9628; www.wmat.nsn.us.

East of Flagstaff

The basin of Lockett Meadow, far left, catches autumn gold below the snowy summits of the San Francisco Peaks. Bonito Park, left, lies ablaze with prairie sunflowers with the San Francisco Peaks beyond.

Robert G. McDonald

Two Kinds of Terrain

• Overview

Ranging eastward out of Flagstaff takes you onto an arid plateau dappled with mesas, boulders and rocky spires, canyons, the ruins of ancient civilizations, and—on the edges—mountains. These places manifest the shapes, textures, colors, and human history from which art is made. Three of the back roads described in this chapter will introduce you to sections of the Navajo Indian Reservation that are not widely used by non-Indians. A fourth trip, east and south of Flagstaff, leads into a completely different kind of terrain that is heavily forested and dotted with lakes. You don't need any special kind of vehicle to make these drives, although a high-clearance vehicle is preferable in one or two spots. With few exceptions, all roads are paved and well-marked.

• The Drives

• Towns and Sites

Flagstaff, Canyon de Chelly, Casner Park, Colorado Plateau, Gray Mountain, Holbrook, Homolovi Ruins State Park, Hopi Indian Reservation, Hubbell Trading Post, Lake Mary (Upper and Lower), Mormon Lake, Munds Park, Navajo Indian Reservation, Petrified Forest, Rock Art Ranch, San Francisco Peaks, Walnut Canyon, and Winslow.

Randy A. Prentice

A female Anna's hummingbird, one of the most common "hummers" in Arizona, tastes a summer wildflower. Neil Weidner

In 1884, a 23-year-old journalist named Charles F. Lummis walked from Cincinnati to Los Angeles to begin his new job as city editor of the *Los Angeles Times*. As he slowly made his way across the country, Lummis sent the newspaper reports on what he had seen. A sensitive observer who loved the unique feel of New Mexico and Arizona in particular, Lummis later wrote an article, "The Artist's Paradise," recalling his trek across the Navajo Indian Reservation east of Flagstaff.

"The atmosphere of the southwest is perhaps the hardest in the world for artists to catch. It is so subtle, so magical, so mixed with witchcraft, that it fools the sharpest eye and laughs at the cleverest palette..." He found, he said, "an air that brings the very rocks to life, that grows and broods upon the desert until strange unrealities fill the world and one sits in the beautiful presence of a dream."

Then as now, a first view of this terrain—a mixture of barren plains and pastel hills—is staggering. With some modification, everything Lummis saw remains visible today in the arid plains of the Colorado Plateau: waves of red-brown and amber sands, black- or ochre-colored hills covered with light green sage, the giant sandstone monoliths and tall cones, the scalloped rocks and limestone arches.

In places the terrain resembles the surface of the moon, a fact which did not escape the space program's notice. In 1971, NASA sent Apollo 15 astronauts Jim Irwin and David Scott to Gray Mountain on the Navajo Indian Reservation to practice driving their moon buggy over the rocky terrain, retrieving rocks, and ferrying them to an imitation of the lunar landing module.

To appreciate the dominant features in this distinctive landscape, picture yourself at a high point in the San Francisco Peaks looking east of Flagstaff. You would see, closest to the city, evergreen forests and the remnants of very old volcanic eruptions in the form of smooth cinder cones. Let your eye drift some 50 miles northeast of the city, and you might pick out the Little Colorado River, which appears as a crack in the barren earth running southeast-northwest. In the distance northeast of the river, you would make out the southern end of Black Mesa, where the Hopi Indians live. If you were to ignore the details and merely scan the horizon like someone looking for rain, there are only two features that appear omnipresent: a capacious sky and an undulating expanse of clay soils where minerals have combined and turned this treeless moonscape into a muted canvas of red, black, and gray hills and ravines. Less obvious, clumps of cedars and cottonwood trees appear on widely separated hillsides and washes.

There are very few towns in this terrain because most of the landscape is part of either the small Hopi Indian Reservation or the gargantuan but largely undeveloped Navajo Indian Reservation. The Navajo reservation covers some

Sunset under a stormy
sky enhances the hues of
Ives Mesa and the Painted
Desert on the Navajo
Indian Reservation.

30,000 square miles in northern Arizona, southern Utah, and western New Mexico and is home to roughly 200,000 people. Dinètah, as the Navajos call this homeland, is a landscape of swirled sandstone mesas and buttes and graceful natural arches, land that completely surrounds the Hopi reservation. The region's distinctive cliffs and pinnacles, the long mesas and squat buttes carved by wind and particles of waterborne silt, are striped and banded like elaborate tapestries, the result of iron compounds leached through the rocks over billions of years.

Interstate 40, like the railroad, runs east-west through this country. The railroad gave birth to the towns of Winslow and Holbrook at the southern edge of the Navajo reservation, and both towns were named for railroad executives. Before Europeans, Anglos, and the railroad builders came to this area, it was home to Ancestral Puebloan Indians (sometimes called Anasazi), the Hopis, and the Navajos.

At Winslow, which was a Hopi settlement long before it evolved into a railroad town, visitors can see how the Ancestral Puebloans, the Hopi's ancestors, lived in the 13th and 14th centuries. A few miles north of the city (Exit 257 when heading east from Flagstaff), Homolovi Ruins State Park preserves the ruins of Ancestral Puebloan pueblos. Homolovi is one of the most beautifully designed of Arizona's state parks, and, while wandering the various archaeological sites in the park, you will see numerous shards, remnants of ceramic vessels many centuries old, lying on the ground or on rocks where visitors have placed them. You can touch these ancient bits and pieces, but it's against the law to remove them from the park.

Robert G. McDonald

Grassy banks rim Ashurst Lake southeast of Flagstaff.

Tourists get in the picture with the statue that marks the song's verse, "Standing on a corner in Winslow, Arizona."

Edward McCain

There are at least three other accessible spots east of Flagstaff where you can find a good connection with the people who preceded you 900 or so years ago.

Walnut Canyon National Monument is 7 miles east of Flagstaff. Take Exit 204 off Interstate 40 and drive south 3 miles to the visitors center. A paved trail makes a steep descent into the canyon and brings you to a cluster of rebuilt cliff dwellings. With binoculars, you can also see the cliff dwellings from the visitors center.

If you're spending some time further east, in the Winslow-Holbrook area, you can visit Rock Art Canyon Ranch near Joseph City. The ranch owner, (928) 288-3260, offers day tours (for a modest fee) into an extensive petroglyph site in a portion of Chevelon Canyon that is on his ranch. Continuing east, you can also see Indian ruins and more petroglyphs in Petrified Forest National Park. From Holbrook, take U.S. Route 180 east 20 miles to the park's southern entrance. Driving north through the park will return you to I-40.

Throughout this area—throughout the West, in fact—North American pronghorn antelope still roam. Experts estimate there are some 8,000 in Arizona alone. Keep your eyes peeled when exploring the plains south of Winslow and Holbrook and you may see herds of them.

Winters in the terrain east of Flagstaff are not quite as severe as they can be in Flagstaff, but the Winslow-Holbrook area can get pretty gloomy about the middle of December. For around six weeks, from the middle of December through January, there's a layer of fog, roughly 400 or 500 feet thick, that hangs in the rolling terrain between the two towns. The fog will settle in the basin along the Little Colorado River and temperatures will drop to 15 or 20 degrees. **AH**

Blooming buckwheat dots a cindered slope at Sunset Crater Volcano National Monument. David Muench

Drive 1

Leupp to Ganado: Paved but Remote

Leave your Jeep at home. This trip is paved from beginning to end, but it will still get you a long way from anything resembling a restaurant or motel. You can pick up snacks at widely separated trading posts (Leupp, Dilkon, and Ganado, for example), but there are no restaurants. You've got to get to Flagstaff to find your way to Leupp, but the route will quickly leave the forested areas at the base of the San Francisco Peaks and drop into the sage-covered plains that constitute a portion of the Painted Desert. Most travelers between Leupp and Ganado, two communities on the Navajo Indian Reservation, are Indians returning from shopping or business trips in Flagstaff. You can forget about heavy traffic.

To begin from Phoenix, head north on Interstate 17 for about 150 miles to the interchange with Interstate 40 at Flagstaff. Take I-40 east to a series of roads leading to Leupp (see Route Finder for detailed directions).

About 3 miles after you get onto Leupp Road, you'll pass a petroglyph site tucked behind a curtain of juniper trees on the right (east) side of the road. Called Turkey Tanks, the site sits within the Coconino National Forest and is not marked. The Forest Service, fearful that vandals will destroy the site, does not publicize it. If you'd like to see it, contact the Coconino forest headquarters in Flagstaff and ask for specific directions (see Route Finder for contact information).

Leupp Road bends from northbound to eastbound and becomes Indian Route 15 as it crosses the boundary onto the reservation. When you're 28 miles along on Leupp Road, you'll find yourself at the gas station and convenience store in Leupp. Not much to see, is there? But this terrain has many stories to tell. Back away from the road are the remains of buildings that were a so-called Japanese internment camp, a relic of World War II hysteria. The buildings were part of an abandoned Indian boarding school.

Between 1942 and 1945, nearly 120,000 Japanese-Americans, almost two-thirds of whom were American-born, lost their homes, possessions, and their constitutional rights because, as Roosevelt's War Secretary put it, you couldn't tell a loyal Japanese from a disloyal one. The government located one of the camps just south of Phoenix on the Gila River Indian Reservation and another at Poston, on the Colorado River Indian Tribes Reservation. Prisoners at those camps, and others, who were seen as troublemakers were shipped to the isolated prison camp at Leupp beginning in April 1943. The site is in the area of Old Leupp, south of Indian 15 near a levee.

As you go through Leupp, you'll cross the Little Colorado River. Continue east on Indian 15 through the scattering of houses and hogans called Bird Springs. About 25 miles east of Leupp, the relatively flat terrain becomes more interesting. In the distance you can see a panorama of cinder cones, buttes, and pinnacles rising mirage-like from the sage-covered fields. You'll drive directly through those pinnacles and buttes as you go east of Dilkon, a major community in the southern end of the reservation.

ENTRANCE
OPEN DAILY ·
8 AM TO 5 PM

Their roots in the past, the entry doors at the Hubbell Trading Post still welcome the public for business.

Like the general stores of the Old West, the Hubbell "bull pen" is where the locals gather to trade and catch up on community news.

George H.H. Huey

From Dilkon it's about 56 miles to the famous Hubbell Trading Post in Ganado.

The Hubbell Trading Post is both an active old-time trading post and a popular stopping point for visitors to the reservation. In addition to being a dry-goods store, which supplies the needs of Navajos in the immediate area, the trading post has a large inventory of Navajo rugs and other crafts. A National Historic Site administered by the National Park Service and managed by Southwest Parks and Monuments Association, the site also includes a visitor center where Navajo weavers can often be found working on rugs. A visitor's loom is also available and anyone can try his or her hand.

Hubbell's is the oldest continually active trading post on the Navajo reservation. It's named for John Lorenzo Hubbell, a Connecticut native who went to New Mexico as a soldier, married a woman of Spanish descent, and eventually learned Spanish and Navajo while traveling through the Southwest. He began trading with the store at Ganado in 1876 and bought out the previous owner in 1878. The Indians called him "Double Glasses" because of his thick-rimmed eyeglasses. Hubbell was in business to make money but, by all accounts, he never lost sight of the welfare of the Navajos who supported him. He once said:

"The first duty of an Indian trader, in my belief, is to look after the material welfare of his neighbors; to advise them to produce that which their natural inclinations and talent best adapts them; to treat them honestly and insist on getting the same treatment from them ... to find a market for their products and vigilantly watch that they keep improving the production of same, and advise them which commands the best price. This does not mean that the trader should forget that he is to see that he makes a fair profit for himself, for whatever would injure him would naturally injure those with whom he comes in contact."

Hubbell ran his trading post for 50 years. When he died in 1930, one old Navajo said:

"You wear out your shoes, you buy another pair; when the food is all gone, you buy more. You gather melons, and more will grow on the vine. You grind your corn and make bread which you eat, and next year you have plenty more corn. But my friend Don Lorenzo is gone, and none to take his place."

Route Finder

• To begin from Phoenix, head north on Interstate 17 to the interchange with Interstate 40 at Flagstaff. Turn east onto I-40, as if heading for Albuquerque.

• Continue on I-40 about 6 miles to Exit 201, Country Club Drive. Turn left (north) and move into the outside lane, following the signs to U.S. Route 89 North.

• Continue on U.S. 89 about 2.5 miles to Camp Townsend/Winona Road. Turn right (east).

• Continue on Camp Townsend/Winona Road for 8 miles to Leupp Road. Turn left (north).

• Leupp Road bends east and becomes Indian Route 15 as it crosses the boundary onto the Navajo Indian Reservation. From the Camp Townsend/Winonoa Road junction, it's 28 miles to Leupp.

• Leaving Leupp, continue east on Indian 15 for 34 miles to State Route 87.

• Cross State 87 and continue east on Indian 15 for 6 miles to Dilkon.

• Continue east on Indian 15 for 17 miles to a T-junction with State Route 77, also called Indian Route 6. Turn left (north) onto State 77.

• Continue 3 miles on 77 to the continuation of Indian 15. Turn right (east).

• Continue for 13 miles on Indian 15 to Greasewood, where there's a trading post.

• Leaving Greasewood, continue on Indian 15 for 17 miles to U.S. Route 191. Turn right (south).

• Continue on U.S. 191 for 6 miles to Ganado and the Hubbell Trading Post.

• Leaving Ganado, drive south on U.S. 191 for 37 miles to I-40 at Chambers, where there's a trading post. Turn right (west) for a 135-mile drive to Flagstaff.

Additional information: Navajo Nation, (928) 871-6647; www.discovernavajo.com. Hubbell, (928) 755-3475; www.nps.gov/hutr.

Petrified logs recline on eroded pedestals at Blue Mesa in the Petrified Forest National Park, near Holbrook. Jack Dykinga

Drive 2

Chinle to Cove:
Into Red Rock Country

If you look at a map of the Navajo Indian Reservation, the prospects of getting from Chinle to Cove don't look very promising. Until 1999, there was no convenient way to get through the Lukachukai Mountains. The dirt road that went through the community of Lukachukai northward over the mountains was unpredictable. At times potholes and ruts so riddled the road that, if you drove it in the summer months without air conditioning, you could figure on getting a sauna and massage in one trip. Then, the Navajos paved the road, and now you can drive it in a sports car with four inches of clearance.

Begin your trip at Chinle, which is a metropolis compared to most communities on the reservation. Chinle has several motels and restaurants, a supermarket, and other services. It is best to known to outsiders as the entry point to Canyon de Chelly (pronounced Duh SHAY), easily one of the most beautiful canyons in all of Arizona and certainly one of the most photographed.

From the Canyon de Chelly visitors center, head northeast on Indian Route 64, which skirts the north rim of Canyon de Chelly (see Route Finder for directions). "Rim" is just the right word for this strip of land. Visitors can drive to various pullouts that appear perched on the edge of an enormous oblong-shaped bowl. At the bottom of this bowl, the Rio de Chelly has carved a route through massive terracotta walls that were occupied by prehistoric Indians for roughly 1,000 years.

When you're not quite 25 miles from the visitors center, Diné Community College appears on the right. Founded in 1968, it was the first tribally controlled community college in the nation. The most prominent building, a six-story glass hogan, contains a museum, art gallery, and gift shop on the third and fourth floors. Although it's difficult to find space during the school year, the college does provide dormitory accommodations for visitors at reasonable rates.

Not long after passing the campus, you'll see the cliffs of the Lukachukai or Chuska Mountains (they blend together in this area) on your right. As you pass through the community of Lukachukai and wind over Buffalo Pass, you enter the heart of the Navajo red rock country, an extraordinarily scenic area dominated by formations of Wingate sandstone that stretches from Rock Point southeast to the vicinity of Cove, which is where you'll be headed once you drive over the pass from Lukachukai. During the 1950s large deposits of uranium were mined throughout this red rock country.

The drive over the top of the mountain—a narrow route over Buffalo Pass that skirts red rock domes and hillocks of sagebrush and piñon pine—will take you to the Red Rock Trading Post. On the outside, this trading post looks like any other in a remote part of the reservation, which is to say it's a small grocery store where, in addition to finding milk and eggs, you can also buy things like bag balm for your livestock or bright Pendleton blankets, favored by Navajos for special occasions, or tools for use on your loom. And then there is the vault. The vault, which most visitors

Aspens forest the slopes
of the Lukachukai
Mountains on the Navajo
Indian Reservation.

are not likely see unless they ask about it, leads to a cave-like museum and arts and crafts shop. The vault is a dark alcove behind a massive steel door. It leads into two windowless rooms that were part of the original trading post constructed around 1890. Spotlights in this hidden museum focus on ancient ceramic pots and baskets, as well as sculptures and traditional silver and turquoise Navajo jewelry. Most of the objects in these eerie rooms are for sale, but some are strictly for display purposes only.

About a mile north of the trading post, turn left (west) onto Indian Route 33 for about a 15-mile drive to the isolated village of Cove. You'll see a terrain filled with magnificent crimson buttes, long mesas, and a towering arch.

As you enter the community turn left onto a driveway and check in at the Cove chapter house—which is a sort of community center or city hall for the surrounding area—before heading down to the arch. The tall graceful arch is only about 3 miles west of the chapter house, but the "road" to it is more like a precipitous goat path.

There is no convenient alternative route to get you back to Chinle from Cove. Your best bet is to return the way you came.

Tom Till

**Lukachukai Arch looms large against its shadow
in the Lukachukai Mountains.**

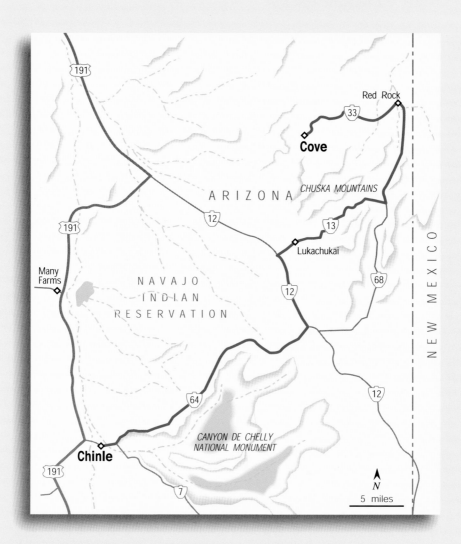

Route Finder

• *Start in Chinle at the Canyon de Chelly visitors center. Drive northeast on Indian Route 64.*
• *Continue on Indian 64 for 23 miles, passing Diné College in Tsaile, to a T-junction. Turn left (north) onto Indian Route 12.*
• *Continue on Indian 12 for 7 miles to Indian Route 13. Turn right.*
• *Continue on Indian 13 through Lukachukai and over Buffalo Pass for 25 miles to Red Rock.*
• *From the Red Rock Trading Post, continue north on Indian 13 for a mile to Indian Route 33. Turn left.*
• *Continue on Indian 33 for 10 miles to Cove.*

• *Return the way you came. Option: At the junction of Indian 12 and 64 in Tsaile, continue straight (south) on 12 for a wonderfully scenic 53-mile drive to Window Rock, from where you easily can reach U.S. Route 191 or Interstate 40*

Additional information: Canyon de Chelly, (928) 674-5500; www.nps.gov/cach. Diné College (dormitory rooms), (928) 724-6611; info@ dinecollege.edu. Indian Route 12 scenic drive, www.arizonascenicroads.com.

Drive 3

Chinle to Canyon del Muerto

The first time I visited Canyon del Muerto on the Navajo reservation, I was struck by what seemed a contradiction: How could a place of such great natural beauty—a miniature Grand Canyon, really—come to be named Canyon of the Dead? Later, when I became more familiar with the lamentable history of this idyllic spot in northeastern Arizona, I realized the name made perfect sense.

High in the canyon walls there are several large caverns, one of which is known as Massacre Cave. Nearly 200 years ago, a brutal confrontation occurred there between well-armed Spanish soldiers and a nearly defenseless group of Navajo women and children.

The record of Spanish colonization in the Southwest is filled with bloody confrontations. In the 16th century, the Spaniards came north from Mexico City and claimed the Indian lands as their own. Then they imposed their religious beliefs on the natives and set out to "civilize" them according to European standards. If the Indians did not cooperate—for instance, when the Spaniards took their sons and daughters as slaves—the Spaniards reacted by killing or mutilating them.

It is also true that the Indians—in this case the Navajos—were not always innocent bystanders. The Spaniards had introduced horses, cattle, and sheep to the Southwest, and for nearly 200 years both Spaniards and Indians stole animals from each other and then fought to regain what each felt was rightfully theirs.

The Spaniards were particularly defensive about the land they had seized, and eventually they began settling in the vicinity of Mount Taylor near the New Mexico village of Acoma. Then as now, the Navajos considered Mount Taylor—also called Turquoise Mountain—to be sacred, and in 1804 several Navajo leaders went to New Mexico Governor Fernando Chacon and made a peaceful appeal for the Spaniards to move away. When that failed, the Navajos declared war on the Spaniards.

By 1805, hostile relations between Navajos and Spaniards had reached a crisis point. In January of that year, the military governor of New Mexico ordered Lt. Antonio Narbona—later to become governor of New Mexico—to go to Canyon del Muerto to find and destroy the Navajo strongholds believed to be located there and to subdue the Navajos forever. Narbona, with a strong force of Spanish soldiers supplemented by Opata Indians from northern Mexico, engaged the underpowered Navajos in battle in Canyon del Muerto. The Navajos, defeated and on the run, concealed their women, children, and elderly in a natural cave high on the face of a sandstone cliff and then tried to lure the Spaniards away from the area.

The Spaniards began leaving and probably would never have noticed the people hidden in the cave, but an old woman, who had once been a slave, evidently could not resist the temptation to say her piece. Thinking the cave impenetrable, she moved to the edge of the precipice and began shouting epithets at the Spanish soldiers far below. Others started throwing rocks and hurling insults at the Spaniards.

The incline from the canyon floor to the cave was steep and treacherous, but not impossible. Narbona ordered some of his men to scale the slope to the cave. The first soldier to get anywhere near the cave encountered a strong and angry Navajo woman. In their scuffle,

Cottonwood trees flagged
with autumn color line
Chinle Wash as it winds
through Canyon de Chelly.

the two slipped off the ledge and fell to their deaths below.

Whether that incident triggered what happened next, no one can say, but the soldiers unleashed a barrage of gunfire, ricocheting bullets off the overhang that formed the top of the cave, until they had killed or wounded enough Navajos to make access to the cave possible.

Historian Raymond Friday Locke described what happened then:

"Entering the cave they finished off the Navajos, the aged, hysterical mothers, and crying babies, to the last person. Then they methodically crushed the skulls of the dead and dying with their gun butts and cut off the ears for trophies."

Canyon of the Dead. No wonder.

Today the scars in the cave walls where the bullets struck are still visible. Narbona said in his report to his superiors that nearly 10,000 rounds were fired that day.

Paul Gill

Canyon de Chelly visitors need Navajo guides to reach Antelope House Ruins.

Visitors on backcountry tours can get near, but not in, Massacre Cave—and along the way see dozens of Ancestral Puebloan, or Anasazi, cliff dwellings—but you must be on a tour or have a Navajo guide. This is not the kind of back road trek you make on your own.

Canyon del Muerto is a branch of Canyon de Chelly (pronounced duh-SHAY). The canyon is about 50 yards wide in some places and a half-mile in others. In both canyons, ocher-colored sandstone walls, often streaked or banded with a black residue, rise as high as 1,000 feet. Canyon del Muerto stretches from a few miles southeast of Chinle northward for some 30 miles to the Lukachukai Mountains near Tsaile.

Jeep tours leaving the vicinity of the Canyon de Chelly National Monument visitors center go east to the junction of Chinle Wash and Tsaile Creek, where both canyons come together. To see Canyon del Muerto, visitors must sign up for a full-day tour which includes both canyons. However, anyone with a four-wheel-drive vehicle can hire a Navajo guide through the visitors center and bypass the commercial tour operators, who charge per person for the all-day tours. Individual guides are paid an hourly rate, which varies from one person to another.

I signed up for the tour at the historic Thunderbird Lodge, just down the hill from the visitors center, and spent the next eight hours traversing a relatively smooth though unpaved thoroughfare (most of it was simply wash bottom). The four-wheel-drive truck I was in had bench seats mounted on the bed, enough to accommodate 24 persons. In the fall and early spring these vehicles are ideal for the scenic tour, but I made the trip in June, and beds in these tour trucks are not shaded.

Which may explain why one of my friends at Tsaile, hearing that I was making trip, said, "Oh, you're going to take the Shake 'n' Bake Express, are you?"

Yes, you do shake, and it does get hot, but it isn't all that bad if you wear a hat and smear yourself with sunscreen. All of the vehicles carry plenty of drinking water, and a box lunch is provided.

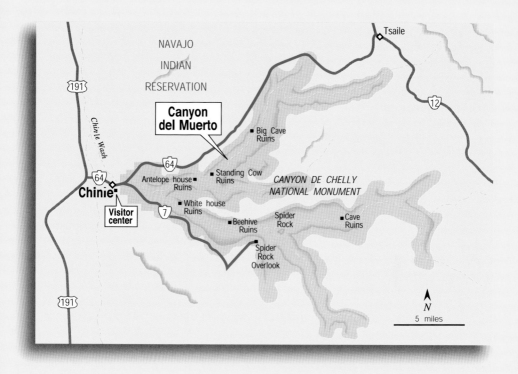

Route Finder

• Begin in Flagstaff on Interstate 40 and drive east to Exit 201, Country Club Drive. Turn left (north) and follow the signs to U.S. Route 89 North.

• Continue on U.S. 89, past Gray Mountain and Cameron, for 61 miles to U.S. Route 160. Turn right (east).

• Continue on U.S. 160 for 10 miles to State Route 264 in Tuba City. Turn right (south)

• Continue on State 264 for 62 miles to State Route 87. Stay left to continue on State 264.

• Continue on State 264 for 26 miles to State Route 77/Indian Route 6.

• Stay left to continue on 264.

• Continue on 264 for 30 miles to U.S. Route 191 just before you come to Ganado. Turn left (north) onto U.S. 191.

• Continue on 191 for 30 miles to Chinle. Turn right onto Indian Route 7.

• Continue on Indian 7 for 3 miles to the Canyon de Chelly visitors center.

• From the visitors center, continue driving east on Indian 64 until it veers away from the canyon, about 11 miles from the center.

• Return to the visitors center and turn left on Indian Route 7 for a drive along the Canyon de Chelly rim until the pavement ends in about 25 miles.

• Return to Chinle.

Additional information: Canyon de Chelly visitors center, (928) 674-5500; www.nps.gov. An excellent map of the Canyon de Chelly–Canyon del Muerto can be downloaded from www.nps.gov/cach/planyourvisit/maps.htm. Tours, Thunderbird Lodge, (800) 679-2473; www.tbirdlodge.com.

End this scenic drive with a round of golf at Pinewood Country Club in Munds Park. Robert G. McDonald

Drive 4

Flagstaff to Munds Park
On the Scenic Route

Munds Park is directly south of Flagstaff on Interstate 17. If you're in Flagstaff, you can easily jump onto I-17 and be there in 15 minutes, but why bore yourself with interstate highway travel? Take this circuitous excursion through the picture-postcard country around Upper and Lower Lake Mary (two lakes) and Mormon Lake. Most of it is paved, but the last 9 miles into Munds Park are dirt (passable with an ordinary car but bouncy in places).

So, begin on Lake Mary Road at I-17's Exit 339 about a quarter-mile south of its interchange with Interstate 40 and go southeasterly (see Route Finder for directions). In a little over a mile, watch for the Coconino National Forest's Mormon Lake Ranger District station on your right. You can get maps and detailed information on the area there.

Four miles later, you'll cross the boundary into the national forest, and the road becomes Forest Service Road 3, and Lower Lake Mary appears on your right as a long rectangle. The Forest Service describes the lake this way: "Sometimes it's a lake; sometimes it's not. Lower Lake Mary ... has a tendency to disappear during the long, dry spells that periodically hit this area. When the lake has water in it, which actually is much of the time, its banks are usually lined with anglers trying to catch the trout [stocked by] the Arizona Game and Fish Department. If it stays full for a year or two, it will pick up a population of northern pike and catfish."

A century ago, the whole area used to be known as Clark Valley before the lakes were formed by two dams. Clark Valley was named for John Clark, a native of Augusta, Maine, who came west and in 1877 established a huge sheep operation in the grassy meadows that are now covered with the waters of the lakes.

In 1907, another Flagstaff pioneer, Tim A. Riordan, hatched the idea of building a lake south of town. The dam was built across a narrow section of what once had been Clark's ranch. Riordan named the lake for his daughter Mary.

A few minutes after passing Lower Lake Mary you'll come to Upper Lake Mary. It's deeper and more consistent on water retention. A scattering of campgrounds and picnic areas can be found near the lake.

When you no longer see the upper lake on your right, start looking for an intersection at which FR 3 continues straight (south), Forest Service Road 651 goes west (right) to Pine Grove Campground a few miles away, and Forest Service Road 81E goes east (left) for Lake Ashurst, a small lake and campground where the fishing is good and shade hard to find. Ashurst, 4 miles off of FR 3, is named for the family of William Henry Ashurst, a sheep rancher who moved to the area in 1876. William's son, Henry Fountain Ashurst, was a U.S. senator from Arizona for 30 years from the time it became the 48th state until 1941.

About 3 miles beyond the intersection, you come to a junction at which West Side Mormon Lake Road (Forest Service Road 90) starts westward to loop around the lake and FR 3 continues along the lake's east side. The two roads come together at the southern end of Mormon Lake.

Lichen-covered boulders
dot the shoreline of
Mormon Lake.

West Side Mormon Lake Road leads in less than 4 miles to the Dairy Springs Campground and to Montezuma Lodge, where rustic cabins can be rented during the warmer months. The area around the Dairy Springs Campground was once a dairy farm run by Mormon settlers.

Continuing southward on the West Side Mormon Lake Road brings you to Mormon Lake Lodge, a facility including cabins, RV park, campground, a steakhouse and saloon, and trail rides. The lodge is open the year round but cuts back to just weekends during the winter.

Mormon Lake is a good example of wishful thinking. Even in a wet year, it will hold very little water. In the summer of 1999, when there were torrential rains, the "lake" was mostly filled with a carpet of yellow daisies.

If you drive to Mormon Lake Lodge, you've passed the road for Munds Park. Turn around and go back about 4 miles and watch for Forest Service Road 240 (sometimes called Mormon Lake Road) on your left just beyond St. Joseph's Camp. Up to this point you've been on pavement, and now you get to pay your dues.

FR 240 is not horrible, but in places it feels like horrible's first cousin. It's a well-used route, and as a result, you'll encounter washboard surfaces and rocky spots that will remind you of the location of your various organs. Still, there's no denying it leads a body into some wonderful forests and wide alpine-like meadows.

After 2 miles, you come to a junction with Forest Service Road 132A, which leads to the right up Mormon Mountain. Stay left, or more or less straight, to reach Munds. A mile later, you'll begin a steep descent down a road so badly ridged it'll make your eyeballs bounce (unless the road grader's been by in the last few days). At the bottom, there's a junction. Go right. In less than a mile you'll come to a signed T-junction. Go left.

When you're 1.4 miles west of the T-junction, you'll drop into one of the most beautiful spots along this route, a big meadow called Casner Park. Parks in the

Boughs of ponderosa pine and Gambel oak arch over Mormon Lake Road.

mountains of the West are not the developed places commonly thought of as parks. Instead, they're usually broad meadows, sometimes just a big grassy field that turns up in the middle of an otherwise dense forest. Casner, named for a horse rancher named Mose Casner who lived in the area in the 1880s, is a wide, green meadow bordered by ponderosa pines.

About 3.5 miles after leaving Casner Park, you're back on the pavement at the edge of Munds Park. The pretty community of Munds looks a little like a suburb in Connecticut or Virginia, a remnant of Norman Rockwell Americana where attractive wooden homes are tucked among the pines and you can get gas, a bite to eat, or play a round of golf.

Once you reach the pavement, you're about 2 miles (slightly less) from I-17. Once you get to the highway, you can go north to return to Flagstaff or south to head for the Verde Valley and Phoenix.

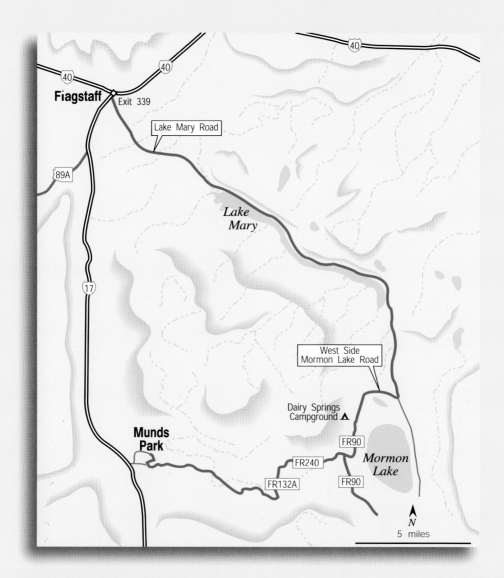

Route Finder

• *Begin just south of Flagstaff on Lake Mary Road at Exit 339 off Interstate 17. The road also is known as Forest Service Road 3.*

• *Continue southeastward on the road, past Lower and Upper Lake Mary, for 28 miles, to West Side Mormon Lake Road (FR 90). Turn left for a southward drive around Mormon Lake.*

• *Leaving the southern end of Mormon Lake, backtrack northward on FR 90 to FR 240. Turn left (west).*

• *Continue for 2 miles on FR 240 to FR 132A. Bear left for Munds. (Going right takes to atop Mormon Mountain.)*

• *Continue on FR 240 for a mile and the start of a long, rough descent. At the bottom there's a fork. Go right.*

• *Less than a mile later, at a T-junction, a sign will read Munds Park. Turn left and follow the road for 5 miles into Munds Park and Interstate 17.*

Additional information: Coconino National Forest Mormon Lake District, (928) 774-1147; www. fs.fed.us/r3/coconino/recreation/mormon_lake/index.shtml. Montezuma Lodge, (928) 354-2220. Mormon Lake Lodge, (928) 354-2227; http://mormonlakelodge.com.

West of
Flagstaff

Paul Gill

A wintry evening begins to dim the San Francisco Peaks, far left, outside of Flagstaff. An aging cabin, left, manages to stay standing beyond the ponderosa pine trees in the Gash Mountain area.

Amid Mountains and Meadows

• Overview

Back roads directly reached via Interstate 40 west of Flagstaff meander among ponderosa pines, beautiful stands of aspen, and wide meadows. Access to the Grand Canyon's South Rim is from Flagstaff or Williams. The Williams depot provides train transportation to the South Rim. The routes offer exhilarating views of the highest peaks in Arizona, flower-filled meadows and peaceful lakes. Summer and fall are the best times to go. Bring a camera or your sketchpad.

• The Drives

• Towns and Sites

Flagstaff, Bill Williams Mountain, Garland Prairie, Grand Canyon, Prescott, San Francisco Peaks, Seligman, Schultz Pass, White Horse Lake, and Williams.

Elias Butler

A Rocky Mountain bighorn ram eyes newcomers warily.
Neil Weidner

If you're one of those people who looks at maps in search of the solitude a good mountain can provide, spare yourself the eye strain and instead take our advice: Head for the Flagstaff area, where you'll find not only high mountains but deep forests, an abundance of wildlife, and a landscape where the symmetry of slope and ridgeline has a softening effect on everything man-made and natural for miles around. Spend a day or a week in the terrain west of the city, and its beauty will haunt you forever.

Within 30 to 40 miles west of Flagstaff, a handful of heavily forested volcanic peaks—Kendrick, Bill Williams, Sitgreaves—tower above wide prairies. Like the San Francisco Peaks at Flagstaff, these mountains were formed by lava and ash spewed out by fiery volcanoes hundreds of thousands of years ago.

During the spring and summer, the emerald meadows west of the city fill with colorful sunflowers, daisies, and wild irises. In the early fall, the changing aspen leaves in the higher elevations provide a stunning prelude to the months when everything sleeps under a deep blanket of undisturbed snow. Most of this terrain is in either the Kaibab or Coconino National Forest, public lands offering seemingly endless opportunities to explore, hike, camp, fish, hunt, or just sit quietly with an engaging book.

The Flagstaff area is on the Colorado Plateau, a massive rock platform covering 130,000 square miles (that's bigger than any of the 50 states except Alaska, Texas, California and Montana) in northern Arizona and New Mexico, western Colorado, and eastern Utah. A large part of the plateau region is dominated by an arid landscape of swirled sandstone cliffs, narrow canyons, and orange walls where time and geologic collision have created a rich canvas. Here and there, on the portion of the plateau within Arizona (the Mogollon Rim is its southern border), there are isolated mountains and ranges that are green, well-forested, and well-watered. But nothing on the plateau is quite like the San Francisco Peaks.

The peaks—they're actually the serrated rim of an ancient volcanic crater—have an appeal that goes beyond anything else in the area, perhaps because they're visible from so many different points in northern Arizona and are such a dramatic contrast to the desolate terrain that covers most of the Colorado Plateau. Humphreys Peak, the tallest of the peaks, is also, at 12,643 feet, the highest point in Arizona. The other peaks are Agassiz at 12,356 feet, Doyle at, 11,969 feet, and Fremont at, 11,940 feet. The numbers vary slightly from one map to another, but the basic message is clear enough: These mountains, remnants of an extinct volcano, are giants.

Both the Hopi and the Navajo Indians, who live on reservations northeast of Flagstaff, attach religious significance to the San Francisco Peaks. For

At the Grand Canyon's
west end of the South Rim,
layered rock rises far above
the Colorado River.

the Navajos, the Peaks are one of four sacred ranges that define Dinétah, the tribe's cultural homeland. For the Hopi, the Peaks have a profound religious significance because they are the winter home of the kachinas, spiritual entities that govern every aspect of Hopi life. Undoubtedly, the Peaks nurture the spiritual life of many non-Indians as well. Every exploration party that passed through the area left journals or reports commenting on the beauty of the mountains.

Not only are Arizona's mountains beautiful, they're abundant. Arizona is a big state, 392 miles south to north and 338 miles east to west at its widest points, and there are more than 200 mountain ranges. One of the biggest challenges faced by both aboriginal Indian groups and European and American explorers in northern Arizona was to find a route between this tangle of steep mountains and deep canyons that would make trade and travel possible. The Grand Canyon, 75 miles northwest of Flagstaff, was the major hurdle to be avoided, although there was no way to do anything but avoid it.

Paul Gill

Their young saplings a favorite food of local elk, autumn aspens rim a meadow near the snowy Hochderffer Hills.

Long before white men came to the area, the Indians figured out that the best way to get to the section of the Colorado River west of Flagstaff and south of the Grand Canyon was to follow a route that ran more or less along the 35th parallel. Hopi and Navajo Indians traded with Hualapai and Mojave Indians using routes they had blazed through the most accommodating passes, in effect creating a primitive highway westward from Flagstaff to the areas around Seligman, Peach Springs, Truxton Canyon, Kingman, and the Colorado River.

The United States acquired much of this country—most of what is now known as the Southwest—from Mexico in 1848. That same year, just 11 days before the Treaty of Hidalgo was signed and the land transferred to the United States, gold was discovered at Sutter's Mill in northern California, an event that would unleash a flood of fortune-seeking prospectors from throughout the United States, Hawaii, Peru, and Chile, among many other places. In 1849, when the migrations were in full swing, travelers tended to follow routes north of the Flagstaff area, in Utah, or further south, along the Gila River, to avoid the nearly impenetrable wilderness in central and northwestern Arizona.

However, the most direct route, assuming one could be developed, was slightly north of the 35th Parallel, passing through what would become Flagstaff, Williams, and Kingman. It did not take long after the 1849 Gold Rush got going for various government survey crews to follow. The California gold was discovered in January of 1848, the rush was on in 1849, and there followed various road and railroad building survey teams: the Sitgreaves Expedition in 1851, the Whipple and Ives Expedition of 1854, and the Beale Wagon Road Expedition of 1857. All of these people were sent west to survey routes through northern Arizona Territory.

The idea was to get people and goods moving east to west and vice versa, to settle the country and build prosperity. That was the 19th-century dream that eventually created the Beale Wagon Road, Route 66, and today's Interstate 40 (not to mention the railroad), one road replacing the other as time moved on, but each following basically the same trajectory through the mountainous region west of Flagstaff.

Today, anyone traveling west or east of Flagstaff inevitably crosses bits and pieces of the wagon road that Lt. Edward F. Beale, aided by 22 camels imported from the Middle East, designed and built in 1857. Beale, a former Navy officer, had been assigned to create a new wagon road to California that would eventually span the country from Fort Smith, Arkansas, to Los Angeles.

During the course of his road building, Beale became a great fan of his camels. His journal entry for Sept. 21, 1857, may be the first love letter written by an American to his camels:

"My admiration for the camels increases daily with my experience of them. The harder the test they are put to, the more fully they seem to justify all that can be said of them. They pack water for others four days under a hot sun and never get a drop; they pack heavy burdens of corn and oats for months and never get a grain; and on the bitter greasewood and other worthless shrubs not only subsist but keep fat; withal they are so perfectly docile and so admirably contented with whatever fate befalls them. No one could do justice to their merits or value in expeditions of this kind, and I look forward to the day when every mail route across the continent will be conducted and worked altogether with this economical and noble brute."

Despite Beale's glowing report on his camels' usefulness, the camel experiment eventually died, not because of anything the animals did or did not do, but because of the Civil War. As Congress was being petitioned for funds to purchase another 1,000 camels, the Civil War escalated and absorbed every politician's attention. Camels took a very low priority. As the historian Odie Faulk wrote:

"...With the opening shots of the Civil War, the Camel Military Corps was disbanded and the beasts sold at public auction. Some were bought to pack ore in Arizona, others to pack salt in Nevada. A few escaped to run wild in the desert where they were shot on sight by prospectors and hunters, who regarded them as pests and nuisances."

With the coming of the railroad, and later the automobile, there was no need for camels. Nevertheless, Beale's prediction that the road he was building would one day be "the great immigrant road to California" turned out to be true. Route 66, with various tributaries, eventually formed a coast-to-coast highway, but the section best known ran from Chicago to Los Angeles. *Route 66* was a TV series, a popular song, and now, in the bucolic towns west of Flagstaff, it's a nostalgic reminder of another era. If you take the route to Garland Prairie described later, you can go into the rural community of Parks and drive remnants of the old Route 66. Go farther west and, between Seligman and Topock, you'll find the longest remaining intact segment of Route 66 in the United States.

One of the most charming remnants of that era of poodle skirts and Formica kitchen counters is the town of Williams, a jumping-off point for two of the back roads described below. In 1984, Williams became the last Route 66 town bypassed by Interstate 40. With doom and gloom on everyone's mind, a historic preservation committee was formed and someone came up with a brilliant idea. Why not sell chunks of concrete from Route 66 for $4.66 apiece? Would anyone believe you could raise $5,000 this way? But it worked. People from all over the United States ordered chunks of the highway, and Williams

A Forest Service trail leads to the eroded amphitheater of Red Mountain Geologic Area, site of an ancient volcanic cinder cone.

Tom Danielsen

used the money to renovate the old Santa Fe depot, which became the town's visitor center.

There's a lot to see and do directly west of Flagstaff even before you leave town for the Williams area. To get a general orientation to the area, spend some time in the Museum of Northern Arizona on U.S. Route 180. The museum provides particularly good introduction to the Indians of the Colorado Plateau and the geological history of the region.

Before you head out to the routes described below, take a short drive up the Snowbowl Road, a paved road that leaves U.S. 180 less than a mile west of the museum's entrance. The road ends at the base of Mount Agassiz. If it's summertime, you can ride the ski lift higher on the mountain for a panoramic view of the San Francisco Peaks and a substantial portion of northern Arizona. Don't forget a jacket. You'll need it.   ᛜ

Drive 1

Schultz Pass: A Back-Road Illusion

If you haven't spent much time around Flagstaff, Schultz Pass will come as a surprise. The road into the pass is only a few miles west of the downtown area, but it feels like it could be 100 miles to the nearest telephone. You'll find elk and deer in abundance among the tall pine and spruce trees that line the route, reinforcing the illusion that civilization is a long way off from this scenic setting.

The road is simple to find from downtown Flagstaff (see Route Finder for detailed directions). As you move north on U.S. Route 180, about 3 miles from downtown, look for the Museum of Northern Arizona on your left (stop in if you have time—it's well worth a visit). Schultz Pass Road is 0.2 of a mile beyond the museum. It's marked with a large sign.

The road is paved for the first 0.8 of a mile as it wraps around the edge of a housing development. The pavement ends as soon as the road enters the tall pines, at which point it is designated Forest Service Road 420. This heavily-used route sometimes is rutted and riddled with potholes, but you never know how good or bad it may be. It's graded from time to time, so it may be smooth when you travel it. Many people drive this road in an ordinary sedan, but a high-clearance vehicle is recommended.

Snow closes the road in the winter. Flagstaff, located at 7,000 feet, sometimes gets its first snowfall in October, and there's hardly a winter when the mountain area doesn't accumulate 35 or more inches. Schultz Pass, which is a cut between the towering San Francisco Peaks and Mt. Elden, tops out at 8,200 feet.

Minutes after you leave U.S. 180 to begin your journey through the Coconino National Forest to Schultz Pass, you are treated to one of the most exhilarating sights in Arizona. Doyle Peak, one of the four San Francisco Peaks, rises in front of you to an elevation of 11,460 feet, well above the crowns of spruce and ponderosa pine trees. In the fall, this route is dappled with the red and gold foliage of maples, oaks, and white-barked aspens.

Schultz Pass is named for Charles Hugo Schultz, a native of Buffalo, New York, who came to Flagstaff in 1880 with a flock of sheep, which eventually grew into one of the largest sheep operations in the state. Schultz retired from the sheep-ranching business and moved to Phoenix in 1911. He died in 1934.

When you've traveled 4.6 miles from the end of the pavement on FR 420, you'll be in the midst of Schultz Pass and will come to a parking area and outhouse at Schultz Tank. Park there and take a walk on the Weatherford Trail, which is across (north) from the parking lot.

In the early part of the 20th century, a Flagstaff hotel owner, John W. Weatherford, stumbled upon an idea that has left its mark on the trail that bears his name. Weatherford concluded that the San Francisco Peaks were so irresistibly beautiful that people would pay to get to the top if a road were built that made it possible. Weatherford was wealthy and enterprising. He'd arrived in Flagstaff in 1886, three years after the railroad, and had started a mercantile store, a livery stable, and built the downtown hotel that still bears his name, among other businesses. But his grandest

The sacred San Francisco Peaks tower beyond the ponderosas and aspens of Kendrick Park.

Downtown Flagstaff bustles at the Hotel Monte Vista.

Edward McCain

dream, according to some accounts, was to build what he called the San Francisco Mountain Boulevard.

Construction of the road started in 1920. Weatherford opened his new toll road in 1926, calling it "The Most Wonderful Scenic Drive in America," a description that's tough to dispute, even today. The trail is the remnant of Weatherford's road.

According to Flagstaff newspaper publisher and historian Platt Cline, Weatherford's scenic road eventually became his albatross. While he received the government permit to construct the road in 1916, natural and man-made problems kept delaying construction. By the late summer of 1924, 7 miles of the 14-mile road had been completed at a cost of $32,000. In Cline's book, *They Came to the Mountain,* he wrote:

"The venture continued to soak up all of his cash and credit. Finally on August 16, 1926, with 10.4 miles of the steep, narrow road completed to Fremont Saddle, he staged a grand opening. The fee admission car count [sic] was 170. He pushed on with construction and by 1928, his best season, he had collected tolls amounting to $5,000 at $2 a car. He struggled on. With the arrival of the Great Depression in the 1930s, the cause became hopeless. His health deteriorated and he died at age 74 in January, 1934."

In 1942 Congress approved $15,500 to purchase all improvements that Weatherford had made on the road, and it was then closed to vehicles. The trail winds around the mountain, climbing steadily for 8.7 miles, and leads to the saddle between Humphreys and Agassiz peaks. During the fall, the trail is one of the best places to hear the elk bugling as they assemble their harems for the breeding season.

A half-mile beyond the Weatherford Trailhead, you'll come to a junction with Forest Service Road 556 to the right. Here you have a choice.

Bear left to continue on FR 420 and State Route 89A in about 6 miles. Or, turn right (east) on to FR556 and continue for about 3 miles to Little Elden Trail, which extends between Schultz Tank and the city of Flagstaff. Continuing east from Little Elden Trail on FR 556 brings you to State 89A in about 2 miles.

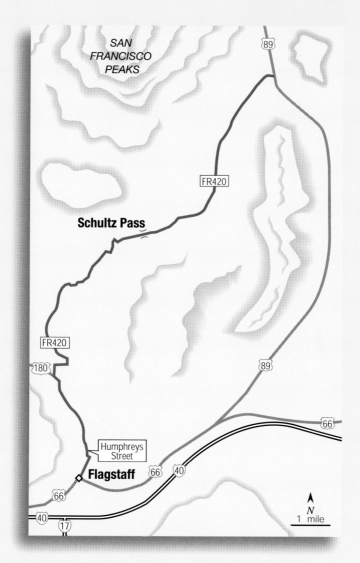

Route Finder

• Begin at the Flagstaff visitors center in the old railroad depot at One E. Route 66, and travel west on Old Route 66 (Santa Fe Avenue) to U.S. Route 180 (Humphreys Street). Turn right (north).

• Continue on U.S. 180 for about 3 miles, passing the Museum of Northern Arizona on the left. In 0.2 of a mile beyond the museum, there's a signed junction with Schultz Pass Road. Turn right.

• In less than a mile Schultz Pass Road is designated Forest Service Road 420 and has a junction with Forest Service Road 557. Bear left to continue on FR 420.

• Continue on FR 420 for about 5 miles to the Weatherford Trail.

• One-half mile beyond the Weatherford Trail, FR 420 has a junction with FR 556. Bear left to continue on FR 420 for a 5-mile drive to State Route 89A. Turn right and return to Flagstaff in about 9 miles.

• Option: Turn right onto FR 556, pass the Little Elden Trail, and continue 2 miles to State 89A. Turn right and return to Flagstaff in about 2 miles.

Additional information: Coconino National Forest, Peaks Ranger District, (928) 526-0866; www. fs.fed. us/r3/coconino/recreation/peaks/rec_peaks.shtml. Flagstaff visitors center, (928) 774-9541 or (800) 842-7293; www.flagstaffarizona.org.

Drive 2

Garland Prairie to Williams: Crossing a Grand Meadow

There are several ways to go west from Flagstaff to the scenic recreation areas south of Williams. One of the most picturesque routes leaves Interstate 40 at Parks and swings south and west through a broad meadow called Garland Prairie. The road crosses and often is parallel to the historic Overland Route, a trail used for centuries by Indians, trappers, and explorers. In the 19th century, the Overland Route connected the Williams area with Chino Valley, near Prescott.

Many people drive this route in an ordinary, low-slung sedan, but it's wiser to have a high-clearance vehicle because, even though the unpaved road is well-maintained, any back road in the forest is subject to change depending on weather conditions. The drive's entire distance is in the southern portion of the Kaibab National Forest. Begin at the interchange of Interstate 40 and Interstate 17 in Flagstaff. Take I-40 west about 18 miles to Exit 178 at Parks (see Route Finder for detailed directions).

When you're about 4 miles south of the interstate, you get your first glimpse of Garland Prairie. About a mile farther, you'll come to a pullout and historical marker on the left, where you can pause for a good view west toward the prairie. The historical sign says:

"In October 1863 a large military expedition paused here, on the edge of Garland Prairie. They had orders to blaze a road from Antelope Springs [Flagstaff] to the newly discovered gold fields along Lynx Creek, and build Fort Whipple near present day Prescott.

"Years after the last gold seeker passed over Garland Prairie, homesteaders began to settle the region. Farmers grew potatoes, hay, oats, and other crops. Life on the high prairies was difficult with harsh winters and little water. Today, the remains of unsuccessful farms dot the landscape, interspersed with homesteads that have endured.

"According to one old timer, 'The only thing those dryland farmers seemed to raise was dogs and kids.'"

Not exactly. They also raised wheat, oats, corn, and turnips, but potatoes were their biggest crop. In 1890, a report noted that over 700 tons of "Bill Williams Potatoes" were shipped from nearby Williams.

A river, a town, and a mountain bear the name of Bill Williams, an eccentric fur trapper and guide who is presumed to have spent some time in the area in the middle of the 19th century. Williams was famous for being a loner much of the time and not telling anyone where he'd been or where he was headed. He didn't keep records. He was known as a reliable guide and trapper, a great marksman, and an incurable drunk. He also argued with his horse. The mountain about 15 miles (as a bird flies) west of Garland Prairie is named for Bill Williams.

Continuing the drive, you come to first Scholz Lake and then White Horse Lake, at an elevation of about 6,000 feet.

In the Kaibab National Forest, clouds loom over the meadow near Dogtown reservoir south of Williams.

Scholz Lake, just a few miles off Garland Prairie Road/FR 141, is an excellent location for wildlife viewing. The area is home to ducks, cormorants, herons, egrets, kestrels, osprey, and passerines. The Kaibab National Forest's Web site has excellent information about viewing wildlife, including elk, mule deer and whitetail deer, antelope, wild turkey, Abert's squirrel and other species (see Route Finder).

White Horse is definitely worth a visit. Just before reaching the lake watch for a parking area and trailhead on the left. This is Sycamore Rim Trail No. 345, which forms an 11-mile loop. But you don't need to hike the entire length—you can hike through the woods to Sycamore Canyon within 2 miles. There's also a chemical toilet at the trailhead.

The White Horse Campground is a fee area. It'll cost you nightly, but you'll find drinking water, boat rentals, rest rooms, and even a dump station for your RV if you're driving one. One area is for tent camping only. The lake primarily has rainbow and brown trout.

Leaving White Horse Lake and backtracking, you'll quickly find yourself driving through a dense stand of quaking aspens, a wonderful blaze of gold and red in the fall. A couple of miles beyond the aspen grove, the road spills out of the forest of ponderosa pines into McDougal Flat, another meadow, filled with an array of wildflowers during the summer months.

Two miles beyond the meadow, there's a turnoff for Dogtown Reservoir, a small lake that holds part of the domestic water supply for the town of Williams. Leaving Dogtown, you're only 4 miles from pavement that will take you into Williams. Or you can skip Dogtown and be in Williams in about the same distance by way of Bootlegger Crossing over the Santa Fe Railroad.

Be sure to visit the restored Santa Fe Railroad depot that serves as the Williams visitor center and ranger station for the Kaibab National Forest. One room is also a small museum where you'll find a good display of artifacts and historical photographs of the Williams area.

Tom Bean

May clouds soften the sky over Scholz Lake in the Garland Prairie area with the San Francisco Peaks in the background.

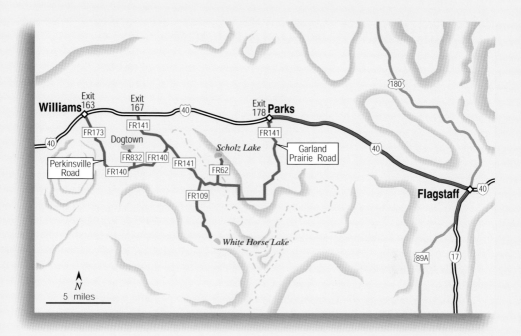

Route Finder

• Begin in Flagstaff at the interchange of Interstate 17 and Interstate 40 and drive west on I-40 for 17 miles to Exit 178 at Parks. Turn left (south) onto Garland Prairie Road, also designated Forest Service Road 141.

• In 7.5 miles, there's a junction where Garland Prairie Road/FR141 abruptly turns 90 degrees to the right (west). Turn right to stay on Garland Prairie Road/FR 141.

• In the next 3.1 miles, the road makes 2 more 90-degree turns first to the right (north) then to the left (west).

• At 1.3 miles beyond the last 90-degree turn, there's a junction with Forest Service Road 62. Turn right (north) for a 2-mile drive into the Scholz Lake area.

• Leaving Scholz Lake, backtrack to Garland Prairie Road/FR 141. Turn right.

• Drive 1.7 miles to Forest Service Road 109. Turn left (south) for Whitehorse Lake.

• Continue on FR 109 for 5.3 miles to White Horse Lake.

• Leaving Whitehorse Lake, backtrack north on FR109 and return to FR 141. Turn left (west).

• Continue on FR 141 through McDougal Flat for 3.3 miles to a Y-junction with FR 140. Bear left (south) for Dogtown Reservoir or continue straight for a short ride into Williams.

• Continue south on FR 140 for 3.7 miles to FR 832. Turn right for a 1-mile drive to Dogtown.

• Leaving Dogtown, backtrack to FR140. Turn right.

• Continue on 140 for 2.8 miles to FR 73, the Perkinsville Road. Turn right for a 4,5-mile drive to the Williams visitors center.

Additional Information: Kaibab National Forest, Williams Ranger Station, 928-635-5600; www.fs.fed. us/r3/kai/contact/williams.pdf. Wildlife viewing guide, www.fs.fed.us/r3/kai/recreation/wildlife. Williams visitors center, 928-635-4707 or (800) 863--546; www.fs.fed.us/r3/kai/visit.

Drive 3

The Bill Williams Mountain Loop

Here we are in Williams, a place that exudes the feel of an era of black and white movies and Formica kitchen tops, of a time when motels were called "travel courts" and Jack Webb was calling women "ma'am." Williams, some 30 miles west of Flagstaff, started life as a cattle ranch and grew into a staging camp for railroad construction crews. But, for anyone younger than 94, Williams is usually remembered as a small and inviting town along old Route 66 where a tourist could catch a train for the short trip north to the Grand Canyon. That's one of the things you can still do here.

U.S. Route 66 sometimes is called "The Main Street of America." Together with roads to which it was linked, it formed a coast-to-coast highway, and there are people around who still remember driving it with their parents in a Model T. Many of the towns that thrived on tourist trade along Route 66 shriveled and disappeared when the interstate highway bypassed them, but Williams was one of the survivors, and today it has turned nostalgia into a cottage industry.

The town is named for Bill Williams, and Bill Williams Mountain forms a large green cushion southwest of town. Bill Williams' name figures prominently in the lore of the area, although that is mainly the result of an error made in the 1800s by a well-intentioned trapper and guide named Antoine Leroux. Leroux was guiding a military survey expedition and when it got to the vicinity of the as-yet-unnamed mountain he noted that his old friend Bill Williams used to trap in that area, and so the mountain was named. But, it turns out Leroux's memory had been faulty, and the area he was thinking of was a long way from the mountain that came to be named Bill Williams.

It doesn't much matter, of course. The people of Williams liked Bill Williams and the aura of the buckskin-clad mountain man, and two organizations eventually were formed to keep that lore alive. They're the Bill Williams Mountain Men and the Buckskinners. If you're in town over the Fourth of July, you'll be surrounded by the Buckskinners' Rendezvous. The whole town looks like something out of 1840, with mountain men in leathers and black-powder gun enthusiasts on every corner.

But, if you don't want to stay in town, there's an easy half-day drive you can make that heads south of Williams and wraps around the base of Bill Williams Mountain and returns you to Interstate 40 about 5 miles west of town. If you have a mountain bike, bring it along. There's a good mountain bike trail along the way.

Start (see Route Finder for detailed directions) at the Williams-Kaibab National Forest visitors center, which is in the renovated Santa Fe train depot in the heart of town, reached from I-40 via Exit 165. There's a little museum there, as well as an information desk for the Kaibab National Forest.

Within 7 miles you be driving on the Bill Williams Loop Road, a relatively smooth, cinder-surfaced route through wonderful ponderosa pine forests in the elevation range of 7,000 feet. You'll see signs along the way with for Dutch Kid Tank (for watering cattle) and, perhaps, Dutch

A mountain biker skims
through a mountain meadow
outside of Flagstaff.

An old-fashioned locomotive leaves the Williams depot
for the Grand Canyon National Park.

Edward McCain

Kid Knoll. If you're wondering who the "Dutch Kid" was, join the club. Forest Service historians
have been unable to trace the origins of most of the place names in this area.

You can drive or ride a bike to an old stage station site. You'll not find much remaining of
the station. Campers carted off and burned most of the wood used to build it. Still, the spot,
about halfway along the loop, is evocative, because it was along the stage route that connected
the Territorial capitol at Prescott with outposts such as Simms and Williams. Simms, west of
Williams, was the original construction camp for the railroad, but everything was eventually
moved to Williams. Williams grew and prospered, and Simms disappeared.

There was not much in this area in the 1870s and '80s, aside from a scattering of sheep
and cattle ranches, and stagecoach travel could be hazardous. The *Prescott Courier* reported
in 1882 that the mountains south of Williams were prime habitat for "professional robbers
and murderers." The paper later deplored the absence of law and order along the railroad
line that ran from Flagstaff through Williams. It described Williams as "the hell hole of the
Territory," a description which at one time or another was applied to several other places in
early Arizona.

Times change. Today there's a ski run on Bill Williams Mountain and wonderful places in
the area to hike and camp.

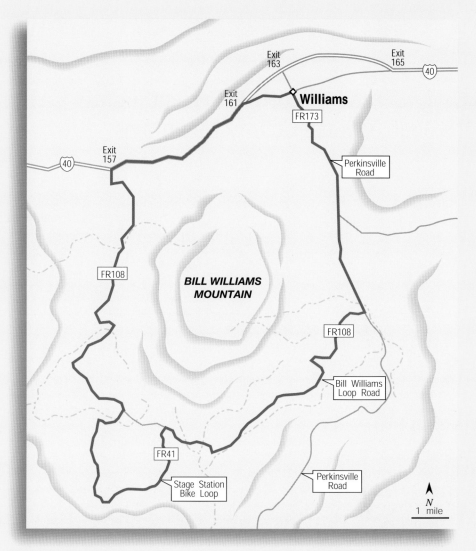

Route Finder

• Begin at the Williams visitors center, 200 W. Railroad Ave. Drive west a few blocks on the one-way avenue to Fourth Street. Turn left (south).

• Fourth Street becomes the Perkinsville Road (also Forest Service Road 173) as it heads south out of the Williams residential area.

• From the junction of Fourth Street and Railroad Avenue, it's 6.6 miles to Forest Service Road 108, the Bill Williams Mountain Loop Road. Turn right (west) onto FR 108.

• Continue on FR 108 westward and southwestward for 8.4 miles to Forest Service Road 41, also called the Stage Station Bike Loop. Turn left (south).

• Continue on FR 41 for 6.8 miles for a loop drive returning to FR108 northwest of the point where you turned onto 41. (You can ride your bike on the portion of the trail.) Turn left (northwest).

• Continue northward on 108 for 9.2 miles to Interstate 40. Turn right for a 5-mile return to Williams.

Additional information: Williams visitors center, (928) 635-1418; www.fs.fed.us/r3/kai/visit/visit. html. Kaibab National Forest, Williams Ranger District, (928) 635-5600.

Named to honor traditional Hopi beliefs, the Kachina Peaks Wilderness in October blazes with turning aspens. Tom Danielsen

Drive 4

Seligman to Prescott: A 'Perfect' Route Through Yavapai County Mountains

For as long as Arizona has been inhabited, people have been trying to find a way through the omnipresent mountains. It doesn't matter whether you're in the rolling deserts in the south or the high plateau country of the north, if you're moving from one place to another in Arizona, sooner or later a jagged mountain with deep canyons and too many creeks or arroyos will block you from your destination.

Because I've spent more than 20 years being lost, found, stranded, and generally perplexed in many of these ranges, it always surprises me to find that one of our ancestors who didn't have an airplane or sophisticated reconnaissance equipment managed to discover what appears—even today—to be the perfect route through a particular block of mountains.

That was, more or less, the deepest thought I could conjure while driving a back road that connects the old railroad town of Seligman with Arizona's Territorial capital of Prescott. I kept thinking: This road will eventually do what every other unpaved back road has done to me. It's going to be smooth and gentle just long enough for me to get overly confident, and as soon as I give it the gas and move faster, it's going to turn into the road from Hades with potholes and ruts and little peaks of frozen mud.

Happily, I can tell you that never happened. The scenic Yavapai County road between Seligman and Prescott, though mostly unpaved, can be comfortably driven in any ordinary sedan. It's a road characterized by large graceful curves and some gentle hills meandering through a portion of the Prescott National Forest, where cattle and horses graze across grasslands sprinkled with juniper, oak, and cottonwood trees.

I started this trip in Flagstaff at the Interstate 17-40 interchange and drove 74 miles west on Interstate 40 to Exit 123, which serves Seligman. Before starting this leg of the drive to Prescott, you can turn right at the end of the exit ramp and drive a few miles into the small town of Seligman, where food and lodging are available. Or, if you're ready to go, turn left and go under the interstate and follow the signs for Walnut Creek and Prescott.

After going under the interstate, turn right at the frontage road (alongside a gas station). The frontage road swings south and becomes County Road 5, an unpaved track that leads to Walnut Creek and the old frontier town of Prescott. As it nears Prescott, the road takes on the name of Williamson Valley Road. The entire route, including a little side trip to the ranger station at Walnut Creek, covers 72 miles one-way, and 50 of those miles are unpaved. But most of the unpaved portion is so well-maintained that it's almost as good as the paved road.

After passing the gas station, continue south 10 miles to where the road comes to a fork. Take the right fork and continue through the junipers and rolling hills. Four miles beyond the fork you'll come to a junction with a ranch road. Bear left and you'll see a sign informing you that you've entered the Prescott National Forest.

The drive ends in Prescott,
and a visit to the Sharlot
Hall Museum includes the
colorful Bashford House.

In another 18 miles you'll come to a junction with County Road 125. A sign says that Prescott is 38 miles straight ahead and Walnut Creek Ranger Station is 2 miles to the right on County 125.

If the ranger at Walnut Creek is available, he can point the way to the site of Camp Hualpai, a onetime cavalry post. Established in 1869 as Camp Devin, then Camp Tollgate, it was finally renamed Camp Hualpai in 1870. The post was located on a mesa above Walnut Creek along the so-called Hardyville Toll Road, one of Arizona's early stagecoach routes that connected Hardyville on the Colorado River (where Bullhead City is today) with Prescott and Fort Whipple. Camp Hualpai was abandoned August 27, 1873.

The Hardyville Toll Road apparently continued to be a major transportation route until railroad lines were completed in 1881. After that most of the freight and passengers were carried on the much faster and more comfortable trains. While they lasted, though, toll roads were a good thing for their owners.

Arizona historian Jay J. Wagoner wrote that the first

Hiking outside of Prescott is a pleasant way to end a drive. Here the Granite Mountain Wilderness extends beyond.

Edward McCain

Territorial legislature granted liberal franchises to six toll road companies. These companies charged very high rates, but some of them also incurred very high costs in building and maintaining the finicky routes through very rough terrain. Wagoner dug out the following information about the cost of traveling one of these toll roads in the 1860s:

"The toll rates established by the legislature ranged from one-eighth cent per mile for each sheep, goat, or pig to four cents per mile for each wagon drawn by two horses, mules, or oxen. There was an extra charge of one and a half cents per mile for each additional span of animals. For each rider on horseback, two and one half cents per mile was assessed."

The route between Walnut Creek and County 5 more or less parallels the old toll road. When you get back to 5, the road swings east and south over a trestle bridge. Fourteen miles later, the pavement resumes, and small settlements begin to appear and Prescott is not far away.

A visit to the Sharlot Hall Museum in Prescott will round out the historical picture of the cattle-and-gold-mining region you just drove through.

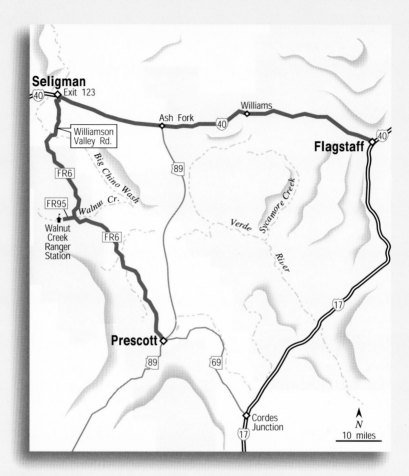

Route Finder

• From Flagstaff head west on Interstate 40 for 74 miles until reaching Exit 123. At the end of the exit ramp, turn right for Seligman, or turn left for the drive to Prescott, following the signs for Walnut Creek and Prescott.

• Pass under the interstate. Turn right onto the frontage road alongside a gas station.

• The frontage road swings south, becoming County Road 5.

• Continue south on County 5 for 10 miles to a fork. Veer right to remain on County 5.

• Continue for 4 miles to a junction with a ranch road. Bear left, entering the Prescott National Forest.

• Continue on County 5 for 18 miles to a sign saying Prescott is 38 miles away straight and Walnut Creek Ranger Station is 2 miles to the right on County Road 125.

• Leaving Walnut Creek Station, backtrack to County 5. Turn right and continue toward Prescott.

• Continue on 5 for 36.4 miles to Iron Springs Road. Turn left.

• Continue for 1.4 miles to a Y-junction with Miller Valley and Willow Creek roads. Bear right onto Miller Valley Road.

• Continue for 0.9 of a mile on Miller Valley Road to where it bears right and blends into Grove Avenue.

• Continue south on Grove for 0.3 of a mile to a T-junction with West Curley Street. Turn left on West Gurley and go about 2 blocks to the Sharlot Hall Museum.

Additional information: Seligman travel information, (928) 422-3939; www.historic66.com/arizona/det-az3.html. Sharlot Hall Museum, (928) 445-3122; www.sharlot.org. Prescott National Forest, Bradshaw Ranger District, (928) 443-8000; www.fs.fed.us/r3/prescott.

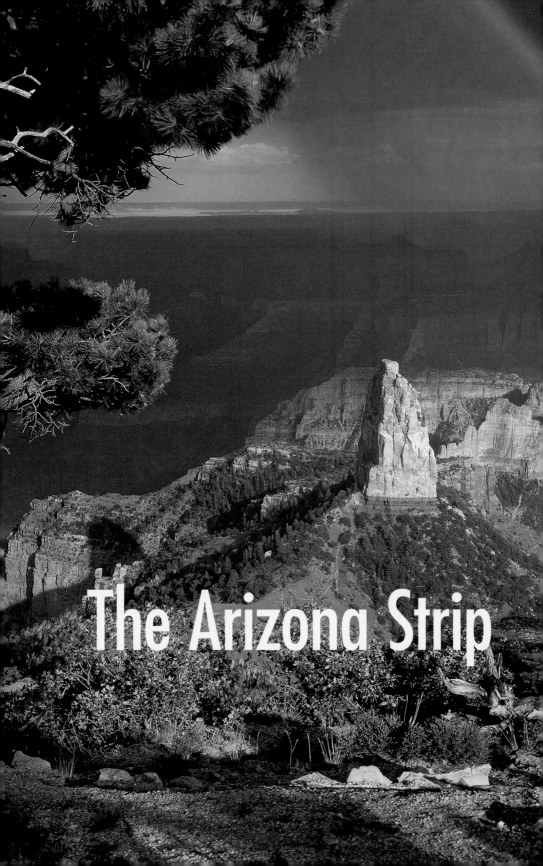

The Arizona Strip

Kate Thompson

Seen from Point Imperial's overlook, far left, on the North Rim of the Grand Canyon, a rainbow stretches over Mount Hayden. A river boat floats in the mist, left, drifting over the Colorado River at Lee's Ferry, before the river enters the Grand Canyon.

A Remote, Startling Region

• Overview

The Arizona Strip stretches in an enormous rectangle west of U.S. Route 89, north of the Grand Canyon, and south of the Utah border. Remote and startling, the terrain is part forest and part barren and desolate, a graveyard for giant rocks and sharp red cliffs that lie in the distance. This is the world between the Colorado and the Virgin rivers, two grinding streams that helped sculpt the lonely plateaus of northwestern Arizona. It remains primitive and largely unpopulated. The drives in this chapter provide excellent access to the North Rim of Grand Canyon. The landscape varies considerably, ranging from the Kaibab Plateau's cool, green forests at elevations between 8,000 and 9,000 feet to arid plains in the valleys east and west of the plateau.

• The Drives

Jacob Lake to North Rim Viewpoints Page 234

Fredonia to Little Black Mountain Petroglyph Site Page 238

Pipe Spring to Toroweap Point Page 242

• Towns and Sites

Colorado City, Fredonia, Jacob Lake, Kanab (Utah), Lee's Ferry, Marble Canyon, Navajo Bridge, North Rim of the Grand Canyon, Pipe Spring National Monument, and St. George (Utah).

Paul Gill

One of the region's ubiquitous jackrabbits pauses to catch a little sun. G.C. Kelley

If you're going to travel the routes described in this chapter, keep in mind that there are no accurate maps of the Arizona Strip. You will find roads on the ground that do not appear on any map, and you will find named roads on the maps that do not appear on the ground. Bring along a Global Positioning System receiver, or at least a compass. Driving in the Arizona Strip can be lonely, confusing, and dangerous. Always carry plenty of water—springs, stores, gas stations, and humans are few and far between. Be certain your tires—including the spare—are in good shape. Rock punctures are common.

If you haven't been scared off by these warnings (and if you take them seriously into your plans), you will be rewarded by views of some of the most astonishing terrain to be found anywhere in the world. Two of these routes will take you to the rim of the Grand Canyon, where you get to see the whole panorama without guardrails or crowds or souvenir shops. If you encounter more than four people at any of these sites, you've arrived on a busy day.

The Colorado River defines the area, which encompasses nearly all of northwestern Arizona. The river flows into Arizona from the north. At the Utah-Arizona border near Page, it bends south and west until it reaches Marble Canyon, 128 miles north of Flagstaff. At that point it bends away from the sandstone walls of the Vermilion Cliffs and takes a sharp turn to the west. For the next 220 miles, the Colorado River, second-longest river in the United States, careens through its most famous feature, the mile-deep abyss called the Grand Canyon.

Once the river turns west, it isolates an 11,000-square-mile rectangle of arid plateaus. This stunning terrain somehow ended up with the boring designation, "the Arizona Strip." Arizona Paradise would make more sense. The Kaibab Plateau is covered with dense forests of pines and aspens (made possible by annual snow and rainfall, which will vary significantly from the northern and southern ends of these cliffs) and wide, green meadows. In early October, the straight white limbs of the aspens on these forested plateaus are crowned with the bright gold of their changing leaves. It won't be long before the first snow falls.

Someone once called this terrain a landscape of splendid isolation, and that certainly seems to fit, especially in the broad, barren plains that separate the plateaus. Cut off from the rest of the state by the Grand Canyon, only four small communities reside in the Arizona Strip—Fredonia, Colorado City, Cane Beds, and Moccasin—and a combined population of about 5,000. That's 5,000 people spread out in an area that covers about 5 million acres. Clearly, in this country, everyone has elbow room.

Because the Strip lies so far from any major population center, hardly anyone goes there unless they're headed for the North Rim of Grand Canyon or to Bryce and Zion national parks in southern Utah.

Touched by the rising sun, the Colorado River runs ribbonlike below the Grand Canyon's North Rim and Toroweap Overlook.

The Grand Canyon stretches from Cape Royal on the North Rim, edged with blooming buckwheat, to the South Rim on the horizon.

Gary Ladd

In a landscape where paradox can be found in almost every direction, the Grand Canyon of the Colorado, an almost ungraspable testament to the power of water in a place where water rarely is found, is the greatest paradox of all. And yet, scarce as it is, water formed the Canyon's sedimentary rocks under ancient seas. and water carved its buttes and mesas into temples and towers and domes and cathedral-like caves.

The Arizona Strip began to take the shape it has today some 30 million years ago when a massive block of the Earth's crust was uplifted and tilted to the northeast. Over time, volcanic eruptions and erosion divided this huge slab into a series of elongated and nearly isolated north-south trending plateaus — including the Shivwits Plateau (the western-most plateau), the Uinkaret Plateau, the Kaibab Plateau, and the Marble Platform. The cliffs along these plateaus range from 200 feet to more than 400 feet in height.

Remote, fractured, densely wooded, and mostly dry, the Arizona Strip has never been an easy country to explore. Some idea of its remoteness can be seen in the remarkable fact that the Grand Canyon's more accessible South Rim was first seen by Spanish explorers when they were led there by Hopi guides in 1540, but it was 260 years later before other Spaniards wandered near the North Rim and crossed a portion of the Arizona Strip. The friars Francisco A. Dominguez and Silvestre Veliz Escalante led Spanish explorers into the Strip in an attempt to find an inland route that would link Santa Fe, New Mexico, to the new Spanish colonies in the vicinity of what is now San Francisco, but hostile Indians and rough terrain forced them northward through western Colorado and central Utah, and they eventually turned back.

Although the Spaniards never found the route they were seeking, they gathered much information on the Arizona Strip. They were the first non-Indians to explore it, the first to describe its topography in written reports, and the first to map it.

Mormon missionaries did the next major exploration of northwestern Arizona, beginning in 1858. Guided by a Paiute Indian, they left southwestern Utah and journeyed southeastward across the Strip, hoping to encounter and convert the Hopis in the pueblos on Second Mesa. They also were looking for new lands to settle. Later, the route followed by these first Mormons developed into the Honeymoon Trail, so-called because Mormon couples would get married at the temple in St. George, in southwestern Utah, and follow a wagon route south and eastward through the Arizona Strip to Lee's Ferry, and eventually into the White Mountains and the Gila and Salt River valleys of central Arizona, where their descendants still live. Until a temple

Near the Utah–Arizona state line, Wahweap Bay overlooks Lake Powell.

was built in Arizona, Mormons also followed the route back to St. George to get married.

One of those pioneers, Jacob Hamblin, was very helpful to John Wesley Powell, the one-armed Civil War veteran who was the first person to navigate the Colorado River through the Grand Canyon. Powell, whose intelligence, stamina, and courage made him a legend in his own time, led two expeditions through the Grand Canyon in 1869 and 1871 and visited the Arizona Strip, with Hamblin's assistance, to learn the fate of two of the men who had abandoned the first expedition at Separation Canyon (both were believed to have been killed by Indians).

The Weather

Summer: At 8,000 feet of elevation, the Grand Canyon's North Rim generally ranges in temperature (Fahrenheit) from the 40s to the high 70s. Afternoon thunderstorms often occur during July, August, and early September. In other, lower, areas of the Arizona Strip the high temperature reaches the 90s or higher.

Spring and Fall: Unpredictable. Be prepared for sudden changes. May and October can be some of the driest months, although snowstorms may occur. The road from Jacob Lake to the North Rim (State Route 67) opens in mid-May and closes in late fall, depending on snowfall. The temperature at night can dip to below freezing.

Winter: Heavy snowfall is the norm along and near the North Rim. State 67 is closed from the first heavy snow in November or early December to mid-May.

On his second expedition through the Canyon, Powell brought along a young geologist named Clarence Dutton (who would later name Point Sublime on the North Rim). In the summer of 1880, Powell, then head of the agency that would later be called the U.S. Geological Survey, sent Dutton and the immensely talented artist/geologist William Henry Holmes back to the plateau country along the North Rim. The result of that trip was a report, *Tertiary History of the Grand Cañon District,* written by Dutton and illustrated by Holmes and another famous artist, Thomas Moran, and published by the Government Printing Office in 1882. (It has since been reprinted, including a printing by the University of Arizona Press.) Not only was the book lavishly illustrated, it was beautifully written. Dutton, who had been a divinity student at Yale before he became a geologist, sprinkled his dry, scientific prose with lyrical description of the Arizona Strip's landscape. The Kaibab Plateau, he wrote, "is a constant succession of parks and glades—dreamy avenues of grass and flowers winding between sylvan walls, or spreading out in broad open meadows..."

Certainly there have been changes in that lonely terrain since those days, but the area remains remarkably primitive. There extend an estimated 6,000 miles of dirt roads in the Arizona Strip, but hardly any people drive them. Roughly 1,200 live in tiny Fredonia, 30 miles northwest of Jacob Lake, and there are park rangers at Pipe Spring National Monument, and a small

Two rocking chairs look ready to rock soothingly in the
Winsor Castle parlor at Pipe Spring National Monument.

George H.H. Huey

community at Moccasin, 14 miles west of Fredonia on State Route 389. The
Kaibab Paiute Indian Reservation has about 250 residents. At Colorado City,
whose approximately 3,500 residents make it the largest community in the
Strip, there is a religious community of polygamous families.

The Mormon heritage remains evident in the Strip. Jacob Lake was named
for the Mormon pioneer Jacob Hamblin; Pipe Spring was, indirectly, named for
his brother, William. Bill Hamblin was a marksman with a rifle. Once, when he
and some friends were camped at the spring, the men bet Bill he couldn't shoot
the bottom out of Dudley Leavitt's pipe from 50 paces. Bill won that bet, and
the place became Pipe Spring.

In a part of the state that is filled with exhilarating vistas, one of the most
engaging sits off by itself some 40 miles (as the raven flies) west of Colorado
City. It is called Little Black Mountain Petroglyph Site (see Drive 2 in this
chapter). Long before any Europeans set foot in North America, the ancestors
of the Ancestral Puebloan people left their mark at this lonely mesa less than a
mile south of the Utah-Arizona border.

This isolated and sometimes perilous land in northwestern Arizona
remains a startling world. Ultimately, the changing light, in a place
dominated by the sky, exaggerates the scale of everything visible. Human
beings, as the petroglyph site indicates, have been here for many centuries,
but in this landscape, it's easy to think they always have been a minor piece
of the puzzle. ⋀⋀

A mule train, left, edges along the North Kaibab Trail in Roaring Springs Canyon of the Grand Canyon National Park. Edward McCain

Drive 1

Jacob Lake to Three North Rim Viewpoints

The trip from Jacob Lake to Timp Point, North Timp Point, and Parissawampitts Point is relatively short but unforgettable. From the community of Jacob Lake, at an elevation of about 7,920 feet, the route meanders south and then west on the Kaibab Plateau between forests of ponderosa pines, aspens, and spruce separated by broad, park-like meadows. Most of the drive passes through terrain reminiscent of Alberta or British Columbia, Canada (minus the lakes and swarming mosquitoes). This drive, however, has a payoff you will find only in this area: You'll be standing on promontories—likely, by yourself—with nothing but the clear, glistening air between you and the Grand Canyon.

After filling your senses with Grand Canyon views, picnicking, and hiking or mountain bike riding, you can return to Jacob Lake on the final leg of an all-day loop, or you can veer northward to Fredonia, the staging point for the next drive in this chapter. A family sedan will do nicely on this trip, unless rain or melted snow has soaked the ground. Before or after the snow season—mid-May to mid-October—is an ideal period for this trip. In October you'll share the back roads with hunters.

Begin this excursion at the North Kaibab visitors center at Jacob Lake, which is 165 miles northwest of Flagstaff (see Route Finder for detailed directions). The so-called lake at Jacob Lake is really a tiny sinkhole buried behind the trees near an RV park. The lake, as one forest ranger put it, "used to be a four-duck pond, but now it's down to two."

At the visitors center, you can obtain free maps and directions to various lookout points. If you don't see the maps on display, ask for them. You can also buy the North Kaibab Ranger District map. Also, if you intend to take advantage of the forest's dispersed camping, ask the rangers for the dispersed camping guidelines.

There's a forest campground (with water and rest rooms) across the road from the visitors center, and a picnic area, also with facilities, directly south of the visitor center on State Route 67.

Jacob Lake Lodge and Restaurant, as well as a gas station with a mechanic, are located at the junction of U.S. Route 89A and State Route 67, just north of the visitors center. Another gas station and convenience store are located about 26 miles south on State 67, the route you'll take on the first leg.

State 67 is an excellent paved highway that connects Jacob Lake with the North Rim of Grand Canyon National Park, and although you head in that direction when leaving Jacob Lake, the trip to the North Rim viewpoints does not require entrance to the national park. In other words, there are no fees to pay.

As 67 heads south from Jacob Lake, watch for the impressive fire lookout tower clearly visible on the left (or east) side of the road. The Kaibab is so heavily forested with tall trees, that the fire lookouts have been built between 100 and 120 feet high to see over them. Also, take advantage of the pullouts along the road with legends telling about the area.

Timp Point and Fire Point,
left, and Steamboat Mountain,
right, frame Grand Canyon
views of Powell Plateau
and Granite Gorge.

Slanting afternoon sunlight sharply defines jagged
rocky outcroppings on the southern face of Locust Point
across Timp Canyon from North Timp Point.

Morey K. Milbradt

Driving south on 67, the first turn-off comes right after you pass DeMotte Campground. A sign right after you make the turn lists the distance to Vista Points (22 miles) and Fredonia (50 miles).

The first viewpoint, Timp Point, puts you face to face with Steamboat Mountain rising from the Canyon floor. Timp also is at the southern end of the Rainbow Rim Trail, which leads to North Timp, Locust, Fence, and Parissawampitts points. A map and other information about the trail is posted at end of the points. The 18-mile trail passes through old-growth ponderosa pine and drops into a number of steep-sided canyons filled with groves of aspens and small meadows.

North Timp Point looks straight out at the majestic dome in Tapeats Amphitheater, a major Canyon formation. The point also lends a view (with binoculars) of Thunder River, a large spring that gushes from an opening in the north wall of Tapeats Canyon.

At Parissawampitts, your view will include Tapeats Amphitheater, Fishtail Mesa, and Great Thumb Mesa.

Leaving Parissawampitts, return to Forest Service Road 22 (the West Side Road) and head north toward Jacob Lake or Fredonia.

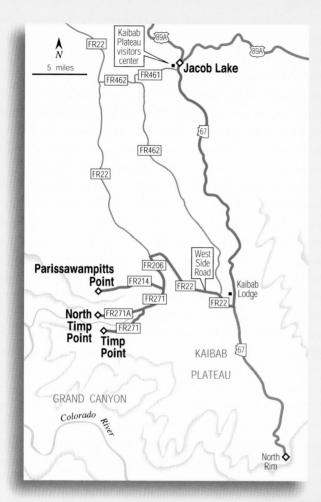

Kaibab Plateau visitors center

Jacob Lake

Parissawampitts Point

North Timp Point

Timp Point

West Side Road

Kaibab Lodge

KAIBAB PLATEAU

GRAND CANYON

Colorado River

North Rim

N

5 miles

• *Continue south 3.5 miles on FR 206 to junction with Forest Service Road 214, which in less than 8 miles leads to Parissawampitts Point. Continue south on FR 206.*

• *In 1.4 miles beyond FR 214, FR 206 veers left (eastward) sharply at a junction. Bear right at this junction and in less than 0.1 of a mile bear left at a fork, leaving you on Forest Service Road 271. (Note: Besides FR 206 and 217, FR 293 and 294 converge within 0.1 of a mile at this point. FR 293 and FR 294 lead to Fence and Locust points, respectively.)*

• *Continue westward on FR 271 for 5.3 miles to junction with FR 271A. Bear left for Timp Point in less than 3 miles.*

• *Leaving Timp Point, backtrack on FR 271 to FR 271A. Bear left onto 271A for North Timp Point in less than 3 miles.*

• *Leaving North Timp Point, backtrack on 271A to FR 271. Bear left onto 271 for return to FR 206. Turn left (north).*

• *Continue north on 206 for 1.4 miles to junction with FR 214. Turn left (west) for 7.7-mile drive to Parissawampitts Point.*

• *Leaving Parissawampitts Point, backtrack on FR 214 to FR 206. Turn left (north).*

• *Continue north on 206 for 3.5 miles to FR 22.*

• *Option: Turn right onto FR 22 to return to Jacob Lake the way you came; or bear left (also onto FR 22) to continue northward toward Fredonia.*

• *If continuing to Fredonia, drive northward on FR 22 for 18.9 miles to junction with FR 462.*

• *Option: Turn right for a return to Jacob Lake; or continue straight onto the paved road for Fredonia.*

• *If returning to Jacob Lake, turn right onto FR 462. At 3.4 miles, bear left at junction with FR 461. Continue on 461 for 5.1 miles to State 67. Turn left for brief drive to visitors center.*

• *If going to Fredonia, continue on the paved road for 21.5 miles to U.S. 89A. Turn left for brief drive into Fredonia.*

Additional information: Kaibab Plateau visitors center, (928) 643-7298; www.fs.fed.us/r3/kai/visit/visit.html. Kaibab National Forest, North Kaibab

Route Finder

• *Begin in Jacob Lake at the Kaibab Plateau visitors center on State Route 67, just south of its junction with U.S. Route 89A.*

• *At 25.4 miles south of the visitors center, continue past turnoff on right for Kaibab Lodge.*

• *Continue south on State 67 for 2.1 miles to Forest Service Road 22 (some maps identify the road as Forest Service Road 422 and the West Side Road). Turn right (west) and note the information/direction signs on the right.*

• *Continue west on FR 22 for 2 miles to junction marked by a directional sign for Fredonia and North Rim view points. Continue straight to remain on FR 22.*

• *Continue 8.5 miles on FR 22 to Y-junction with Forest Service Road 206. Turn left (south).*

Drive 2

Fredonia to Little Black Mountain Petroglyph Site

Where did they come from? Where did they go? Why did they come to this broken hill on the Arizona Strip? My thoughts were swimming in a place without water, 500 miles, it seemed, from the nearest answer.

Little Black Mountain Petroglyph Site barely lies within Arizona, although it feels like it's barely in the world. The "black mountain" looks more like a red sandstone mesa. The 500-foot-high mesa rises 14 miles southeast of St. George, Utah, a mere 0.3 of a mile south of Utah's border with Arizona. The human population went away centuries ago and left only its enigmatic symbols and drawings scraped in the enduring rocks.

At this particular spot, they left some 500 pictures of bighorn sheep, snakes. spirals, stick figures, bear paws, lizards, turtles, and strange designs that could mean anything. The only thing anyone can say with any certainty about these pictures is that Indians from different cultural groups made them over a period of approximately 5,000 years.

The federal Bureau of Land Management's plaque at the site says, in part:

"The Little Black Mountain Petroglyph Site is probably a religious ceremonial and calendar watching location. The majority of the glyphs [figures] have a religious or seasonal meaning. The

Steve Bruno

Animal figures intermingle with sunlike glyphs on this
rock wall at the Little Black Mountain site.

Little Black Mountain rises from the Arizona Strip's high desert floor, barely south of the Utah state line.

The immense solitude of the Arizona Strip heightens the mystery
of the petroglyphs at remote Little Black Mountain.

Steve Bruno

relative isolation of the site lends itself to the performance of secret ritual acts/vision quests and many of the glyphs—snakes, handprints, and sheep—are indications of sacred locations. Seasonal or calendar indicators depend on the interplay between light and shadows and are deliberately placed to indicate changes between seasons. The glyphs indicating calendar watching include spirals, circles, bisected circles, plants, baskets, and constellations."

The site's more than 500 individual rock art designs decorate cliffs and boulders at the base of a 500-foot mesa. They are associated with the cultures of the Great Basin, Western Anasazi (or Ancestral Puebloan), and Lower Colorado River, a suggestion of the many cultures that have been this way. Some of the representations of turtles, lizards, and bear paws may be symbols with social or religious meanings now lost in time.

Getting to this site takes a long time on a network of secondary roads and one dirt road, but all are in good shape. The major roads in this network—one flows into the other—are U.S. Route 89A and State Route 389 in Arizona, and State Route 59 and Interstate 15 in Utah (see Route Finder for detailed directions).

Starting in Fredonia, you'll cross into Utah and return to Arizona just a few miles from the site. As you draw nearer to the site, you'll be atop a hill from which you can look south into the most isolated portions of the Arizona Strip and for miles see nothing but folds of mountain ranges and haze-blue mesas.

There are no facilities at the site other than a picnic table, a gravel trail, and brochures in a metal box. The area includes a portion of the BLM's Dutchman Trail for bicycles. The riding is over relatively flat, or gently sloping, roads.

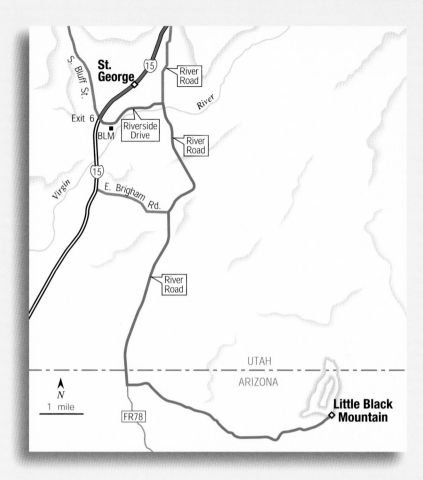

Route Finder

• Starting in Fredonia for an 80-mile drive to St. George, Utah, go west on State Route 389 for 15 miles to Pipe Spring National Monument.

• Leaving Pipe Spring, continue west on State 389 for 19 miles to the Utah border at Hilldale.

• Crossing the border, the road becomes Utah Route 59.

• Continue on Utah 59 to Hurricane. Turn left (west) onto Utah Route 9.

• Continue on Utah Route 9 for 9 miles to Interstate 15. Turn left (south) for 12-mile drive to St. George.

• Continue on I-15 in St. George to Exit 6, Riverside Drive. Turn left (east).

• 0.4 of a mile from I-15, Bureau of Land Management (BLM) office is on right on Riverside Drive.

• 1.2 miles beyond BLM office, Riverside Drive has junction with River Road. Turn right (south).

• Continue south on River Road (also labeled BLM 1069), crossing the Virgin River, for 4.2 miles to Arizona border. Pavement ends here.

• Continue south 0.4 of a mile to junction with narrow dirt road on left (east). Turn left. About 100 feet along on the dirt road, you'll see a BLM sign for Little Black Mountain.

• Continue on BLM road for 0.4 of a mile to bend. Bear right (south).

• Continue south for 4 miles to a cattle guard. En route, you gradually climb a hill. Reaching bottom on the other side, ignore dirt road on left. Continue straight for the cattle guard.

• Cross the cattle guard, go through a gate (close it after passing through), and arrive at the site in 1.9 miles.

Additional information: Pipe Spring National Monument, (928) 643-7105; www.nps.gov/pisp. Little Black Mountain Petroglyph Site, (435) 688-3200; www.blm.gov/az/asfo/culture.htm.

Drive 3

Toroweap, the End of the Road

Toroweap Point, a rocky, North Rim ledge overlooking Vulcan's Throne and Lava Falls in the Grand Canyon, is one of the most isolated spots in the United States. It is also one of the most sublime. At the end of the road, you can sit on great slabs of sandstone and watch the Colorado River meander through the narrowest portion of the Grand Canyon. There are no guardrails and hardly any people here. If you suffer from vertigo, stay well back from the rim.

To reach this patch of isolation, you'll drive a minimum of 100 miles roundtrip on unpaved and sometimes unpredictable roads. The final 5 miles are the roughest. The single-lane road becomes very rocky, narrow, and steep in places.

You'll find no food, water, gas, lodging, emergency services, or human habitation anywhere near Toroweap Point. Carry plenty of water—it's a hot place in the summer months—and bring tools: Make sure you have a good spare tire and a working jack.

Toroweap has stirred emotions and inspired many descriptions from adventurers. Here are a few:

"Set at the end of a washboard road, Toroweap is the most isolated destination in Grand Canyon National Park. No place I have visited underscores the fragility of life and the mortality of man like the precipice here. It is here that gravity becomes the most urgent of all physical laws, and the consequences of a misstep loom large."—Photographer George Stocking, writing in *Arizona Highways*.

"So isolated is this land that the people of the now-deserted village of Mount Trumbull had to travel 278 miles through three states just to reach their county seat at Kingman."—Arizona Official Historian Marshall Trimble, writing in an earlier *Arizona Highways* back roads book.

"Incredible ... spiritual ... held onto my kids and later had nightmares, but I loved it."—A visitor who wrote her impressions in the visitors register at the site.

"Stupendously big ... spell-binding"—Wayne Ranney, author of *Carving Grand Canyon*.

"First I walked boldly up to the edge, peered over, and then quickly retreated. I removed my hat and put a rock on it, lest the wind carry it into the chasm far below. Then I cautiously crawled up to the edge on all fours for another look. The only sound was the wind rushing through the Canyon and the distant roar of Lava Falls, some 3,000 feet below."—Marshall Trimble.

"It has been described as the wettest, coldest, hottest, driest place on Earth—it sometimes seemed that way, too."— The late John Riffey, who was the ranger at this spot for many years.

This area is known as both Toroweap and Tuweep. The National Park Services notes that Toroweap is a Paiute term meaning "dry or barren valley" and refers to features including the geologic formation and fault, the valley, and the overlook. Tuweep, a Paiute term referring to the "earth" or possibly "long valley," describes a settlement (now abandoned) and the NPS ranger district.

Physical features includes places like the Kanab, Uinkaret, and Shivwits plateaus; Hurricane and Main Street valleys; Mount Trumbull, Mount Logan, and Paiute wildernesses; and the Grand

An lone juniper stands dark against a vivid sunset in Hurricane Valley on the Shivwits Plateau in Arizona's extreme northwestern corner.

Canyon-Parashant National Monument. The first people likely were hunter-gatherers living a nomadic life in what was a milder climate. The Ancestral Puebloans (Anasazi) arrived about 2,000 years and remained for 12 or 13 centuries. The most recent American Indian group to live here is the Paiute, who have a reservation to the north. Evidence of past human presence here includes dwellings and rock art, including the Nampaweap Rock Art Site.

There are three major routes leading to and from Toroweap—Sunshine, Main Street, and Clayhole. Directions in the Route Finder describe the way in via the Sunshine Route and the way out via the Main Street or Clayhole routes. The Bureau of Land Management (BLM) publishes one of the most current, detailed maps of the Arizona Strip (see Route Finder for information).

Before starting the drive, spend some time in the Pipe Spring National Monument-Kaibab Band of Paiute Indians Visitor Center and Museum. The facility features exhibits about the people and cultures who have lived in this region for centuries. The center also provides information and maps for visiting other nearby public lands, including Grand Canyon National Park and Grand Canyon-Parashant National Monument. Besides the museum, Pipe Spring includes Winsor Castle, built by Mormon pioneers, and its surrounding grounds, which include historic buildings (including a spring house), farm animals, an orchard and garden, and a half-mile trail.

Within 5 miles of leaving the paved highway, County Road 109 virtually coincides for a few miles with the Dominguez and Escalante Historic Trail, forged by an expedition led by two Spanish padres. Then, for 30 more miles their trail will be a few miles to your right.

After leaving 109, you'll soon see an unnamed hill, 5,921 feet high, which marks the area of black lava rocks known as the Witches Water Pocket. In 1872, a Paiute Indian told Colorado River explorer Maj. John Wesley Powell that witches haunted the area. Clarence Dutton, a protégé of Powell's, later mentioned this spot in his *Tertiary History of the Grand Cañon District*:

"About a mile from the valley we find the Witches Water Pocket. In every desert the watering places are memorable, and this one is no exception. It is a weird spot ... jagged masses of black lava still protrude through rusty, decaying cinders."

About 4 miles beyond this spooky area, the road forks. A sign says Toroweap is 14 miles straight ahead and Mount Trumbull is 6 miles to your right. When you're not quite 6 miles south of the sign, the melancholy remains of tin-roofed Tuweep Church appear on the left, a lonely remnant of the 1920s when settlers tried homesteading in this desolate country.

It's less than a mile from the church to the boundary of Grand Canyon National Park, Tuweep Area. About 0.75 of a mile beyond the boundary lies the Tuweep Ranger Station. While a ranger is stationed at Tuweep, someone is not always there. The 5 miles that separate the ranger station from the Toroweap Campground get rougher as you get closer to the Canyon. If you ignored the warning about taking a motor home or large trailer on this road, this is where you'll be forced to turn around. At one spot the boulders on either side of the road make it impassable to larger recreational vehicles.

At the Toroweap Campground (there are no fees), you'll find picnic tables, fire pits (though wood-gathering is prohibited) and clean, composting outhouses. Walk or drive 0.9 of a mile south of the campground to Toroweap Point, and the Colorado River will be visible in a narrow gorge some 3,200 feet straight down. Wander westward along the rocks, and you may be able to hear Lava Falls, one of the most famous rapids in the canyon, about a mile downstream.

For a real thrill, try to make your trip during the time of the full moon. Watching the full moon come up over the eastern cliffs of the Grand Canyon, especially from a spot as dramatic as Toroweap, makes a memory you'll not soon forget.

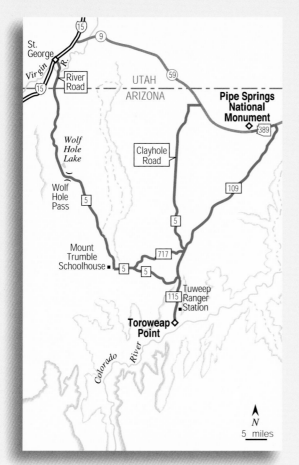

• Continue on County 115 for 7.6 miles to Tuweep Ranger Station, located less than a mile south of Grand Canyon National Park boundary.

• Continue south on 115 for 3.4 miles to a fork. Bear left for Toroweap campground and overlook in 1.2 miles.

• Leaving Toroweap, backtrack on 115 to junction with 5. Turn left (west).

• Continue westward on 5, along south side of Mount Trumbull Wilderness, for 13.1 miles to junction with County 717. Stay left to remain on 5.

• Continue on 5 for 6.2 miles to old Mount Trumbull (locals call it Bundyville) town site and schoolhouse.

• Backtrack on 5 to junction with County 717. Bear left (northeasterly) onto 717.

• Continue on 717 for 16.5 miles to County 5. Note: 4.2 miles along 717, the road turns 90 degrees to right (east). At junction with 5, turn left (north).

• Continue on 5 for 39 miles to State 386. Notes: This part of County 5 is also known as Clayhole Road; 27.7 miles along County 5 you'll cross County Route 30; in another mile you'll pass under a power line; in another 7.2 miles the road turns 90 degrees right (east). From there, it's 3 miles to State 389.

• At State 386 turn right for Pipe Spring and Fredonia, or left for Colorado City and St. George, Utah.

• Option: To leave the area by the Main Street Route, continue north on County 5 from the old schoolhouse for 54 miles to the southern end of St. George, Utah. En route, the road changes designation. At 6.7 miles, cross Hurricane Wash. At 11.5 miles, pass junction with County Road 103 (Mount Dellenbaugh Road) on left. At 22.5 miles, pass junction with County Road 30 on right. At 26 miles, go through Wolf Hole Pass. At 29.5 miles, pass junction with County Road 101 on left. At 30.3 miles, pass Wolf Hole Lake on right. About here, the road becomes BLM 1069. At 39.5 miles, cross into Utah and the road becomes River Road. At 54 miles you'll be in the southern part of St. George.

Additional information: Bureau of Land Management, Arizona Strip Field Office in St. George, Utah, (435) 688-3200; www.blm.gov/az/st/en/fo/arizona_strip_field.html. National Park Service, Toroweap information, www.nps.gov/archive/grca/grandcanyon/tuweep; backcountry permits, www.nps.gov/grca/planyourvisit/permits.htm

Route Finder

• From Pipe Spring National Monument, turn left (east) onto State Route 389. Drive 5.2 miles (between mileposts 24 and 25) to County Road 109, the Sunshine Route. Turn right (south).

• At 7.2 miles south of State 389, continue past junction on right with BLM 1067.

• At 10.4 miles beyond BLM 1067, County 109 veers right and then left, changing direction from southwest to northwest to south within 0.4 miles. In this stretch, you'll pass two BLM roads on right.

• Continue on County 109 for 22.5 miles beyond the second road to County Road 5. At this point you are 40.5 miles from State 389. Turn left (south) onto County 5.

• Continue on County 5 for 6.3 miles to County Road 115. Stay left to get onto County 115. A directional sign for Toroweap is at this junction.

A couple and their dog work their way through sand dunes in the Little Painted Desert, near Winslow. Edward McCain

Index

Inside back cover:
Wet Beaver Creek flows in the Verde Valley. Randy A. Prentice

Back cover, top:
The Arizona Strip's Mount Hayden points to a rainbow. Paul Gill

Back cover, bottom from left:
The Superstition Mountains flank one side of the Apache Trail. Willard Clay
Ives Mesa in Navajoland is named for Lt. Joseph Ives. George H.H. Huey
Moonlight accentuates the sacredness of Baboquivari Peak. David Muench
Oak Creek reflects Cathedral Rock near Sedona. David Muench